New Brewery
Cooperage
Pumping Station
Infirmary
Fire Brigade Sta.
Christ Church
Vicarage
Chapel
Schools
Saw Mill
Brewery
Maltho.
M. R.
Market Place
Market Hall
Sunday School
Grave Yard
St. Modwen's Church
(Vicarage)
St. Modwen's Hole
Manor House
Abbey
(Remains of)
The Abbey
Boat House
Soho
Ward Bdy.
Bond End
Peel Croft
Football Ground
Pavilion
Grammar School
Mission Room
School
Liable to Floods
Floods
Sheffield Street
James Street
Green Street
Trent Street
Corporation Depôt & Workshops
Refuse Destructor
Argyll House
Smithy
Broadfield House
Laundry
F.B.

BURTON UPON TRENT

A HISTORY

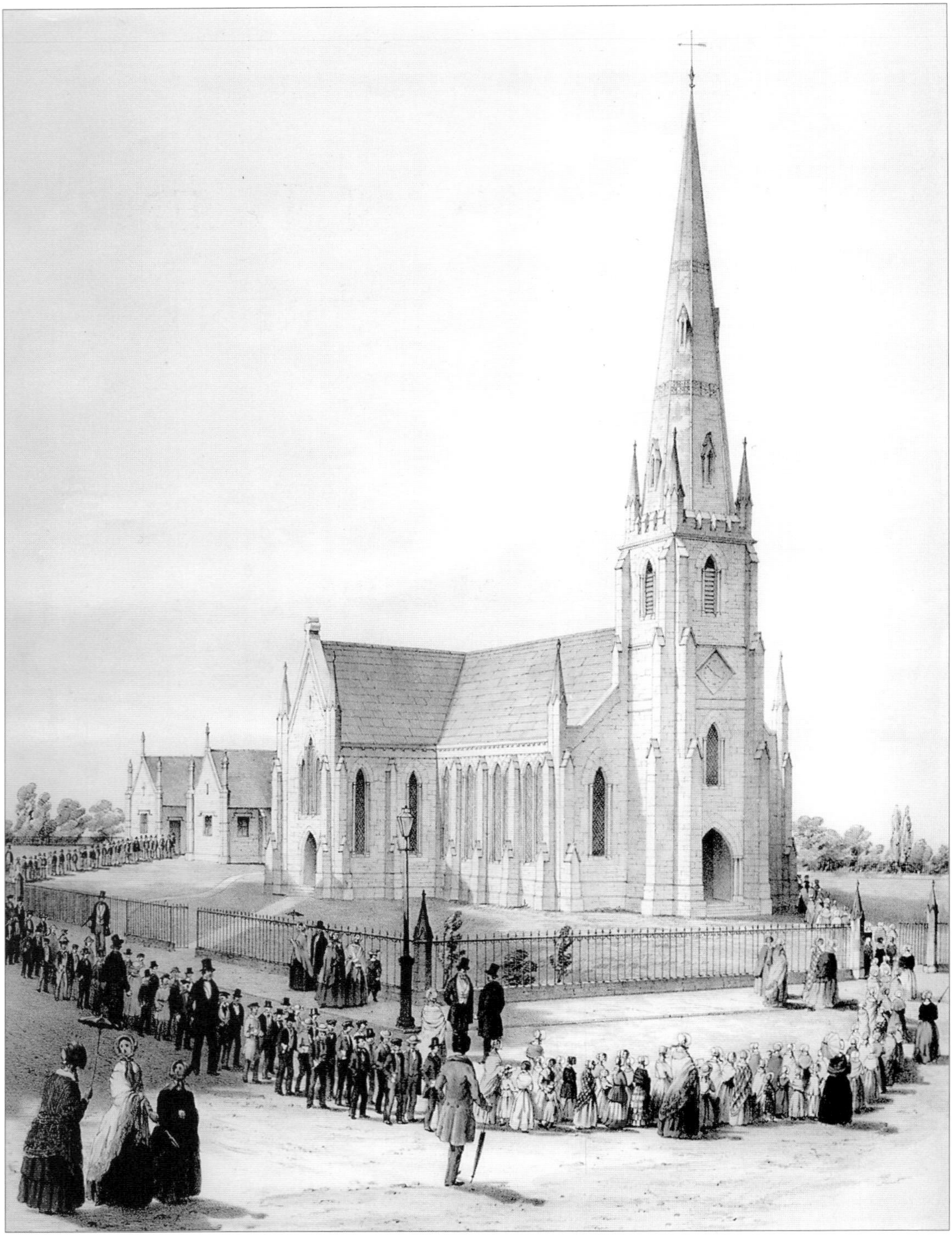

Christ Church, Moor Street with the National School behind (1857) (from an engraving by Rock and Co.).

BURTON UPON TRENT
A HISTORY

Richard Stone

Phillimore

2004

Published by
PHILLIMORE & CO. LTD,
Shopwyke Manor Barn, Chichester, West Sussex, England

ISBN 1 86077 312 5

Printed and bound in Great Britain by
THE CROMWELL PRESS LTD
Trowbridge, Wiltshire

Contents

For Penny and Helen

List of Illustrations

Acknowledgements

Burton is my town. I was born here. A lifetime of interest in its history has led to a collection of snippets of information and items of local interest. Although I have attempted to track down sources, I am aware that I am indebted to many people I am unable to name.

My thanks to Burton upon Trent Civic Society for allowing me access to their photographic archive and to Acorn Photography for permission to reproduce pictures from a collection that includes original glass plate negatives and spans generations of Burton photographers past and present. Also to Burton upon Trent Public Library for access to a range of material including maps and directories held in their local studies collection, and the Coors Visitor Centre & the Museum of Brewing.

Special thanks are due to Valerie Burton, Councillor Tom Dawn, Dr Robin Trotter and Catherine Lister for their helpfulness, and also to A.M. Campbell (Dentists) and Mike Osborne Properties.

I am grateful to Karen Lanchester (photographs 46, 55, 69, 75, 86, 94, 150, 151); Pauline Howell (illustration 111 by A.S. 'Sid' Howell); Dr Robin Trotter (photographs 74, 87); Dorothy Greening (photograph 136); Bob Mitchell (illustration 138); Bennett Lovatt & Associates (dustjacket); and to Acorn Photography for the author photograph.

As ever, Helen Stone has done a splendid job interpreting my diagrams, doodles and footnotes to produce illustrations and line drawings (5, 6, 8, 9, 10, 11, 12, 13, 21, and 47).

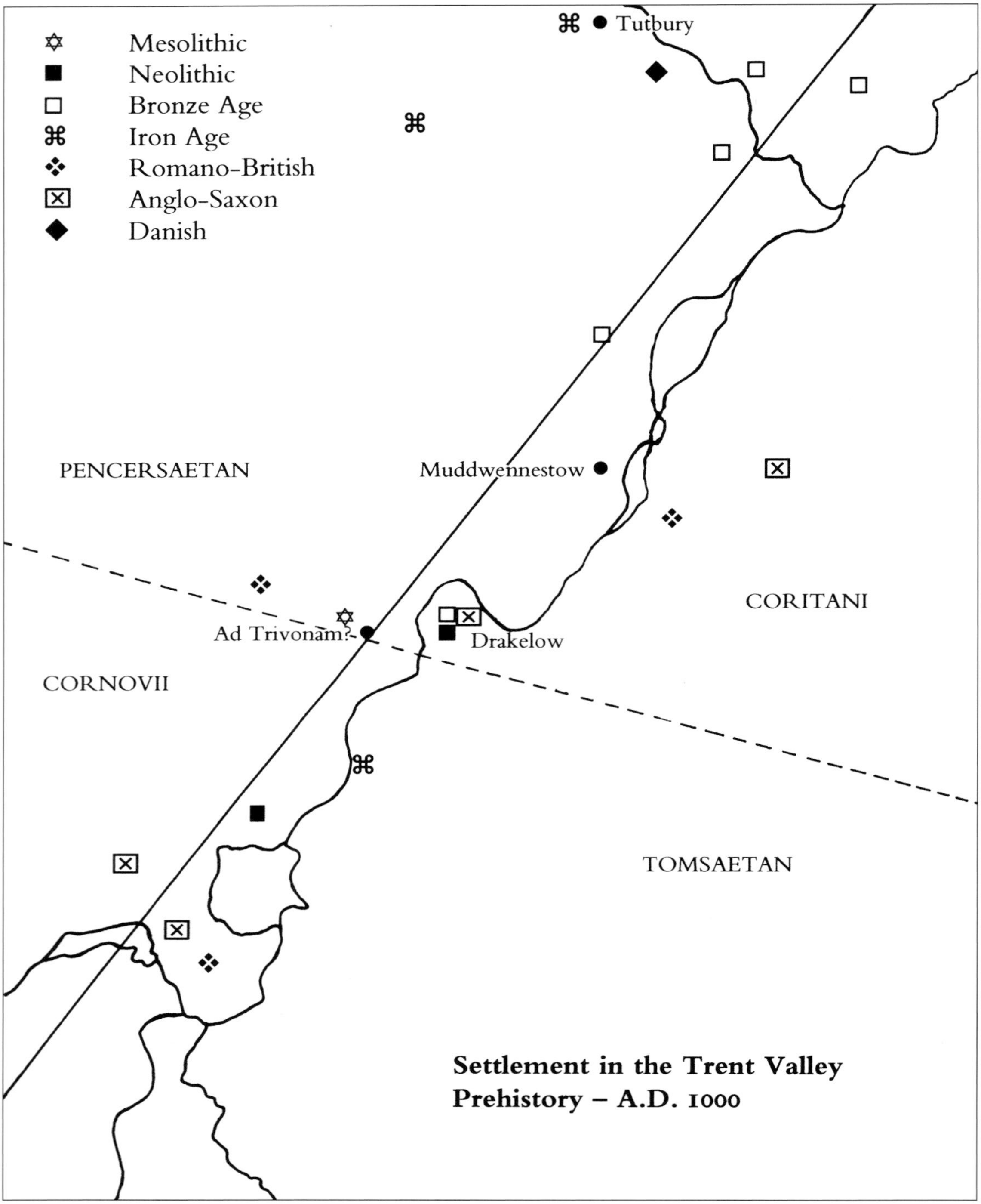

1 *A scatter of archaeological finds in the Trent Valley close to Burton reveals evidence of human settlement throughout the ages.*

ONE

Settlement:
From the First Footsteps to the Foundation of Burton Abbey

Around 1002, Wulfric Spot, a Saxon noble, establishes a monastery beside the River Trent at Byrtune. His endowment of the abbey includes extensive estates stretching across Staffordshire and Derbyshire into Leicestershire, Warwickshire and beyond. Land brings wealth and authority. Wulfric's gift places the abbot at the head of a feudal empire. For the next five centuries the monastery will dominate life in the local area.

The foundation of the abbey begins the story of Burton, a settlement shaped by spiritual and temporal control growing in the shadow of the monastic precincts. But what was here before? What was the area like? Why was the site chosen? In order to answer those questions we must sift the evidence of archaeological record, balancing myth and legend with fragmentary Dark-Age sources.

Knapped flint hand axes and other primitive stone tools have been discovered in the gravel beds of the Trent Valley. Distinct layers of deposits in the river terraces exposed by quarrying and natural erosion reveal signs of human presence dating back 250,000 years. Successive glacial periods have totally reshaped the landscape since the first Neanderthals left their traces.

When the last ice age ended around ten thousand years ago, Britain was still connected by a land bridge to the rest of continental Europe. As the ice sheets retreated people followed. Tundra was replaced by forest. Small nomadic groups foraged along the waterways and woodland fringes. These hunter-gatherers of the Mesolithic period, or middle Stone Age,

2 *Knapped flint tools and weapons dating from tens of thousands of years ago have been discovered in the gravel beds of the Trent Valley.*

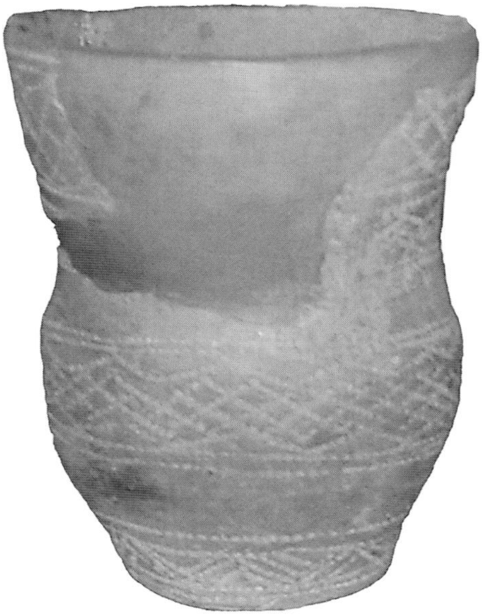

3 *Distinctively shaped pots, known as 'beakers', appeared around 4,500 years ago. They were used as drinking vessels and also as burial urns for cremated remains. A beaker pot 18cm. in height was excavated at Catholme.*

lived in temporary shelters: simple bivouacs for overnight stays, small round huts of bent and woven hazel saplings covered with foliage for seasonal use. They carried their few belongings with them as they travelled, leaving little trace behind. Sites of the period are extremely rare. All those discovered so far occur in river valley environments.

In 1943, the bucket jaws of a digger opening a gravel quarry close to Branston exposed a human skeleton preserved in a layer of peat. Forensic investigation identified the bones as those of a young woman perhaps 23 years of age. Major J.L. Auden, the East Staffordshire coroner, officially pronounced them 'ancient remains'. A wooden trackway uncovered nearby led to a birch-branch platform fastened down with pegs of alder and hazel. Associated finds including the business end of an alder spear, stone scrapers, animal bones that had been split to extract nutritious marrow and nutshells all support the interpretation that this was the floor of some kind of dwelling. However, there were no postholes or timbers left to indicate an overhead shelter and no sign of a hearth, although there was a scatter of charcoal.

A soil column cut through the various layers of peat on the site was sent to Professor Harold Goodwin of Cambridge University. At the time, dating soil samples by pollen analysis was a new technique. Professor Goodwin was the country's leading expert. His results produced a date for the finds of approximately 8000 B.C. How far this can be accepted without corroborative evidence is hard to say. If accurate, it makes the Branston trackway the oldest in Britain by over 4,000 years. Wetland may seem inhospitable to us but it was a far less hostile environment than the wildwood and provided significant resources. Wildfowl, fish, reeds for thatching and a starch staple in the rhizomes of reedmace were all readily available and plentiful. The presence of charcoal opens up an interesting possibility. Did the Stone-Age people of the Trent Valley practise controlled burning, clearing swathes of reed to encourage new growth and attract grazing animals into the open where they were visible and vulnerable?

By 3500 Britain had long been an island but waves of immigrants continued to cross the sea from mainland Europe. The new arrivals were farmers. Sheep, goats and cattle were domesticated. Polished and hafted stone axes allowed trees to be felled, creating land for crops of wheat and barley. Cultivation meant permanent settlement, the establishment of territorial rights and a whole new connection with the land. Visible symbols of communal occupation began to appear on the landscape. A timber henge monument discovered a few miles south of Burton at Fatholme was built by some of the first farmers around five thousand years ago. Here the community might have gathered to feast and perform ceremonies aimed at ensuring a successful crop. A series of ring ditches excavated nearby produced pottery fragments, flint scrapers and arrowheads.

A beautifully finished Neolithic axehead of a type mass-produced at Great Langdale in the Lake District was found at Warren Farm, Drakelow. Its journey to the Trent Valley is an indication of the extent to which trading routes were established in prehistoric times. The River Trent was a natural highway. An oak log boat found at Shardlow in 1998 with a cargo of stone still on board turned out to be 3,500 years old.

Contact and communication helped spread ideas. Around 2400 B.C. distinctively flared drinking pots known as 'beakers' appeared across Europe and became so characteristic and widespread they gave their name to a whole culture. Beaker People buried their dead in round burial mounds or barrows, cremation gradually replacing inhumation. Crop marks visible from the air identified two features at Tucklesholme Farm between Walton-on-Trent and Barton under Needwood that proved to be barrows flattened by centuries of erosion and ploughing. Subsequent excavation revealed cremated human remains placed in cinerary urns. Similar sites have been investigated between Egginton and Willington. The settlements where these people lived, typically a few thatched roundhouses surrounded by storage pits for grain, have proved elusive.

Smelting copper and tin to make bronze allowed the manufacture of more efficient tools and weapons. A bronze palstave dating to around 1000 B.C., the middle of the Bronze Age, was unearthed close to the junction of Derby Road and Eton Road. A bronze spearhead was pulled from the riverbank at Drakelow. Decorative personal objects show a more cultural side to life 3,000 years ago: part of a beaded bronze necklet thought to have been made in eastern Europe was found at Clay Mills.

Technological advances in metal working made iron available, more durable than bronze and capable of retaining a sharper cutting edge. Ploughing with oxen was introduced. From small beginnings communities grew in size and land increased in value. Security became an issue. Hillforts surrounded by defensive ditches and banks topped with wooden palisades were constructed on high

4 *Cremation gradually replaced inhumation during the Bronze Age. Pots similar to this containing calcined bones and ashes were found during gravel extraction between Egginton and Willington.*

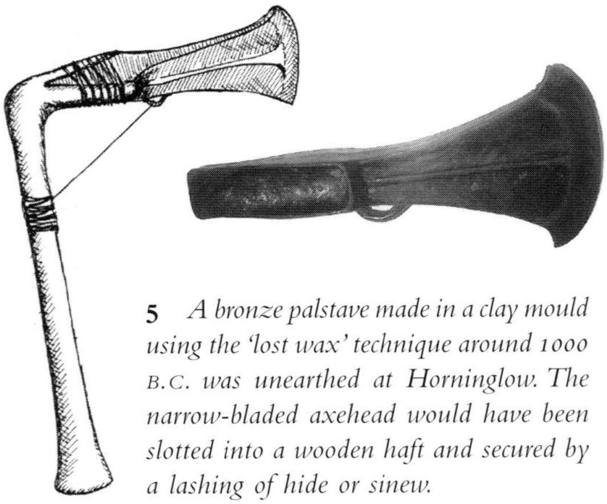

5 *A bronze palstave made in a clay mould using the 'lost wax' technique around 1000 B.C. was unearthed at Horninglow. The narrow-bladed axehead would have been slotted into a wooden haft and secured by a lashing of hide or sinew.*

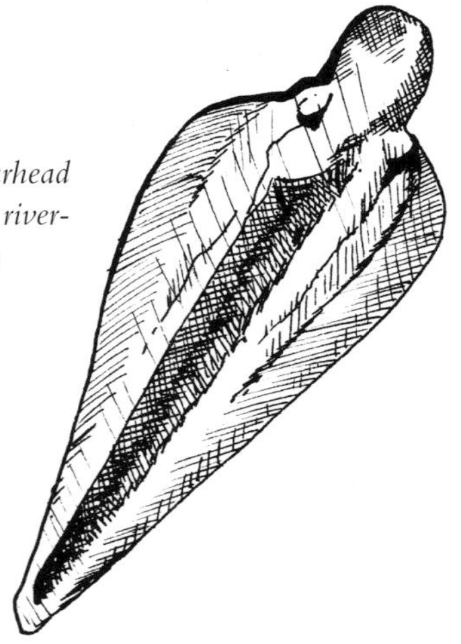

6 *A bronze spearhead discovered in the river-bank at Drakelow.*

7 *A fragment of beaded, bronze necklet found at Clay Mills in 1944 shows a cultural side to life 3,000 years ago. Thought to have been made in eastern Europe and possibly of Balkan origin.*

ground to provide a defendable refuge and meeting place. For safety, communal granaries were moved inside these fortified enclosures. Near Burton, the earthworks of a hillfort at Borough Hill, Walton are still traceable on the landscape. A hillfort once occupied the rise where Tutbury Castle now stands.

By 250 B.C. two powerful Celtic tribes dominated this part of the Trent Valley. North and west the land belonged to the Cornovii; south and east the Coritani held sway. It is possible a smaller tribe occupied a kind of buffer zone, an independent group sandwiched between the rival interests or part of a Coritani confederacy. A chunky gold-alloy torc found in Greaves Wood, Hanbury in 1848 confirms the presence of an important chieftain in the area. Torcs, worn as a collar around the neck, had both symbolic and ritual significance and were a badge of leadership among Iron-Age tribes.

Clan rivalries were suppressed when the seasoned, disciplined campaigners of the Roman XIVth and XXth legions arrived. By A.D. 48, military camps had been established and in the years that followed a raised roadway of stone slabs laid over gravel and compacted clay was built. North and south of Burton the route is approximately that of the current A38. Where the modern trunk road now loops around the north-west fringes of the town from Branston to Stretton, the Roman road followed a more direct line across open moorland to a ford or bridge over the River Dove at Clay Mills. At five metres wide it was broad enough to allow two marching columns to pass. Known as Ryknield Street, it linked the Fosse Way in the Cotswolds with Ermine Street in Yorkshire, part of an arterial web of communication criss-crossing the country.

The route of another major Roman road in the area, the *Via Devana* from Leicester to Chester, is uncertain. Traces discovered at Stanton suggest it crossed Ryknield Street at Branston. *Ad Trivonam*, a lost Roman settlement known to have been halfway between the military station at Wall near Lichfield and the fort at Littlechester, Derby may have been sited at the junction.

A hoard of 32 Roman gold coins was found at Callingwood. Money was a novelty in an economy largely based on barter and often in short supply. British minted copper versions of first-century Roman coins have been discovered near Grange Street and at Stapenhill.

In 1881, workers digging clay at the brickworks of Chamberlain and Ballard beside Stanton Road, Stapenhill uncovered a Romano-British cemetery containing five cinerary urns and 31 burials. Sherds of locally made pottery and Samian ware imported from Gaul were found together with beads of glass, amber and terracotta, and bronze clasps, brooches and buckles. The finest finds were beside the skeleton of a middle-aged woman. Among the more unusual items was an engraved disc of red deer antler. Size and shape suggest a spindle whorl used to weight a stick on which combed raw wool was teased, twisted and spun into yarn. Weaving was a basic task and every household had its own loom for weaving cloth. But spindle whorls are usually plain and made of fired clay or stone. The use of antler, the carefully incised decoration and its presence in the grave open up the possibility that this was a treasured belonging. Perhaps a gaming piece, even a talisman or lucky charm. A square enclosure uncovered on the same site contained pottery spanning the entire period of Roman occupation.

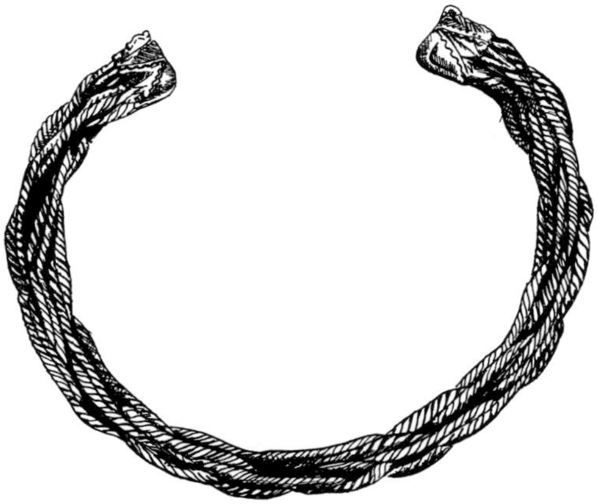

8 *Torcs were worn around the neck as symbols of status and leadership. This gold alloy example found in Greaves Wood, Hanbury weighs 440g. and has been tentatively dated to the second century B.C. Similar finds elsewhere in the country suggest these incredibly valuable items were sometimes deliberately buried and may have been intended as a 'sacrifice' to Celtic deities.*

9 *Among the finds excavated at a Romano-British settlement on high ground beside Stanton Road, Stapenhill was a cinerary urn containing human ashes and a string of 36 beads (21 of blue glass, 14 of terracotta and one of amber).*

Law, order and civil administration were swamped in the unrest that followed the withdrawal of Roman forces early in the fifth century. A market economy that had brought prosperity and stability disintegrated. Britain's wealth and vulnerability attracted waves of Angles, Saxons and Jutes, under pressure in their Germanic homelands from an expansionist Frankish Empire. Last of the mini-kingdoms carved out by the new arrivals was Mercia and the area around Burton was at its heart.

10 *Decorated earthenware drinking vessel 14cm. high found beside the 1.8m-tall skeleton of a middle-aged woman at Stapenhill.*

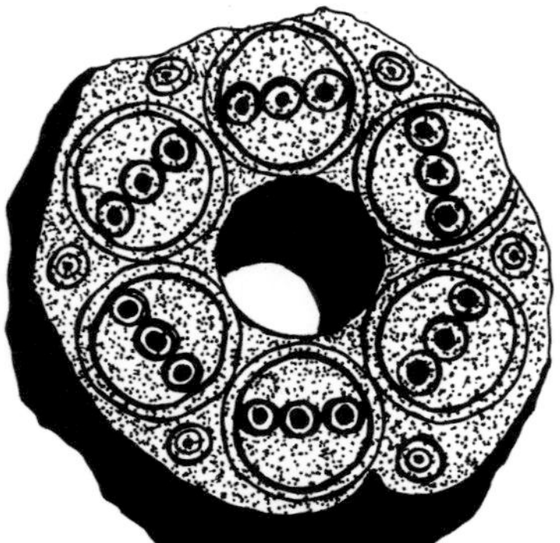

11 *A finely engraved disc of red deer antler from the Romano-British settlement at Stapenhill may be an unusually decorative spindle whorl, a gaming piece or even a lucky charm.*

Anglo-Saxon culture was soon in the ascendant, probably as much by assimilation as by conquest. One Anglian folk group, the Tomsaetan, settled the land of the Coritani while another, the Pencersaetan, established itself alongside the Cornovii. Brooches belonging to the earliest Anglo-Saxon period have been found at Wychnor and Brizlincote. A complex of buildings excavated north of Catholme Lane at Barton show evidence of occupation from the fifth to the tenth centuries. A small sixth-century decorated earthenware bowl 6cm. high discovered at Drakelow is of a type usually associated with burials and intended for use in an afterlife. In this instance there was no sign of human remains. The bones of six Anglo-Saxon warriors were discovered between Wychnor and Catholme in 1899. Iron spearheads and shield bosses had survived from the weapons that had been buried beside them.

In the seventh century, under the warrior ruler Penda, Mercia was the dominant Anglo-Saxon kingdom. Penda's eldest son Peada converted to Christianity as a precondition of his marriage to a Northumbrian princess in 653. After the wedding, four monks returned to Mercia with the couple. From a base at Repton they began to spread the gospel. One of the monks, Diuma, was designated Mercia's first bishop.

It is around this time that the legend of St Modwen has its origins. According to tradition, Modwen and two companions, Athea and Lazar, were undertaking a pilgrimage to Rome. On their way they established a religious community on an island in the River Trent, dedicating a church they built there to St Andrew. The site became known as St Andrew's Isle or 'Andresey'. On the return journey a second church was consecrated in honour of St Peter and St Paul on the opposite side of the river at the foot of Calvecliffe (Scalpcliff Hill). Athea stayed in the local area. Modwen travelled on to Scotland where, according to some accounts, her brother Ronan lived and worked as a missionary. When she died her body was returned for burial on Andresey.

Sainthood in the early Christian Church depended on public acclamation rather than any process of papal ratification. Modwen's reputation soon attracted pilgrims. Miracles were reported. When the monastery was built overlooking Andresey three centuries later, Modwen's remains were transferred to a shrine in the abbey church. But who was Modwen? Where did she come from? Did she even exist? These questions exercised Geoffrey, elected Abbot of Burton in 1114, who recorded:

> For a long time I had felt a burning desire to find out something certain about the homeland, family, life and virtues of the most holy virgin Modwenna and I often prayed to her about this with an eager heart.

Extensive research led him to Ireland and a tenth-century chronicle attributed to a writer known as Conchubranus, telling the story of Monenna, a sixth-century Irish abbess who founded a monastery at Newry. Monenna provided a convenient background for Modwen and Abbot Geoffrey incorporated her story into his own account of the life of Modwen. Later elaborations make Modwen the daughter of King Mochta and relate how she pursued Prince Alfrid of Northumbria to England to demand the

12 *Incomplete sixth-century bronze brooch with silver gilding found at Wychnor in 1926 and approximately 16.5cm. in length (partly reconstructed here for illustrative purposes). Brooches were used to hold clothing together but were clearly also meant to be decorative. Gilding the bronze helped prevent tarnishing and kept the brooch shiny.*

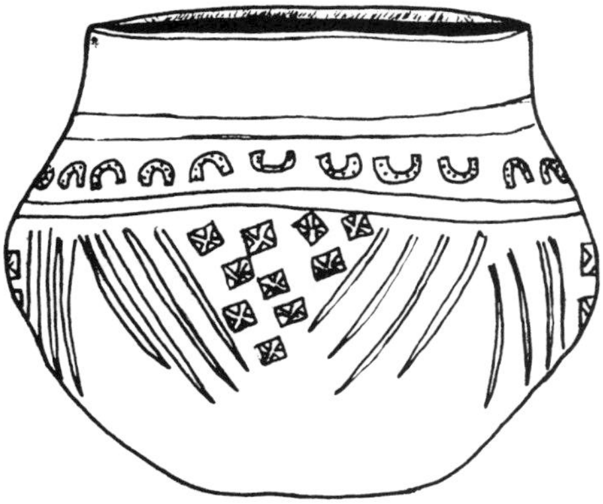

13 *Sixth-century grey-brown earthenware votive jar 6 cm. high discovered at Drakelow and of a type usually associated with burials. Drakelow is recorded in a land charter of 942 as* Dracan Hlaw *(Dragon Low), indicating a burial mound, but no human remains were found with the vessel.*

14 *Central iron bosses, similar to this example, survived from wood and leather shields buried with their Anglo-Saxon warrior owners at Wychnor in the sixth century. Shield bosses were used aggressively to batter and push back enemies. The distinctive 'button', attached by a rivet, was used to trap an opponent's blade in combat.*

return of items taken from her convent by the Irish King Finnachta as a parting gift. If the tales must be treated as myth, we still have the association of Modwen's name with Burton by tradition and early record. The existence of a shrine and the presence of physical relics all point to a flesh and blood woman of faith and charisma.

Towards the end of the eighth century, towns along the English coast suffered raids from Scandinavian Vikings. In 865 a Danish army arrived with serious longer-term intentions. A campaign of conquest began with the subjugation of East Anglia. As pagan forces penetrated westwards, King Burgred of Mercia fled to Rome. In 873/4 a large Danish force over-wintered at Repton from where they ravaged the surrounding countryside. Christian sites were particularly targeted. Any church on Andresey, almost certainly a wooden structure like most Anglo-Saxon buildings, would have been destroyed.

England rallied under Alfred, King of Wessex to win a significant victory in 878 at the Battle of Edington. A politically expedient treaty was agreed between Alfred and the Danish king, Guthrum. Under its terms the land was divided. Guthrum accepted baptism and the Danes were allowed to settle in eastern England. Derby, Leicester, Lincoln, Nottingham and Stamford, known collectively as the Five Boroughs, came under Danish administration. The Rivers Trent and Dove marked the boundary between the 'Danelaw' and Anglo-Saxon-held territory. Homesteads along the Trent Valley were now perched on a fragile frontier.

Guthrum's acceptance of the Christian religion triggered wholesale conversion amongst his followers. A Danish wheel-headed cross from this period has stood outside St Mary's Church at Rolleston since 1897. Sir Oswald Mosley rescued it from the floor of the porch at St Michael and All Angels, Tatenhill. Where the cross came from originally we cannot be sure. Place-names with the suffixes 'by' and 'thorpe' (Bretby, Ingleby, Donisthorpe, Oakthorpe, for example) indicate several Danish settlements locally. 'Holme', a Danish word for island, is tacked on to many of the islets and water meadows that interrupt the River Trent as it flows through the area.

Alfred organised the Saxon regions into shire counties divided into three, four or five units each of approximately 100 hides. A hide, roughly 120 acres, was a measure based on the amount of land needed to support a household. Every hide was required to supply one man for military service whenever danger threatened. East Staffordshire was in Offlow Hundred.

Edmund I, grandson of Alfred the Great, reconquered Danish Mercia in 944. Succeeding Saxon rulers faced with further Viking incursions employed a mix of armed resistance and bribery. By then many second- and third-generation Danish settlers had been assimilated into English life but they were still viewed with suspicion as the enemy within. On 13 November 1002, St Brice's Day, a terrible plan to kill every man, woman and child of Danish extraction was unleashed. Wulfric Spot of Mercia, a prominent and influential member of King Aethelred's inner circle, may have led the massacre.

It was the same Wulfric Spot who founded the abbey at Byrtune. The suffix 'tune' or 'ton' is common in place-names. It can mean a town or village but often signified little more than a homestead. The picture that emerges from the archaeological record is of a chain of small settlements in East Staffordshire and South Derbyshire strung out along the Trent Valley, sheltered by hills to the east and west. Anglo-Saxon Byrtune or Muddwennestow (the 'holy place of St Modwen') was probably little more than a hamlet distinguished by a saintly connection. But if the homestead at Byrtune belonged to Wulfric, well placed at the centre of the vast Midlands estates he owned, it would have been a fortified manor of substantial size. There may even have been a small religious community attached to a rebuilt church on Andresey, possibly even a minster. Privileges later enjoyed by the abbey, not having to pay for chrism, the right of the abbot to preside over his own court, and exemption from sending a representative to synod, for example, show a level of spiritual independence commonly associated with a minster church.

An existing holy place was an attractive site for a monastery but earthly considerations also played a part in the decision. Convenient natural resources included a plentiful supply of river water for drainage, timber from Needwood Forest and red sandstone from a quarry at Winshill. Unusually there was no fresh water supply within the precinct, but drinking water may have been available nearby from a well on Andresey. After the depredations of the Vikings in Northumbria, the abbey at Burton was for many years the only monastic institution north of the River Trent.

15 *The legend of St Modwen has its origins in the latter half of the seventh century when large-scale conversion of Anglo-Saxon Mercia to Christianity began. According to tradition, Modwen founded a religious community and dedicated a church to St Andrew at Burton. This striking wind sculpture of St Modwen on the Trent Washlands is by John Fortnum.*

16 *Early tenth-century Danish wheel-headed cross rescued from the porch floor of St Michael and All Angels Church, Tatenhill and re-erected in 1897 outside St Mary's Church, Rolleston.*

In an age of religious conviction, absolution had a price. It has been supposed that the abbey was Wulfric's penance for the blood on his hands. If so, his view of events differed from that of his king. Aethelred publicly declared it 'a most just slaughter' and church leaders actively encouraged the action by promising forgiveness in advance. But the timing is suggestive. Aethelred's confirmation of Wulfric's will in 1004 makes clear the new abbey was already in existence at that time. A separate bequest to Archbishop Aelfric shows the will could not have been written before 1002, the year of Aelfric's appointment.

Some sources suggest Wulfric died of wounds received fighting the Danes at Ringmere near Ipswich in 1010. Although he may have taken the precaution of obtaining King Aethelred's confirmation of his grant while he was still alive, at least two other bequests had taken effect by 1006 making it more likely that Wulfric died before 1004.

The prominence of Wulfric and his brother Aelfhelm at court together with the extent of their lands suggests a family connection to the ruling elite. A tenuous trail of inheritances, charter references, and recurring personal name elements convincingly identify Wulfric Spot's mother as Wulfruna, the founder of Wolverhampton. Wulfruna was a relative, possibly the daughter of Wulfsige the Black. One conjecture is that Wulfsige was related to Alfred the Great, either directly or by marriage, through Alfred's daughter Aethelfleda, the 'Lady of the Mercians'. Wulfric's daughter, referred to as 'my poor daughter' in his will and perhaps suffering from some form of disability, was among other beneficiaries of his will.

Saxon society may have been class-ridden but within each strata there was considerable equality between men and women. Wulfruna owned vast tracts of land, Aethelfleda ruled Mercia, and Godiva (famed for her legendary naked tax protest in Coventry) was lady of the manor at Branston. Wulfric Spot's rank is underscored by the status of the witnesses adding their names to the king's on the charter ratifying his will. Signatories include Aethelred's six sons, two archbishops, ten bishops, 12 abbots, three ealdormen and 22 thanes.

One of those murdered on St Brice's Day was the sister of King Sweyn of Denmark.

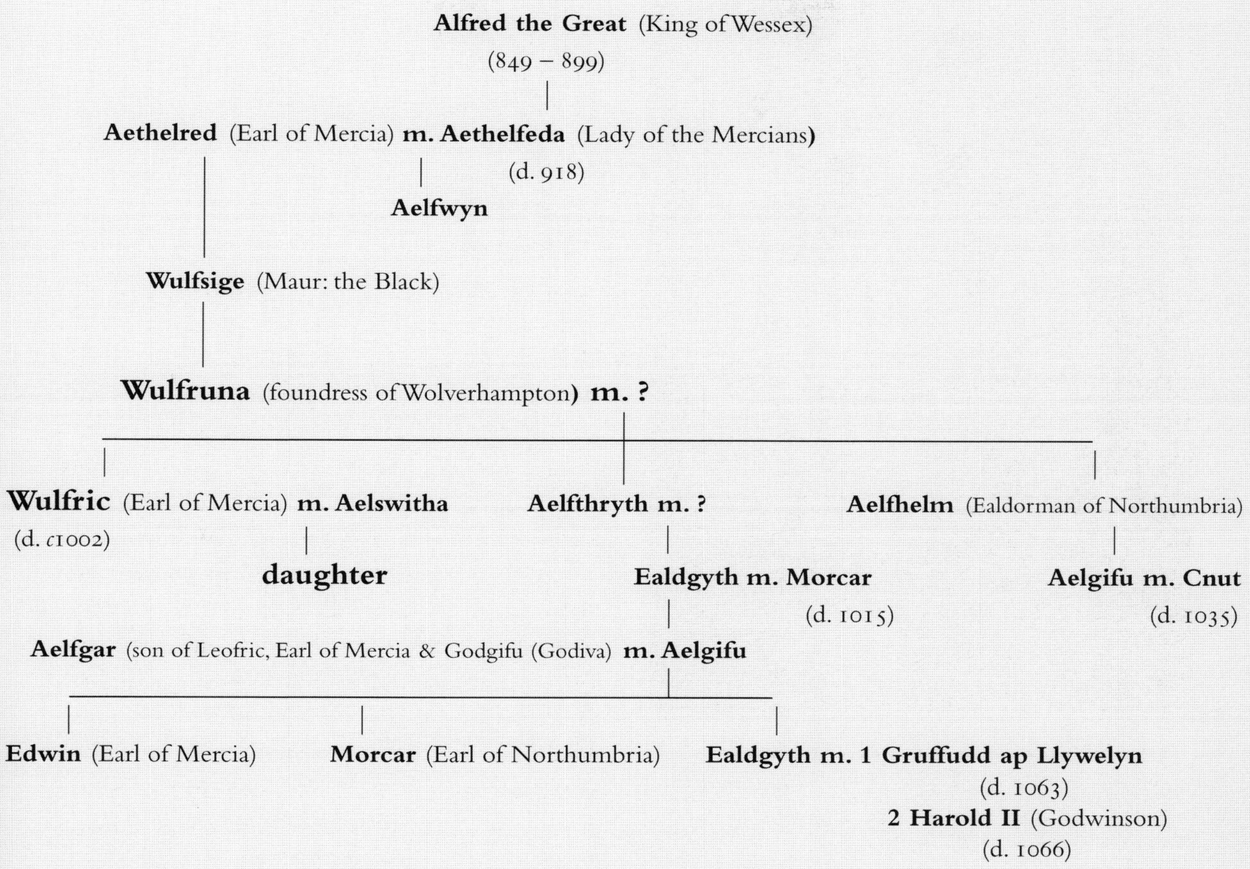

17 *Conjectural family tree of Wulfric Spot, founder of Burton Abbey and a prominent member of King Aethelred's court. Previous ownership of some 80 estates mentioned in Wulfric's will can be traced back to Wulfruna (foundress of Wolverhampton) and Wulfsige the Black. In a charter of 995 Wulfric is referred to as the son of Wulfruna.*

Retaliation was swift and bloody. Conflict continued until, with the death of Edmund Ironside in 1016, Sweyn's son Cnut was recognised as king of England. Cnut consolidated his position with a diplomatic marriage to Edmund's widowed mother Emma and the appointment of the Saxon earls Godwin of Wessex and Leofric of Mercia, husband of Lady Godiva, as his chief advisers. But rivalry between the Earls of Mercia and the House of Wessex was to lay Saxon England open to a new threat.

TWO

Township:
Boundaries, Bridges and Burgages

The building of the abbey makes Burton the focal centre of the area. Travellers are drawn by the promise of hospitality. Routes are diverted. A wide new road, the 'Broadway', leads from the old Roman crossroads at Branston past the abbey gates to a crossing point on the River Trent where a number of trackways from the east converge. A bridge soon replaces the ford. Wulfgeat, a monk from St Swithin's, Winchester is appointed as the abbey's first abbot, the head of a self-sufficient religious community and lord of the manor with both administrative and judicial responsibilities.

For ordinary people life is a constant struggle for survival. There is little to spare. Every winter brings with it the threat of starvation. After a particularly bad harvest, Abbot Leofric is reduced to stripping gold and jewels from the shrine of St Modwen to buy supplies and alleviate famine. More than a hundred and fifty peasant families are at the core of the large, interdependent rural enterprise that is Burton Abbey. Day-to-day operations require a supporting infrastructure of servants, suppliers and craftspeople. Outside the monastery walls a cluster of dwellings appear forming the nucleus of a small township.

There was little love lost between Edwin, Earl of Mercia and Harold Godwinson. Edwin refused to be drawn into the dispute between Harold and William, Duke of Normandy, leaving them to sort out their differences alone at Hastings in 1066. By the time William began treading on Edwin's toes and parcelling out chunks of Mercia amongst his nobles it was too late. Edwin's revolt of 1069 was brutally put down. Much of Staffordshire was laid waste.

In the years after the Norman Conquest land was redistributed. Burton Abbey made some gains, including Branston, but overall suffered a net property loss. After Hugh d'Avranches was created Earl of Chester, Henry de Ferrers replaced him at Tutbury as the major secular landowner in the area, one of around two hundred knights established as tenants-in-chief by King William in return for military service. Nigel de Stafford, ancestor of the Gresley family of Drakelow, was an under-tenant of de Ferrers.

From its foundation, exchanges, acquisitions and gifts of land had taken place consolidating the abbey's property portfolio. In 1008, King Aethelred accepted two small Gloucestershire estates in return for Rolleston on the abbey's

18 *The medieval 'Great Bridge' of Burton followed a gently curving line across three separate arms of the River Trent, one of which has since silted up. The earliest references to a bridge at Burton date from the 12th century but it is probable that stone footings were laid soon after the foundation of the abbey.*

doorstep. Wetmore was bought from the king four years later. Stapenhill and its church were acquired from Edward the Confessor, lost after 1066 and regained in 1190.

Clauses in the charter relating to the purchase of Wetmore suggest it once included Horninglow, Shobnall and Outwoods. In an abbey survey of 1114, the land owned by William of Shobnall is recorded as within Wetmore. Estate boundaries have a tendency to remain in place throughout changes of ownership. Natural and man-made features typical of Anglo-Saxon charters define the limits of *Wihtmere* (Wetmore) and make a hypothetical interpretation possible. The text begins: 'from the *trente* where the thieves hang [gallows in medieval times stood close to where Scalpcliffe Road now meets Stapenhill Road] to the middle of *bere fordes holme* [Beresford Holme, now Broadholme, the island crossed by Burton Bridge] direct to the *lewe* (low or mound, possibly the original Horning 'low') beside *fif lan* (five 'lands' or cultivated strips)'. The boundary charter continues: 'from the lands to the *sich* (a stream, the Walsitch is now culverted beneath Horninglow Street near the junction with Hawkins Lane)'. The next features described: a *maere thorne* (boundary thorn), an *æcer* (an acre of arable land) and a *hæge* (hedge) are not traceable. Assuming a line more or less due east across what would have been rough common allows us to pick up the next boundary landmarks: following a *broce* (Shobnall Brook) and a ditch (Shobnall

Dingle) to *ansydelege* (Anslow). From here along a *stræte* (Outwoods Lane) to a *stubbe* (tree stump) then following a ditch to a *stræte* (where Tutbury Road now meets Longhedge Lane and Anslow Lane) to *ebrocan* (wet ground) and on to another ditch. From here the directions are: straight on to a stream that runs by *chese wælle hylle* (Beacon Hill?) and *hunger hill* (Beam Hill?) to the boundary with *stretones* (Stretton). The charter concludes: 'to a ford along a stream back to the *trentan* and along the river back to where the *theofes hangad*'.

An intriguing alternative possibility is that the boundary extended along the river from Broadholme to a mound at Fivelands (*fif lan*), Stapenhill (between Holly Street and Saxon Street). Then followed a lost watercourse along the line later adopted as the borough's western boundary to an area near Lawns Farm, Branston known as the Thorns. A boundary post stood beside the footpath here until recent times. This reading of the charter would place Burton as an enclave at the centre of Wetmore.

TERRA SCÆ MARIÆ DE BERTONE.
ABBATIA S MARIE de Bertone ten in uilla Stadford
unã hid 7 dimid . Tra . ē . II . car . Ibi ſunt in dñio . 7 IX . uilli
hñt ibi . II . car . Ibi . XVI . ac pti . Silua dimid leuu lḡ.
7 tntđ lat. T.R.E. ualb LX . ſol . Modo . LXX . ſolid.
Ipſa abbatia ten BRANTESTONE . Godeua comitiſſa tenuit T.R.E.
Ibi . ē . I . hida 7 dimid . Tra . ē . V . car . In dñio . ē una 7 dim.
7 V . uilli 7 III . bord cũ . III . car . Ibi . XXIIII . ac pti . Silua
dimid leuu lḡ . 7 tntđ lat. Valuit . LX . ſol . Modo . XL . ſol.
Ipſa abbatia ten WITMERE . Ibi . I . hida 7 dim cũ append
ſuis . Tra . ē . VII . car . In dñio ſunt . II . 7 VI . uilli hñt . II.
car . Ibi . IIII . ac pti . Silua una leuu lḡ . 7 alia lat.
T.R.E. ualb . IIII . lib . 7 poſt . XX . ſol . Modo . L . ſol.
Ipſa abbatia ten STRATONE . Ibi . I . hida 7 dimid . Tra . ē . II.
car . In dñio . ē una . 7 VIII . uilli 7 II . bord hñt . V . car . Ibi
XXVIII . ac pti.
T.R.E . ualb . LX . ſol . 7 poſt . XX . ſolid . Modo . XL . ſolid.
Ipſa abbatia ten BRYNLEGE . Ibi dimid hida cũ append.
Tra . ē . I . car . Ipſa . ē in dñio . 7 pbr cũ . I . uillo 7 uno bord
hñt . I . car . Silua ibi . II . leuu lḡ . 7 una lat.
Valuit . X . ſolid . Modo . XX . ſol.
Ipſa abbatia ten DERLAVESTONE . 7 duo hões de ea . Ibi . III.
virg træ . Tra . ē . II . car . Ibi ſunt . II . uilli
Ibi . VI . ac pti . Silua . II . qrent lḡ . 7 una qrent lat.
T.R.E. ualb . XXX . ſolid . 7 poſt . X . ſol . Modo . XXVII . ſol . 7 II . den.

19 *An extract from the entry for Burton Abbey in Domesday Book. Compiled from a nationwide audit carried out in 1086 to settle issues of land ownership and provide a basis for taxation, the survey records details of land held by the abbey in 18 manors across Staffordshire and Derbyshire.*

Domesday Book was compiled from a nationwide audit carried out in 1086 or shortly afterwards, designed to settle issues of land ownership and provide a basis for taxation against which there was no appeal. It records land owned by the abbey in 18 different manors ranging across Staffordshire and Derbyshire. In contrast to the comprehensive level of detail characteristic of Domesday Book for most counties, entries relating to Staffordshire are brief, incomplete and riddled with inconsistencies. One and a half hides listed under the holdings of Burton Abbey in Stafford should probably read in 'Staffordshire'. Reference to a castle belonging to Henry de Ferrers at Burton is almost certainly a mistake for his stronghold at Tutbury.

A small number of villagers are recorded on the abbey's local estates: nine at Burton, 12 at Stapenhill, eight at Stretton, six at Wetmore and 10 at Winshill. In addition to five villagers, Branston also has three smallholders.

Villagers, who made up the bulk of the population, held land, commonly around thirty acres, in return for working one or two days each week on the abbey estates and contributing produce and other services. According to Abbot John of Stafford, speaking after a dispute over the duties owed, villagers possessed 'nothing but their bodies and their stomachs', a contemptuous put down to any

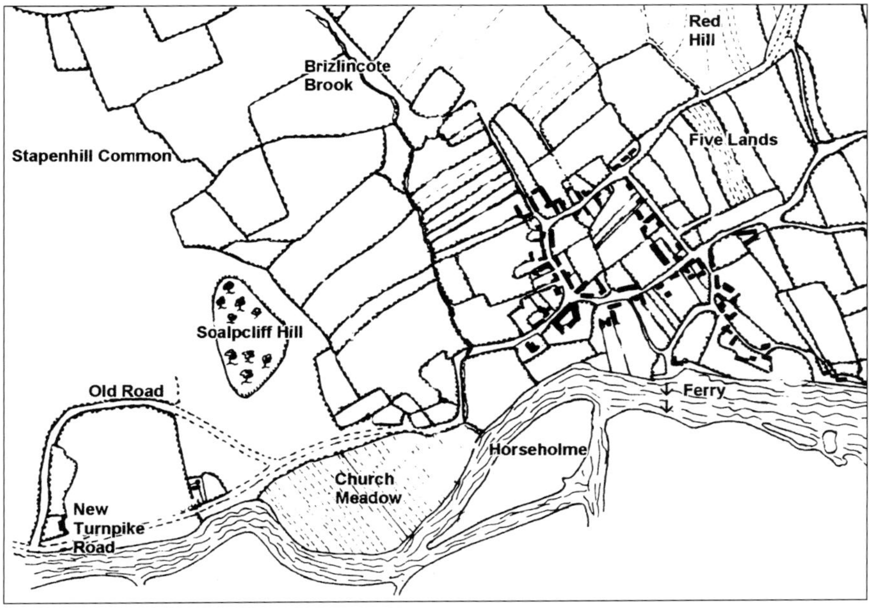

20 *Stapenhill c.1757 redrawn from a map by William Wyatt, steward to the Earl of Uxbridge. Stapenhill and its church were acquired by Burton Abbey from Edward the Confessor, lost along with other property after the Norman Conquest, and regained in 1190.*

member of the peasantry daring to think for themselves and a learned allusion to the Rule of St Benedict which emphasised the difference in status of a monk who at God's disposition possessed 'their body and will'. At certain times of the year tenants were expected to graze their livestock on the abbey's fields so that even the droppings of their animals became the abbots' property as fertiliser. Smallholders had similar obligations to villeins but tenanted smaller plots, sufficient perhaps to pasture an ox that they might be expected to contribute to a communal plough team or provide to haul a waggon.

Sixty plough teams worked the abbey lands. Each team had up to 16 oxen yoked in pairs and ploughmen worked with an assistant to guide the lead animals.

Domesday Book's snapshot describes a feudal rural economy at its most basic. Internal abbey surveys conducted on his appointment by Abbot Geoffrey (1114-50) just a generation later reveal a much more complex economic structure. The number of freemen shown on the abbey estates had increased from five to thirty-three. A new class of *censarii* appear, rent-paying tenants owing only irregular service to the abbot (duties such as mending fences or the seasonal loan of a plough) but committed by sworn oath to defend the abbey

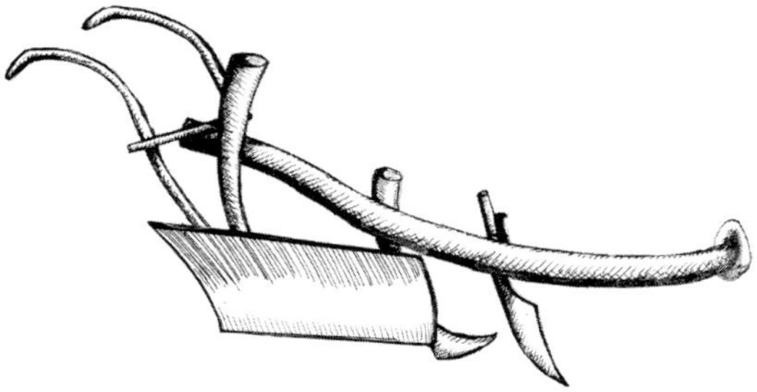

21 *Sixty plough teams were employed on the abbey lands in the 11th century. More and more land was brought into productive use in succeeding centuries. Teams of up to 16 oxen pulled simple ploughs. A beam of weathered ash fitted with a coulter, share and mouldboard cut vertically and horizontally before turning the earth.*

22 *Wulfric Spot's endowment of the abbey included a corn mill beside the River Trent. Newton Road Mill, wrapped around the ghost of the Saxon mill, was still using water power to grind flour when it closed in 1991 and became the subject of a protracted wrangle between conservationists and prospective developers.*

23 *When Modwen died near Dundee witnesses claimed to have seen her soul carried to heaven by a pair of swans. Her body was brought to Burton for burial at the church she founded on Andresey.*

and its property. For a lord of the manor committed by religious vocation to a life of peace and goodwill it made practical sense to build up a network of loyal supporters as a counterbalance to predatory and ambitious baronial neighbours. A population of 50 villagers listed in Burton and the immediate district when Domesday Book was compiled remained unchanged at the time of the abbey surveys. But in addition there are at least 70 *censarii,* 20 *bovarii* (ploughmen or oxherds) and 38 *cotseti* (cottage tenants). Some of the *censarii* have significant land holdings, others combine cultivating small plots with jobs as labourers, abbey servants (grooms, cooks, etc.) and craftspeople (dyers, tanners, bakers, carpenters, tailors, masons and shoemakers for example).

Wulfric Spot's endowment of the abbey included a corn mill beside the River Trent at Winshill. A horizontal wheel, simply geared to turn a grindstone set on an upper storey via an upright drive shaft, would probably have supplied the power. Three local mills owned by the abbey in the Domesday audit have become six by the 12th-century surveys. In addition to the mill at Winshill there is now one at Stapenhill, two in Burton itself and two in Stretton. Lepsi the miller pays the sum of 50s., grinds the abbey corn for free and hands over the fish caught at the weirs in return for a four-year rental of two mills. Mills were an important source of revenue. All tenants were required to take their grain to one of the abbey mills for grinding, a percentage of the yield being retained by the miller.

Kinship was important. Being well connected enhanced your prospects. Abbot Geoffrey leased land at Branston to his nephew Herbert in one of many deals made over the years by abbey officials whose relatives benefited from vows of poverty and celibacy that precluded direct heirs. Abbots Geoffrey Mauland (1085-94) and Robert (1150-9) were both dismissed for irregularities involving land belonging to the abbey.

The extent of the abbey's land holdings made boundary disputes and neighbourly tension unavoidable. Henry I was forced to intervene in a long-running argument between the abbey and Robert de Ferrers over rights of pannage in part of Needwood Forest. Matters escalated when Osmund, a forester in the service of de Ferrers, rounded up and slaughtered pigs from the monastery found foraging in the disputed area. The Bishop of Chester and William Peveril were sent to knock heads together. Under pressure to compromise, de Ferrers agreed to pay rent to the abbey for the woodland in question, but to allow the abbey to collect firewood and be a 'friend and guardian' of the monks in return for their prayers.

When two peasant tenants of the abbey defected to Roger the Poitevin at Drakelow, Abbot Geoffrey Mauland ordered the confiscation of the runaways' meagre grain stores and demanded the return of his tenants. Roger defied the abbot's request and sent a force of armed men to raid the abbey's granary in retaliation. A bitter feud ensued during which the monks resorted to extreme measures. St Modwen's holy relics were taken from the altar in the shrine behind the choir of the abbey church, and ritually 'humiliated' by being placed on the floor, while the monks wailed lamentations in a bid to alert their patron to the seriousness of the problem. Shortly afterwards Drakelow was abandoned after ghostly visions were reported and the village was struck by disease.

24 *A seal was used to authenticate official abbey documents. The earliest surviving seal dates from the time of Abbot Geoffrey (1114-50) and shows the abbey church from the west with towers either side of the entrance and a large central tower at the crossing. The almond shape is typical of medieval seals.*

The cult that had grown up around the legend of St Modwen attracted pilgrims in search of healing and divine intercession. King William himself had knelt before the holy relics at Burton. Shrines were big business, attracting prestige and generating income. Those who came to pray brought offerings. Stories of miraculous events, of which the colourful episode at Drakelow was one among many, added to a shrine's reputation.

Not long after his involvement in the affair of the abbey's pigs, Osmund the forester was found guilty of an unrelated criminal incident and sentenced to be blinded. Abbot Geoffrey was quick to claim the punishment on behalf of St Modwen, declaring it the result of divine intervention. Geoffrey's account also includes a premonitory visit by St Modwen in which she appears to Osmund in a dream and warns him of his fate. The abbot's promotional spin was not a totally cynical ploy. Religious belief in medieval England was no abstract concept but a reality and the hand of God a constant physical presence in everyday affairs.

As lord of the manor the abbot exercised considerable judicial power. He, or his representative, presided over local courts. Henry I, youngest son of William the Conqueror, confirmed the extent of the abbots' legal authority, including the right to hang thieves, in a grant to Abbot Geoffrey (1114-50). Although the more serious cases were referred to the Shire or Hundred Court, where guilt was deemed indisputable, the abbot had the power to invoke the ultimate penalty. Three sets of gallows – on the approaches to the town at Branston, at Derby Turn and east of the main river crossing on the border of Stapenhill and Winshill – awaited those convicted.

A Court Leet met at Easter and Michaelmas (29 September) to enact by-laws, elect officials and deal with manor business. Attendance was compulsory for all tenants aged between 12 and 60 years of age, who were required to renew formally their oaths of allegiance to the abbot. Business took all day and food was provided. Early meetings were probably held in the chapter house. By the end of

25 *Stone from the medieval bridge (demolished in 1876) was used to build features along the riverside walk and in the municipal gardens at Stapenhill.*

26 *Fragments of the medieval 'Great Bridge' survive beneath Meadow Road.*

the 12th century, when Abbot Nicholas was catering for a hundred people, the nave of the abbey church is likely to have been the only building large enough to cope. The Court Baron took place at the same time and dealt with civil matters such as feudal services owed by tenants, probate, debts, claims for damages and property transactions. A Manor Court met at three-weekly intervals on a Saturday to deal with criminal offences. At the Assizes of Bread and Beer a fine, public shaming in the stocks or a whipping at the pillory might be ordered for minor transgressions such as selling underweight loaves or disturbing the peace.

With a new main road leading past the abbey gates, a more convenient crossing of the River Trent than the several fords that allowed access at various points was essential to the establishment of an influential religious centre and a viable settlement. Stone footings for the 'Great Bridge' of Burton were probably laid soon after the founding of the abbey. Eventually, 36 arches carried a 5m. wide causeway for 500m. across three separate arms of the river. Approaching Winshill, a gently curving line was introduced following a natural bend along the Derbyshire bank and across the Trundle Hole, a lagoon-like inlet that silted up completely in the 19th century. Stone for the

27 *A ferry across the River Trent was probably operating in the 13th century, when William 'the shipman' was recorded living at Stapenhill. A regular service continued until the Ferry Bridge opened in 1889.*

28 *A sculpture above the main entrance to the Market Hall (built in 1883) commemorates King John's grant, during a visit to the abbey in 1200, of the right to hold a weekly market and annual fair.*

bridge was brought from a quarry downstream between Winshill and Newton Solney.

A watercourse, known as the 'Silver Way' in more modern times, was dug to provide a direct link from the main arm of the River Trent to the smaller channel of the Fleet and increase the water supply to the abbey. A ferryboat was probably operating between the Derbyshire and Staffordshire banks at Stapenhill. William 'the shipman' is recorded living at Stapenhill in 13th-century records.

Travel was a hazardous business. Kings, bishops, abbots and other dignitaries only took to the road with large retinues. When Cardinal Nicholas, legate of Pope Innocent III, arrived at Burton Abbey in 1213 (part of a tour of inspection after King John agreed terms with the Pope to end almost six years of excommunication), around fifty mounted men were in attendance. For safety, traders and merchants looked for fellow company on journeys. Road surfaces were poor, progress slow, hospitality uncertain and robbery with violence a constant threat. A cross at the east end of the bridge reminded travellers of the advisability of prayer. One of the earliest bridge chapels in England, dedicated to St James, was strategically placed to pull in passing traffic. It dispensed food, comfort and spiritual care in return for alms for those keen to receive the reassurance of an official blessing for their journey. The money collected helped pay for the upkeep of the bridge, a responsibility that fell to the abbey. A bridge keeper holding land at Winshill in return for his duties appears in the monastic records of the early 12th century.

In order to grow, Burton needed to attract business. Trading was restricted to boroughs, places with an officially supervised market where activities were strictly supervised. Reeves or bailiffs collected tolls and taxes, enforced weights and measures standards and checked the quality of goods offered for sale. At the time of the Norman Conquest, Stafford, Tamworth and Tutbury were the only boroughs in the county. At Tutbury 'in the borough around the castle are 42 men who live only by their trading' recorded the Domesday Book clerk.

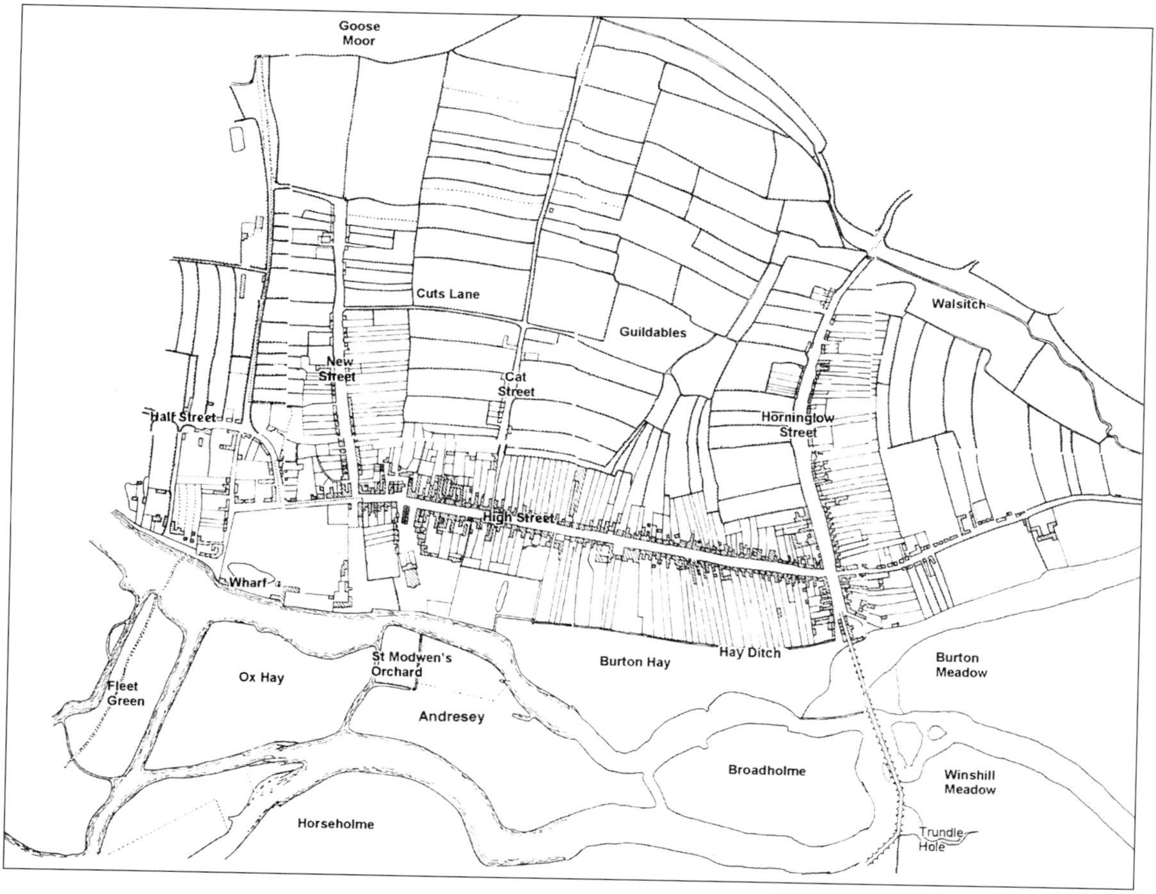

29 *Map redrawn from the earliest large-scale map of the town by William Wyatt, steward to the Earl of Uxbridge c.1760. It shows burgage strips surviving from the first 'street of new buildings' or 'Newbuggyng' (Horninglow Street) and subsequent expansion of the borough.*

30 *Market c.1920. Brisk business in the open-air market.*

References to Burton as a borough first appear in a 12th-century charter of Henry I confirming various rights of the abbots of Burton. Abbot Nicholas (1187-97) created the first burgage plots. It was not until 1200 that formal licence to establish a borough, linked to the right to hold a weekly market and an annual three-day fair to celebrate the feast of St Modwen, was conferred by King John while he was a guest at the abbey. Abbot William Melburne was quick to exploit his new authority. Burgage plots, narrow parcels of land 24 perches long and four perches wide (approximately 120m. by 20m.) with a narrow frontage facing the road, were laid out in 'Newbuggyng', a 'street of new buildings'. The area for development stretched for approximately 700m. from the Great Bridge to a new bridge across the Walsitch. Plots were available at a fixed rent of 12d. a year for use as locations for the workshops and tenements of traders. Freedom from feudal obligations, tax breaks and the right, subject to some restrictions (for example, the buyer had to be a Burtonian and a Christian), to sell the property or pass it on to heirs, was a valuable privilege, providing further incentive for small business enterprises.

The difficulties and dangers associated with moving goods around restricted the catchment area of a market to those places that could be reached, business transacted and the return journey completed in daylight. In 1222, Abbot Richard de Lisle (1122-9) obtained royal licence to create a borough at Abbots Bromley, followed five years later by permission for a market and fair there, without fear of the competition having any noticeable impact on trade at Burton.

The foundations for growth and township were laid. But wealth and prosperity would not be easily won.

THREE

Growth of the Borough:
Fire, Flood and Feud

Life is precarious in 13th-century Burton. For most, it is squalid. Hard labour and unremitting toil take their toll. Disease is endemic. Disasters, both natural and unnatural, are never far away. Fire sweeps through the town in 1254 followed by flood as the River Trent bursts its banks. Persistent heavy rain again leads to flooding in the early 1280s. Bad management, manorial responsibilities and a series of property disputes involving costly litigation leave the abbey teetering on the verge of insolvency

In 1256, the sheriffs of Derbyshire and Staffordshire held a joint inquiry aimed at resolving responsibility for maintenance of the bridge at Egginton where the old Roman Ryknield Street crossed the River Dove. A bridge of some description, possibly a timber structure on Roman foundations, appears to have been in poor condition and may have been damaged beyond repair by recent flood-water. The sheriffs failed to reach a conclusion but shortly afterwards building began of a new stone bridge. Known as Monk's Bridge, it has been attributed to John of Stafford, Abbot of Burton Abbey from 1260-81 but at the time serving as prior. The abbey itself was in no position to fund such a major capital project and John may have diverted an inheritance. William of Stafford, probably John's father who owned land at Stretton and Egginton, had been a benefactor of the abbey. Monastic vows would have prevented John from accepting any money left in his father's will directly. A bridge would have been a permanent memorial. Bequests to the Church were common. In return, prayers were offered for the soul of the donor. Religious conviction ran deep: purgatory, graphically and horribly depicted in medieval church wall paintings, was a certain expectation after death. Belief that the prayers of the living eased the passage of the soul made putting preparatory arrangements in place a prudent and responsible act of personal insurance.

Since it was first built, Monk's Bridge has been widened and heavily restored. Most of the current structure dates from the end of the 18th century. Viewed from below, three of the four arches show their medieval origins. Three ribs distributing weight evenly across the semi-circular barrel vaults are typical of 12th-century church architecture, where their use had been pioneered. A wooden framework would have been necessary to support the arches until each stone was in place. The

31 *The building of Monk's Bridge across the River Dove at Egginton is attributed to John of Stafford, monk and prior of Burton Abbey before being elected abbot in 1260.*

outer ribs are decoratively chamfered, useful inside a building to admit additional light but an aesthetic indulgence beneath a bridge. A master mason as designer, architect and project manager clearly took pride in building Monk's Bridge.

Upkeep of bridges was a costly business. If Burton Abbey seems to have accepted an early responsibility for maintaining the Great Bridge at Burton, attempts were later made to share liability with the townspeople. After flood damage in 1284, John of Norfolk, referred to as a monk but most probably from an order of a lay hermits (a hermitage once stood opposite St James's Chapel), was granted the king's protection to appeal for funds to pay for repairs to be carried out. A century later a group of trustees successfully applied for a grant of pontage (the right to charge a toll) in order to help defray the expense of maintenance. A bridge 'monk', presumably the bridge keeper, is mentioned in records for 1396 but by 1441 a layman holds the post.

Early in the 14th century, Burton found itself at the centre of a national power struggle. Thomas, Earl of Lancaster dominated the political landscape. When Edward II attempted to reassert his authority there was rebellion. In February 1322, both sides began to raise armed support. Lancaster retreated to Burton, destroying a bridge across the River Trent at Wychnor and digging in behind a barricade blocking the approach to the Great Bridge while he waited for reinforcements. The Earl held a powerful position. The river was in flood, the next nearest crossing was a day's march away, and he had a direct supply line to his castle stronghold at Tutbury. An attack by an advance troop of the royal forces was repulsed on 5 March. Edward himself arrived at the scene of the stand-off five days later. The key to unlocking the stalemate was a little local knowledge. The King was shown a ford at Walton. Robert Waters, one of Edward's commanders, kept the Earl's forces occupied with a contingent of archers while the King led his main force through the shallow crossing unobserved. Taken by surprise, Lancaster and his troops retreated to Tutbury leaving Burton ablaze. Discovering his expected reinforcements had defected, Thomas abandoned the castle and continued north with King Edward's levies in close pursuit. The two sides faced each other again at Boroughbridge in Yorkshire on 16 March. In a decisive battle, the rebels were defeated. After a summary trial, Thomas of Lancaster was sentenced to death and beheaded.

The Earl of Lancaster was an enormously wealthy man. His flight and capture triggered a looting spree. Over a hundred cases stemming directly from the breakdown of law and order in the aftermath of the Battle of Burton Bridge were outstanding when the king's justices arrived the following year.

One of the accused was Abbot William Bromley (1316-29). Thomas of Lancaster had probably lodged at the abbey during the siege. The abbot denied a charge of appropriating silverware belonging to the Earl but was found guilty and fined £300. With hard times and the abbey in deep financial trouble the temptation was probably just too great. Given a further opportunity to come clean, William Bromley confessed that he and other monks had indeed held on to some of the Earl's belongings. A lenient view was taken. Abbot Bromley received a full pardon and by way of compensation for the depredations suffered by the town was granted the right

32 *Much of the present structure of Monk's Bridge dates from the 18th century when it was widened and heavily restored. Viewed from beneath, three of the four arches show where widening took place in 1775. The medieval masonry is of high quality. Chamfered ribs were first used in 12th-century church architecture to distribute weight equally across a vault.*

33 *After being driven from Burton by Edward II the rebel Thomas, Earl of Lancaster was captured and beheaded. This painting of the execution, completed shortly after the event, is in the church of St Peter ad Vincula, South Newington, Oxfordshire.*

to appoint clergy to posts at Tatenhill and Hanbury churches.

Details of cases heard by the courts give an insight into the lavishness of the Earl's lifestyle. In addition to gold, jewels and livestock, the goods allegedly stolen included silver saltcellars and candelabra, barrels of sturgeon, saffron, carpets, curtains, robes, and rolls of rich fabric.

Many of Lancaster's Staffordshire and Derbyshire knight-tenants who had fought at his side were fined, including John Mynors of Blakenhall, the man responsible for destroying the bridge at Wychnor. Others managed to postpone facing justice by volunteering for military service abroad. An extract from the Plea Rolls for Easter 1325 provides a typical example:

> The jury of the Hundred of Offlow had presented at Tutbury *Coram Rege* [before the king] that John de Leybourne, knight and many others were at the Bridge of Burton assisting the Earl of Lancaster against the King. The said John not appearing the sheriff had been ordered to produce him at Michaelmas, on which day the case was made a *remanet* [postponed], John having set out for the Duchy of Aquitaine in the King's service in the suite of John of Fulton and for which he had letters of protection for a year dated 17 June 1324.

In some instances, those accused managed to delay their arrest long enough to have the charges against them dropped when Edward II was overthrown in 1326.

At the time of the Battle of Burton Bridge the population of Burton was close to two thousand. Horninglow and Wetmore were still separate hamlets. Abbot John of Stafford extended the borough in 1273 from its beginnings in Newbuggyng (Horninglow Street) along part of the Broadway (High Street) and past the abbey gates. Burgage plots on the west side of High Street were bounded at the rear by the Hay Ditch, an artificial channel originally dug to feed fresh water to the abbey fish ponds.

Throughout the 13th century more and more land was brought into productive use but three consecutive wet summers ruined harvests across Europe and led to widespread famine in 1286. Perhaps as a socially inspired work creation scheme, Abbot Thomas Packington chose that year to enlarge the borough along Norreys Street (named after John le Norrey's house that stood on a corner). This was later called Cat Street before becoming Station Street.

An abbey rental survey of 1319 lists 303 burgages and a further 75 rented properties in a borough that now includes Cuts Lane (Union Street) and New Street. Some burgage strips have been subdivided into half, third or quarter plots.

Temporary stalls for the weekly market were set up in an open space just outside the abbey precinct between the market cross on the Broadway and the west door of the church. There was no physical boundary or town wall but the borough limits were clearly defined. 'Bond End', where many abbey servants or 'bondmen' lived, and other streets outside the township were known collectively as Burton Extra. Broadway was the one through road. Eight other central streets mentioned in the 1319 survey all culminated in footpaths leading out across moor and common land. One track, Butterwoman's Causeway (Casey Lane), the route from Outwoods regularly used to bring in produce destined for the market, was paved. In times of epidemic or flood when movement in the town centre was restricted the causeway may have provided an alternative market area. Apart from the further development of New Street in the latter part of the 14th century, the shape of the town changed little over the next five centuries.

Bubonic plague reached Europe in 1348 and spread rapidly. By summer it would have reached Burton. There was a recurrence in 1361 and further outbreaks in succeeding decades. London was worst hit but few places escaped. Half the population of England died. Prices rose. Destitute families turned to the Church for help.

An increase in the number of people clamouring at the abbey door for handouts put further pressure on the monastery coffers. A feudal system based on the availability of plentiful, cheap labour creaked under the strain. Skilled craftspeople were able to double and treble their prices. Even the poor wage labourer found himself in demand and able to negotiate for his services. The Statute of Labourers (1351) vainly attempted to reverse the laws of supply and demand. Under its regulations landowners were banned from competitively bidding up wages and the feudal obligations of peasants were reinforced. But it was both unpopular and unworkable and led to the Peasants' Revolt.

34 *Seal of John of Stafford, abbot of Burton Abbey from 1260-81.*

35 *Station Street, 1860. Station Street was first laid out in 1286 when Abbot Thomas Packington extended the borough and created Norrey's Street (after the house of John le Norrey that stood on the corner). It was soon known as Cat Street before becoming Station Street in the 19th century.*

No major uprising took place locally but there was an unprecedented challenging of authority. In 1367 some of the abbey tenants thumbed their noses at the abbot and refused to take their grain to be ground at the abbey mill. Millers were always suspected of sharp practice and the tenants were perfectly capable of grinding their own flour on hand querns. Ten villagers in Stretton refused to give up their time to help harvest the abbey's crops. It was the beginning of the end for the tyranny of feudalism.

If growth apparently stalled it did not mean life in Burton stood still. The crumbling of a feudal system that had kept everyone in their place and the labour shortages caused by the Black Death created opportunities. Social mobility was possible. Those with ambition, energy and drive found opportunities to prosper.

The beginnings of a more diverse economy appear as the 14th century progresses. On the abbey's estates sheep farming and wool production became economically important. Six granges were established locally by 1327. Shobnall Grange was under the direct management of the abbey (in 'demesne') with tenants in charge at Burton, Branston, Stretton, Stapenhill and Winshill. Surplus wool was exported as far as Florence. In 1343, a corn mill was converted for fulling, a process in which woollen fibres are soaked and pounded with water-powered hammers to produce felt cloth.

In an age of descriptive surnames Richard and John the 'Peyntours', a term associated with decorative alabaster work, appear in the abbey survey of 1319. Alabaster carving was already established in South Derbyshire at Chellaston. There were local quarries at Fauld and Tatenhill. Norman masons were responsible for the earliest known architectural use of alabaster when they incorporated it in an arch of the west doorway of St Mary's Church, Tutbury (*c.*1160). In later years Burton gained a reputation nationally for sculptural alabaster. Richard and John Peyntours may have been among the first local practitioners, possibly producing small statuettes of St Modwen for sale to pilgrims.

Beer was a dietary staple and considered a healthy option. Brewing was a cottage industry. The abbey had its own brewhouse and most households brewed their own ale. Some no doubt sold any surplus but the fame of Burton's beer was still in the future. John of March is recorded as a taverner in the abbey survey of 1319. The first written reference to an inn, the *Swan on the Hoop*, appears in a property deed of 1425. By 1498 the attractions of local hostelries were proving so irresistible that the Bishop of Lichfield and Coventry found it necessary to issue a formal ban on the monks of Burton frequenting them.

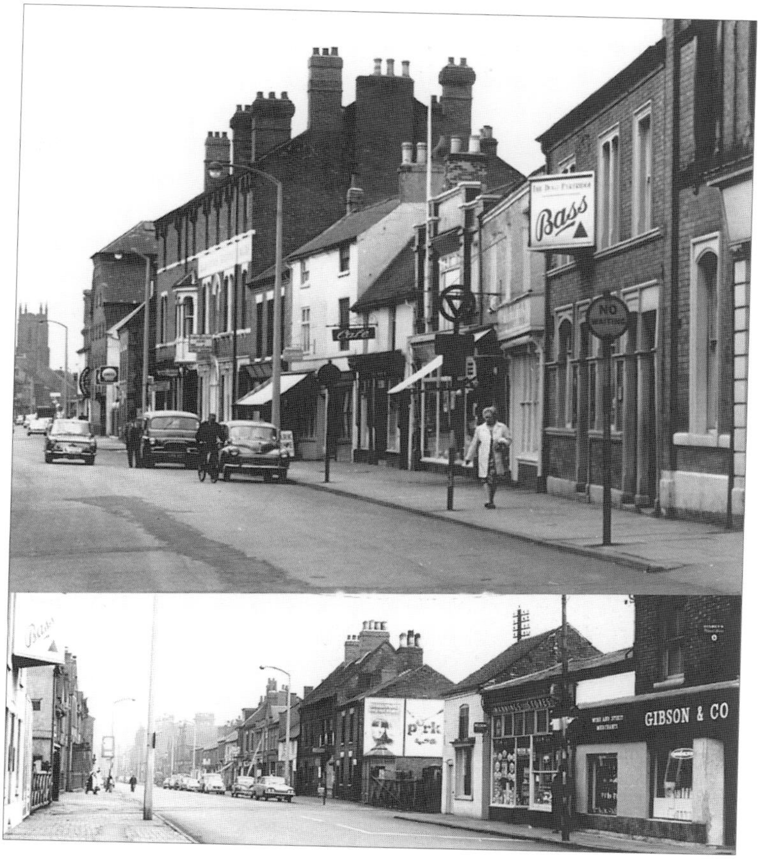

36 *New Street, 1962. New Street was developed as an extension of the borough in the latter half of the 14th century.*

37 *Shobnall Grange, one of six local farms belonging to Burton Abbey, was the only one directly managed by the monks and not by a tenant.*

38 *From the 14th century, alabaster was used to sculpt detailed monuments. Local quarries supplied a number of workshops in the town. The earliest known external use of alabaster architecturally is in the second arch of the west doorway of St Mary's Church, Tutbury, built c.1160.*

Renewal and rebuilding were a constant theme. As townspeople prospered, sophisticated box-framed houses of pit-sawn timbers infilled with a basketwork wattle and daubed with mud plaster began to replace crude hovels. Steep roofs were safely raised to two storeys or more using tie beams with central vertical crown posts and cross braces to stiffen the framework. Laying floor joists flat side down caused unacceptable instability and whippiness. Extending the beams out over the lower storey as a projecting jetty solved the problem. This had the added advantage of increasing room space upstairs and became an essential architectural feature of late-medieval timber-framed buildings. Narrow passageways led to courtyards at the rear of properties. Business was commonly transacted from a stall set up outside or on a counter lowered from a window.

Overhanging jetties often ran along adjoining sides of a building, mitred where they met at the corner by a bisecting 'dragon' beam supported on a 'teazle' post. An elaborately carved example known as 'Finney's post' was rescued when a house in High Street was demolished. According to legend, pallbearers were carrying Mrs Finney, a wife with a reputation for nagging, to her last resting place when the coffin accidentally knocked the teazle post, waking the poor woman who was merely comatose. A rhyme tells the story:

> This post, as Finney's legend saith,
> awoke a scolding wife from death;
> But when at last she ceased to breathe
> And honest Finney ceased to grieve
> 'Oh shun,' he said, as borne along
> With solemn dirge and funeral song,
> 'Oh shun that cruel stump
> That gave my dear so hard a bump.'

The abbey church served the whole community but the high altar and upper church were reserved exclusively for the monks. A separate parish altar with its own chaplain stood in the nave for use by the townspeople. Lay use of the nave was limited. Baptisms probably took place in a porch at the west doorway. Most marriages were recognised simply by mutual consent, with any religious ceremony limited to a nuptial mass if the service could be afforded.

In the absence of any significant evidence to the contrary we must assume relationships between the burgage holders and the abbey were generally good. No serious disputes are recorded despite the imposition of continual rent rises. Unlike the situation in most boroughs, the burgesses did not play a high-profile role in the administration of town affairs.

Matters were less cordial with neighbours. After his park at Abbots Bromley had been broken into and a number of deer taken, Abbot Thomas Southam (1366-1400) was bullied into increasing the payments requested by Sir John Bagot in return for his 'protection'.

In 1499, long-running problems with tenants from Barton, Tatenhill and Rolleston led to a court case. The tenants disputed Abbot William Flegh's authority to fence off Rough Hay, traditionally regarded as common pasture, and to charge tolls for livestock driven along Butterwoman's Causeway to Burton market. The court upheld the abbot's right to enclose the land but ruled the toll illegal.

39 *Projecting upper-storey jetties (a feature of late medieval timber-framed houses) running along adjacent sides of a building were mitred at the corner around a dragon beam supported on a decoratively carved teazle or corner post. 'Finney's post', rescued from a house in High Street, is made from an upside-down tree trunk.*

40 *The former Marketstede and Bank Square, demolished in the 1960s, was once at the commercial heart of the borough.*

In many boroughs local merchants formed guild associations. Their aims were partly economic, a business 'club' where useful contacts could be made and mutual interests protected, but they also pursued social objectives, encouraging education and carrying out charitable work. Importantly they had a religious purpose. Reference to a guild at Burton appears for the first time in a bequest of 1462. There are clues suggesting a much earlier foundation. In the mid-13th century, William 'at the Guildhouse' owned land at Branston. An area of pasture known as the 'Guildables' was named in a document of 1462. This and other land at Morrey near Yoxall appear to be two of several endowments made to provide the guild with an income and in order that prayers would be said for the soul of the benefactor. The abbey survey of 1319 records four priests in the town and there are 15th-century references to four guilds. It is likely that the priests were originally attached to monastic chantries, later taking on parochial responsibilities for different areas of the town under a guild association. Guild priests also led services in the bridge chapel.

Edward IV visited Burton in 1468 and granted an additional three-day fair to be held annually from 17-19 October to celebrate the feast day of St Luke. This may have been for the benefit of a guild. Guilds often had their own chapel within a parish church. A whole row existed at St Michael's in Coventry. A two-storey Guildhall built in the Market Place by Abbot Thomas Feld (1473-93) had a chapel dedicated to St Luke. Upstairs was a room where meetings and quarterly fund-raising dinners could take place. On the ground floor were 20 shops and a nearby row contained chambers for the guild priests.

41 *An incised, 14th-century coffin lid with a floriated cross from St Modwen's churchyard, possibly the sepulchral slab of a priest, is now in the south porch of the parish church.*

Medieval Burton may have seen the emergence of an identifiable business community and an increasingly independent urban middle class, but real power and influence still lay with the abbey.

FOUR

The Benedictine Abbey of St Mary and St Modwen

The Abbey of St Benedict and All Saints occupies 14 acres of land beside an arm of the River Trent known as the Fleet. Wooden buildings are soon replaced by more substantial structures of locally quarried red sandstone. In Domesday Book, the dedication is recorded as St Mary's. St Modwen's name has been added by the beginning of the 12th century. A representation of the saint appears on the abbey seal during the time of Abbot Nicholas (1187-97).

St Benedict of Monte Cassino wrote his *Little Rule for Beginners* in the early part of the sixth century. In it he set out a code for living a communal religious life that formed the basis of western monasticism. It was introduced to England by St Augustine, the founder of Canterbury Cathedral, on his mission of conversion in 597. Benedict advocated dividing the day into discrete periods devoted to prayer, study ('sacred reading') and work, declaring idleness 'the enemy of the soul'.

By the time Burton Abbey was founded the manual labour element had largely disappeared. Life for the brothers was structured around eight religious services, beginning at 1 a.m. in winter or 2 a.m. in summer with Vigils. Other services (Lauds, Matins, etc.) were observed at regular intervals throughout the day and ended with Compline at either 6 p.m. or 7 p.m. according to the season, followed by a light supper and bed.

St Benedict's Rule was an austere discipline. Monks took vows of poverty and celibacy. Personal possessions were banned. Talking was discouraged ('at all times monks ought to strive to keep silence'). Guests were 'to be welcomed like Christ', a commitment to hospitality that frequently placed a strain on resources.

The layout of the monastery buildings followed a typical pattern. Guest accommodation, dining hall, kitchen, monks' dormitory and chapter house surrounded a cloister from which two doors, one at each end of the north range, gave direct access to the church. Tradition holds that Wulfric Spot was buried beneath the door to the upper church and his wife Aelswitha beneath the door to the lower church. Other buildings – for example stables, granary, barns, brewhouse and infirmary – were set outside the immediate claustral precinct. Next to the infirmary was a chapel. Ministering to spiritual needs was considered as important

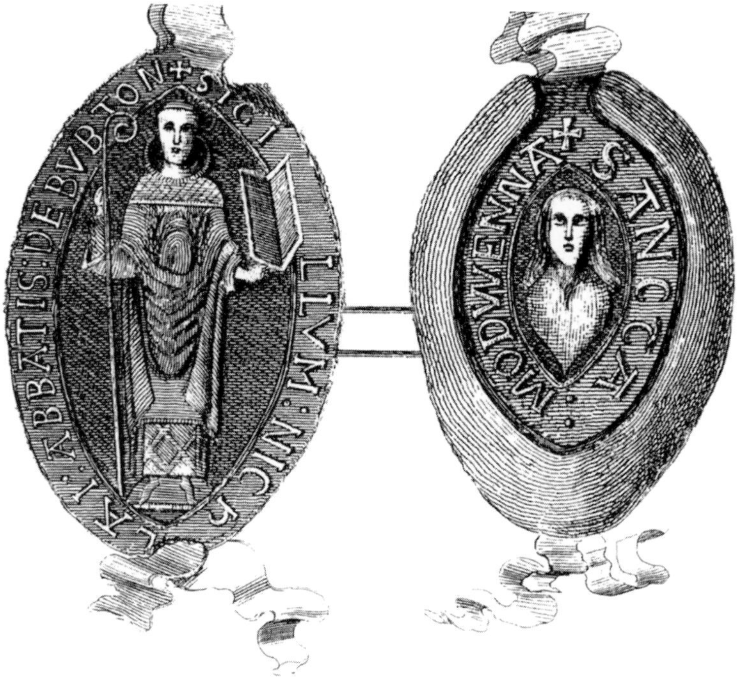

42 *The shrines of saints attracted pilgrims in search of spiritual or material help through divine intercession. St Modwen's reputation grew steadily during the 12th century and Abbot Nicholas (1187-97) incorporated her image on the reverse of his seal.*

43 *Remnants of the abbey at the rear of the Market Hall include elaborately carved stone door jambs. This was once the entrance into the chapter house from the east cloister, rebuilt in the 14th century under Abbot Robert Longdon and his successor Robert Brickhill.*

for an individual's welfare as any medical care they might need.

North and east wings of the cloister were reserved exclusively for the monks. Here small desks were set up in stone recesses for work and study. A door from the eastern arm led into the chapter house. Running alongside the eastern range was the monks' dormitory. Single cells were set either side of a central passageway. At the north end of the range, stairs led into the church for use when attending night services. At the opposite end of the dormitory were toilet facilities beneath which a drainage channel flushed waste back into the river.

Meetings were held in the chapter house at 9 a.m. each day. Here the monks gathered to deal with the day-to-day administrative business of running the abbey and to hear a reading from the works of St Benedict.

Monasteries were bureaucratic institutions. At the head of the organisation was the abbot, usually nominated by the monks of the chapter, a powerful position of considerable status. The abbot and chapter were subject to a degree of supervision including 'visitations', a kind of annual audit conducted by the Bishop of Lichfield and Coventry, but by definition in the 'peculiars' of Burton, Abbots Bromley and Mickleover they enjoyed privileges free of episcopal intervention. In the time of Edward I, and in the early years of Edward II's reign when Thomas, Earl of Lancaster held the strings of state, the abbot of Burton was frequently invited to attend Parliament or sit on national commissions. The abbot's personal seal, embossed in beeswax and attached by strips of cloth or parchment, authenticated official documents.

When it came to domestic affairs the abbot was supposed to make decisions in consultation with his fellow monks of the chapter. This did not always take place. In 1306, the prior (the abbot's deputy with responsibility for spiritual affairs) took the opportunity of a newly elected abbot, John of Burton (1305-12), to present a list of regulations drawn up by the chapter aimed at ensuring more constitutional decision-making and better financial accounting procedures.

Democracy in the community was subject to erosion. At first all the monks shared the same simple lifestyle. By the close of the 13th century, the abbot had his own apartments and kitchen and a house for the almoner had been provided. Other senior officers were soon maintaining separate accommodation. A house near the abbey gate was reserved for the chamberlain, who looked after the organisation of the abbot's household. Senior monks had first sitting at table. Novices and more lowly members of the community were only allowed leftovers.

Abbeys were centres of learning. Seventy-eight manuscripts are listed in the abbey library by the late 12th century. The *Annals of Burton*, written by the monks, provide a commentary on local and national affairs spanning a period from foundation to 1262 and amount to a considerable scholarly accomplishment.

The almoner combined responsibility for distributing food to the poor with running a school where the sons of well-to-do gentry were sent to be educated. Boys sang in the choir and assisted at private masses. A *custos puerorum* or warden of the boys is mentioned in the abbey records for 1390.

Visiting dignitaries expected the abbot to entertain them personally. In order to do so in style, Abbot William Bromley (1316-29) built a 'great hall by the water of the Flete', most probably next to the infirmary chapel.

ABBOTS OF BURTON ABBEY

Wulfgeat	*c.*1004 - 1026	monk (Winchester)	died
Brihtric	1027 - 1050	monk (Winchester)	died
Leofric	*c.*1051 - 1066	monk (Winchester)	died
Brihtric	*c.*1066 - 1085	abbot (Malmesbury)	died
Geoffrey Mauland	1085 - 1094	prior (Winchester)	expelled
Niel	1094 - 1114	sacrist (Winchester)	died
Geoffrey	1114 - 1150	prior (Winchester)	resigned
Robert*	1150 - 1159	monk (Winchester)	expelled
Bernard	1160 - 1174/5	abbot (of Cerne)	died
Robert (*reinstated)	1176 - 1176/7	abbot	died
Roger Malebranche	1177 - 1182	prior (Great Malvern)	died
Richard	1182 - 1187	prior (Rochester)	died
Nicholas	1187 - 1197	prior (Abingdon)	died
William Melburne	1200 - 1213	monk (Reading)	died
Roger the Norman	1214 - 1216	prior (Winchester)	died
Nicholas of Wallingford	1216 - 1222	prior	died
Richard de Lisle	1222 - 1229	prior (Bury St Edmunds)	elected abbot of Bury St Edmunds
Laurence	1229 - 1260	kitchener	died
John of Stafford	1260 - 1281	prior	resigned
Thomas Packington	1281 - 1305	prior	died
John of Burton	1305 - 1316	prior	died
William Bromley	1316 - 1329	cellarer	died
Robert Longdon	1329 - 1340	prior (Tutbury)	died
Robert Brickhill	1340 - 1347	cellarer (prior?)	died
John Ibstock	1347 - 1366	almoner	died
Thomas Southam	1366 - 1400	abbot's chaplain	resigned
John Sudbury	1400 - 1424	sacrist	resigned
William Mathew	1424 - 1430	almoner	resigned
Robert Ownesby	1430 - 1433	monk (St Albans)	resigned
Ralph Henley	1433 - 1455	monk	resigned
William Bronston	1455 - 1473	cellarer	died
Thomas Feld	1473 - 1493	monk	died
William Flegh	1493 - 1502	kitchener	died
William Beyne	1502 - 1530/1	prior	died
William Boston	1531 - 1533	monk (Peterborough)	elected abbot of Westminster
William Edys	1533 - 1539	sub-prior	surrendered post on Dissolution

Previously at Burton Abbey unless otherwise stated

44 *The abbots of Burton Abbey were at the head of the most important monastic community in Staffordshire, with extensive administrative and secular responsibilities. As lord of the manor, the abbot or his representative presided over local courts and had the right to hang thieves.*

45 *Behind an 18th- and 19th-century façade a wing of the Manor on Abbey Green has an exceptionally high quality medieval roof that identifies it with the personal chambers and guest house added by Abbot John Ibstock (1347-66). Arched wind braces protect the roof from wind pressure on the gable end.*

Abbot John Ibstock (1347-66) added a guest house with rooms attached for his own use at the southern tip of the west cloister range.

The abbey had its own gardens, one near the abbey kitchen to the south of the main buildings and another north of the church. A wide range of fruit and vegetables as well as culinary and medicinal herbs were grown. Both gardens contained fishponds. Freshwater fish including bream, carp, pike and tench were 'farmed' for the table and in demand for religious fast days when meat was not allowed. Eels and other fish caught in traps at the weirs controlling the flow of water to the abbey mills were the property of the abbot. There was also a fishpond at Shobnall Grange. Pigeons, an important source of winter protein, were kept in dovecotes in the abbey gardens and at Shobnall.

The number of monks was never large, generally between fifteen and thirty. With abbey officials headed by the steward, bailiffs and abbey gatekeeper, domestic servants and a large number of lay people or confratres, who in return for gifts or endowments shared in abbey life, the total community was around three hundred and fifty.

In common with the rest of the monastic buildings, the church went through phases of restoration and remodelling. Extensive alterations begun by Abbot Niel (1094–1114) probably saw most of the Saxon building replaced in austere Norman style with thick walls of dressed stone filled with a rubble core and deeply recessed arched doorways. His successor, Abbot Geoffrey, added a tower over the central crossing. Richard de Lisle, previously a monk at Bury St Edmunds, built a chapel dedicated to St Edmund, Abbot Laurence (1229-60) added a Lady Chapel and Abbot Robert Longdon (1329–40) a chapel of the Confessors. By the middle of the 15th century, there was a bell tower at the corner of the lower church. In 1474 the central tower collapsed and had to be replaced.

At the east end of the church was the high altar. Other altars stood in side chapels and in the nave was the parochial altar of the Holy Cross.

An agreement between Abbot Ralph Henley and Sir Thomas Gresley in 1536 allowed lead pipes to be laid from an abbey well at Stapenhill across land owned by the Gresley family in order to provide the abbey with fresh drinking water.

A lack of hard evidence makes it difficult to construct a really accurate picture of Burton Abbey at any time during its five hundred years. At the Reformation many of the monastic buildings were already in a poor state of repair. The abbey church became the parish church but by 1600, and possibly much earlier, only the nave was in use. The eastern end of the church that once stretched almost to the river was in ruins and had been walled off at the chancel. All physical remains of the church vanished when it was demolished in 1718 and a replacement built. A drawing dated 1643, purporting to be by the 17th-century engraver Wenceslaus Hollar, has been exposed as a much later forgery probably based on Hereford Cathedral. A genuine Hollar illustration of 1661, used by William Dugdale in his *Monasticon Anglicanum*, provides clues but is something of a jigsaw puzzle with important pieces missing. Trees hide the west entrance and the crossing is absent, leaving the south transept disconnected. A ground plan of the abbey is reproduced in Stebbing Shaw's 1798 *The History and Antiquities of Staffordshire* but the measurements do not tally with either of two detailed inventories carried out after dissolution and appear to refer to somewhere else.

46 *Font, St Modwen's Church. The octagonal bowl, an immersion font of late medieval date, stands on a stem inscribed 1662 and with the initials of William Middleton (curate 1662-5), TH and TW (presumably churchwardens at the time).*

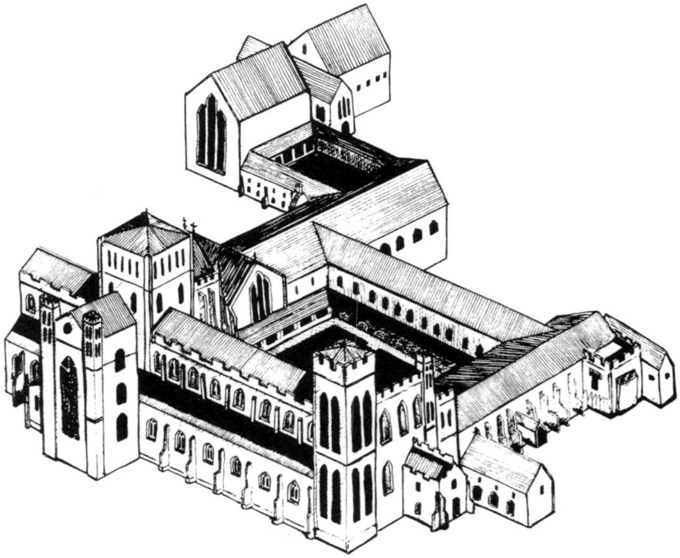

47 *All Benedictine abbeys followed a similar layout. This interpretation shows Burton Abbey as it may have looked in the late 14th century, with Abbot William Bromley's 'Great Hall' next to the infirmary linked by a cloister to the rest of the monastic complex. The abbey church was over 90m. long.*

Royal patronage was a mixed blessing. Although the abbey was not a royal foundation, a succession of rulers treated it as such and expected the abbey to provide a corrody, a kind of pensionable post, for a member of the royal household. Corrodies were also purchased by individuals as annuities, a way of making provision for security in old age or widowhood, and became an established part of monastic life. Burton seems to have pioneered the idea. Some of the earliest known corrodies in England occur in the abbey records of the early 12th century.

A close relationship between the abbey and the owners of the manor of Shobnall ('Scopenhal' in 12th-century deeds) led to a series of agreements by which land transferred to abbey ownership. In deeds dated 1247, members of the Shobnall family – Walter, son of Ralph, Hawise, daughter of Jordan and Eva, and Matthew of Shobnall – all gave land to the abbey in return for corrodies. In Walter's case the deal included his land and 'capital messuage'. In all likelihood these various grants of land added up to the 520 acres of Seyne Park containing the dwelling later known as 'Sinai Park House'. Walter of Shobnall was made keeper of the abbey gate, given a burgage in Burton (formerly belonging to Alan of Wetmore) and the same food, drink and clothes allowances of a monk plus meat from the abbots' kitchen and provisions for his groom. Welcoming guests to the abbey was an important position. Walter's appointment was for life and his position as gatekeeper hereditary, an arrangement that required renegotiating after three generations when Maud of Shobnall was widowed in 1295 with only an infant son, Ralph. A new arrangement was reached by which Maud and Ralph were provided for in return for giving up the family rights as guardians of the abbey gate. Close links with the family continued. In 1441, the abbey appointed William of Shobnall as bridge keeper.

Sinai Park House stands on a prominent ridge in a commanding position overlooking the Trent Valley. Reference to a 'place surrounded by a dyke' in Shobnall ('Shopenhale') Park is made in the time of Abbot William Bromley, in the early part of the 14th century. The site, surrounded by a rectangular moat, is typical of 13th-century manor houses. We may imagine the original house as a large communal hall, open to the roof with a central hearth from which smoke was left to find its own exit through thick thatch. At one end, a screened service area; at the other a raised dais for the high table with a private chamber behind. Once acquired by the abbey, the house was used as a retreat and convalescent home for the monks. Abbot William Bromley authorised five days' rest at Sinai after the monks had been subjected to bloodletting. This medieval therapy was believed to be preventative as well as curative. Even a monk in good health was bled by the abbey infirmarer, usually from the elbow, three or four times a year. Before the use of Sinai Park House as a sanatorium, bloodletting would have been followed by light duties at the abbey, permission to sit during services, extra rations and additional rest. Abbot John Ibstock extended the recuperation period to seven days.

Seyne Park is first mentioned by name in 1410 when the Bishop of Lichfield and Coventry writes to confirm his agreement to a request by Abbot John Sudbury for services to be held in the oratory, a small private room set aside for reading or prayer, at the manor there.

48 *The porter's lodge built on the foundations of the former abbey gatehouse was demolished in 1927. Welcoming guests to the abbey was an important job and the gatekeeper held one of the senior lay positions. The borough was extended along Broadway (High Street) and past the abbey gates in the 13th century.*

49 *Sinai Park House probably occupies the site of the 'capital messuage' given by Walter of Shobnall to the abbey in 1247. Used as a sanatorium by the monks, it was substantially rebuilt by Thomas Paget as a hunting lodge in 1572. Most of the current structure is 16th-century but the central hall range is on earlier foundations.*

Abbey income was derived from rents, market tolls, the profits from fairs, mills, fisheries, demesne farm produce and woodland, the shrine of St Modwen, tithes in cash and kind, endowments and gifts, and from trade, most notably in wool. There was no central accounting. Individual officials and discrete branches of abbey activity had their own direct revenue streams allocated from different sources. Lack of control and mismanagement led to a series of financial crises. Papal intervention was necessary when 12th-century changes in rental practice backfired. Instead of the customary lease of property for a term of two lives, a number of fixed rate open-ended agreements had been made, leaving the abbey out of pocket as land values rose.

Despite the richness of its assets, financial incompetence forced the abbey in and out of the hands of royal commissioners appointed at regular intervals throughout the 14th and 15th centuries.

Trouble was not limited to monetary affairs. Any picture of poor unworldly monks out of touch with the material world is far from reality. Religious standards began to be questioned in 1323. Under the rule of Abbot John Sudbury (1400-24), a noted academic and Bachelor of Canon Law who had risen through the ranks at Burton from monk to sacrist and prior before his election as abbot, the most incredible catalogue of misdemeanours is recorded. To be fair, Abbot Sudbury inherited a poverty-stricken institution. Abbey finances were so bad when Thomas Southam resigned that Henry IV remitted the standard £40 penalty levied for every month the post of abbot remained vacant. And even by the low standards of the 15th century, his was a particularly lawless time. In the first five years of Henry's rule the country was torn apart by rebellions led by Owen Glendower in Wales, Richard Scrope, the Archbishop of York, and Henry Percy, Earl of Northumberland. Perhaps a streak of ruthlessness was necessary for survival. Sir John Bagot of Abbots Bromley had harassed Sudbury's predecessor Thomas Southam, extorting what amounted to protection money. John Sudbury went on the offensive, forcefully repossessed land he believed rightfully belonged to the abbey and defied Bagot to take him to court.

Repeated allegations of sexual misconduct against Abbot John Sudbury included charges of adultery, entertaining women and, specifically, ravishing Margery Taverner in his chambers on Christmas Day. He was also accused at various times of rustling (20 cows belonging to John Hondesacre of Stapenhill), poaching (game from Needwood Forest), and assault (on Sir Thomas Gresley's chaplain). An example of John Sudbury's willingness to resort to robbery with violence occurred in 1404. The abbot was in charge of collecting tariffs on behalf of the king. A number of tenants from Stapenhill refused to pay. Sudbury simply waited until they came to trade at Burton market and took the outstanding sum by force.

Faced with the impossibility of sorting out a tangle of accusations and counter-claims and keen to ensure loyalty, Henry IV issued Sudbury with a royal pardon on 1 May 1412. The terms of amnesty were 'for all treasons, insurrections, rebellions, felonies, misprisions, offences, impeachments, transgressions and contempts', a fairly standard list for such documents, though no doubt in this case much was applicable. 'Murders and rapes of women' were not included in the pardon. National concern about civil strife is evidenced by the inclusion of a clause to the effect that the pardon is subject to the abbot behaving in future and not supporting 'Owin Glendourey of Wales or Thomas de Trumpyngton or other of the King's adversaries'.

Just three years later, Abbot John Sudbury was in need of another pardon, and this time murders, rapes and rebellion were included in the deal. Henry V was keen to wipe the slate clean on his accession and issued such pardons fairly liberally in an attempt to unite the country. His pardon was subject to its recipients not becoming involved in counterfeiting, one of the few crimes not to have tainted the abbot's reputation.

John Sudbury resigned in 1424. Under his rule essential church maintenance had been carried out and a new shrine built to house the remains of St Modwen. If his successors lacked the same aura of uncompromising toughness and energetic purpose they pursued his example in other ways. Abbot Ralph Henley received a general pardon from Henry VI in 1446. After the death of abbey servant William Cooper in 1448, Henley along with two monks, Thomas Norton and

50 *Fragments of sculpture rescued from the abbey have been incorporated in the remains of the east cloister at the rear of the Market Hall.*

51 *The Grammar School endowed by Abbot William Beyne c.1528 was demolished along with the master's house and replaced by new school buildings on the same Friars' Walk site in 1834.*

William Stapenhill, faced charges of accessory to murder. A second reprieve was sought and obtained. Persistent drinking, gambling and poor management led to Abbot Henley's suspension. The offer of a generous pension persuaded him to go quietly and he resigned in 1455.

Henry VI ordered the chapter to elect a replacement 'devoted to God' and 'useful and faithful to the realm'. They chose William Bronston but immorality continued. Prostitutes visited the abbey regularly. By 1465, another royal amnesty was necessary and was duly issued by Edward IV.

Matters improved marginally under Abbots Thomas Feld (1473-93) and William Flegh (1493-1502). But not until Abbot William Beyne (1502-30/1) were proper order and discipline restored. One of Abbot Beyne's achievements was to endow a grammar school. But by now it was too late. A rising class of businessmen and administrators increasingly resented the power of the Church. Owing allegiance to the Pope in Rome as well as to King and Realm raised questions of loyalty. Corruption ran deep. Change was on its way and the abbey that so dominated the area would soon be swept away.

FIVE

Dissolution of the Abbey:
Pagets, Parish and Protestantism

Burton Abbey's record of mismanagement, immorality and lax discipline is mirrored, in many cases exceeded, elsewhere. It provides moral justification for reform of the Church. There is further impetus for change when the Pope refuses to comply with Henry VIII's request for divorce from Catherine of Aragon. From 1525 the pace gathers, orchestrated by the King's right-hand man and chief minister, Thomas Cromwell. A series of politically influenced appointments, among them Roland Lee as Bishop of Lichfield and Coventry and William Boston elected Abbot of Burton in 1531, provide a network of support for Cromwell's proposed reforms within the Church. Boston is rewarded in 1533 when strings are pulled behind the scenes to secure his promotion to the abbacy of Westminster.

William Boston's replacement at Burton was William Edys. Not Cromwell's first choice as abbot but, nevertheless, a man sympathetic to his cause. Cromwell was an efficient fixer. A Royal Commission set up to investigate the monasteries uncovered plenty of evidence to confirm maladministration on an epic scale. Its findings helped steer a raft of legislation through Parliament that removed papal authority. In 1534 Henry was named Supreme Head of the Church in England. Anglicisation of the liturgy began. English versions of the Bible became available from 1535 and proved hugely popular.

In 1536, commissioners were despatched to put a value on every religious house in the country. Those with an annual income below £200 a year faced immediate closure under the Act of Dissolution. Tutbury Priory bought time by paying £100 for special licence to continue but bowed to the inevitable in 1538. Sir William Bassett of Meynell Langley, an ally of Cromwell whose brother Francis was a member of Cromwell's staff, leased the priory site.

In 1538 the abbey church became the parish church. Provision was made for a curate, priest, clerk and organist. Churchwardens took over responsibility for registering baptisms, marriages and deaths. The Bassett brothers were instructed to destroy the shrine of St Modwen. A statue of the saint, clearly an object of considerable value to warrant special attention but now an unacceptable idolatrous reminder of a discredited pre-Reformation Church, was dispatched to London on Cromwell's direct orders. It was never seen again.

The decision to surrender Burton Abbey and its possessions to the king's commissioners was formally taken in the chapter house on 14 November 1539. In its place a Collegiate Church of Christ and St Mary was constituted. In 1541, a rental lease for the abbey buildings was agreed with the Crown and William Edys was chosen as dean. Four former monks and some of the lay servants also took up posts at the college. Seven remaining monks and other staff were given pensions. Edys died in 1544 and was replaced as dean by Robert Brokke but the college was only to survive another year. Stipends, alms for the poor, pension liabilities and responsibility for road maintenance inherited from the abbey, together with running costs, proved an unmanageable burden. In 1545, the college was wound up. One of the canons, Robert Baslowe, replaced parish priest Bartholomew Kirkby as curate of the parish church. Other members of the college were awarded pensions, found alternative jobs or paid compensation. A former petty canon of the college, John Bradshaw, was the church organist in 1557 and had probably been given the post when the college was dissolved. Abbot William Beyne's endowment ensured the Grammar School survived, safe in the hands of trustees. Robert Harman, the schoolmaster when the college folded, was not on the list for recompense and presumably continued in post. In 1549, and probably from its inception, the school was in Church Lane, later known as Friars' Walk.

52 *Seal of the short-lived Collegiate Church of Christ and St Mary, formed in 1541 after the dissolution of the abbey and wound up in 1545.*

Despite its burden of debt, the commissioners' estimate of a gross annual revenue exceeding £500 had shown Burton to be the wealthiest abbey in Staffordshire by a big margin. It was a rich prize. In January 1546 it fell to Sir William Paget who took over as lord of the manor of Burton and lay rector of the parish church. The tithe income due to the parish church was probably sufficient to pay the stipends for the curate and a preacher (delivering a sermon was one of the new practices introduced by the Reformation). But with accommodation, clerical vestments, bread and wine for the sacrament, and copies of the new Book of Common Prayer to provide he would have been out of pocket on that particular deal.

John Paget, William's father, was probably born in Staffordshire. From humble beginnings he rose to the post of serjeant of the mace in London. Officiating at city ceremonies paid well enough to enable his son to study

John Paget

William (1st Baron Paget of Beaudesert) **m. Ann Preston**
(1505 – 1563)

Henry (2nd Baron) **m. Catherine Knevitt**
(d. 1568)

Thomas (3rd Baron) **m. Nazaret Newton**
(1543 – 1589)

William (4th Baron) **m. Lettice Knolleys**
(1572 – 1628)

William (5th Baron) **m. Frances Rich**
(1609 – 1678)

William (6th Baron) **m. Frances Pierrepont**
(1637 – 1713)

Henry m. Mary O'Rorke

Henry (7th Baron, 1st Earl of Uxbridge) **m. Mary Catesby**
(d.1749)

Thomas m. Mary Whitcombe

Thomas m. Elizabeth Egerton
(1689 – 1741)

Henry (8th Baron, 2nd Earl)
(1719 – 1769)

Sir Nicholas Bayly m. Caroline Paget
(1707 – 1782) (d. 1766)

Henry (9th Baron, Earl of Uxbridge) **m. Jane Champagné**
(1744 – 1812) (second creation)

Henry (1st Marquess of Anglesey) **m. 1 Caroline Villiers m. 2 Charlotte Wellesley**
(1768 – 1854)

Henry (2nd Marquess) **m. 1 Eleanora Campbell**
m. 2 Henrietta Bagot
m. 3 Ellen Burnand
(1797 - 1869)

Henry (3rd Marquess)
(1821 - 1880)

Henry (4th Marquess) **m. Blanche Curwen**
(1835 – 1898)

Alexander m. Hester Stapleton-Cotton

Henry (5th Marquess)
(1875 – 1905)

Charles (6th Marquess) **m. Marjorie Manners**
(1885 – 1947)

Henry (7th Marquess)
(b. 1922)

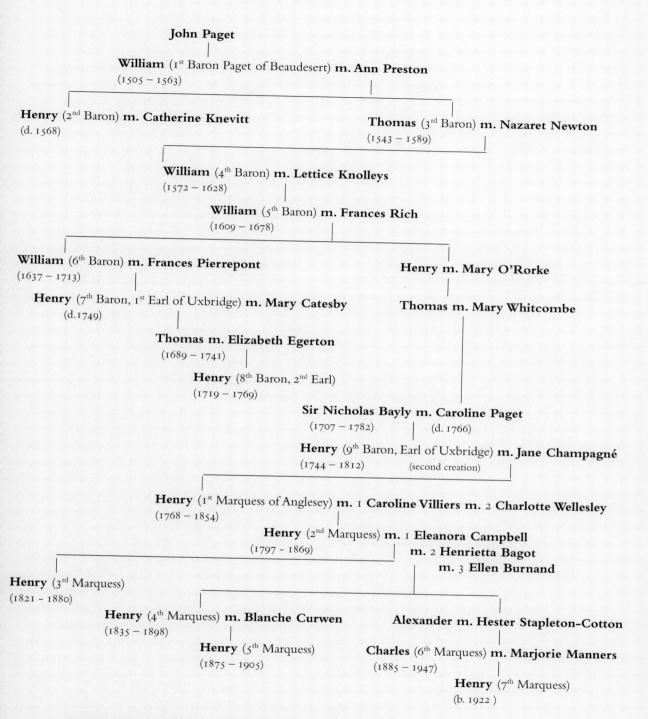

53 *Sir William Paget took over as lord of the manor of Burton in 1546. Three years later he was created Baron Paget of Beaudesert. After Henry (9th Baron and 2nd Earl of Uxbridge) died a bachelor, the titles passed to Henry, son of Caroline Paget and Sir Nicholas Bayly. The 10th Baron became Marquess of Anglesey in 1819.*

54 *A wintry scene on Stapenhill Road c.1910. Road maintenance was a parish responsibility from 1555 and all residents were expected to contribute. Many roads were in poor condition, particularly in the winter season when surfaces became deeply rutted and muddy.*

civil law at Cambridge. William was clever enough to take advantage. After graduating, employment by the Boleyn family brought him connections at court. He was soon in the king's service and rose rapidly to become a principal secretary of state and was named as an executor in Henry VIII's will. During the regency council of Edward VI headed by Edward Seymour, Duke of Somerset, Paget was made a Knight of the Garter and created Baron Paget of Beaudesert. When Somerset was toppled in 1551, Paget was caught up in the hotbed of suspicion and rivalry that was the Tudor court and imprisoned in the Tower of London. In his official duties Paget was a pragmatist, a man of straightforward expediency and certainly no conspirator. He was pardoned the following year and appointed Lord Privy Seal by Queen Mary. After the accession of Elizabeth I in 1558 he chose to retire from public life.

William Paget's position at court had left little time for him to put into practice any plans for the monastic precinct at Burton. Some conversion of the abbey buildings aimed at making it more suitable for residential use was underway, but it was Paget's agents who supervised the work. Sir William owned property elsewhere and had made Beaudesert House, near Longdon on

Cannock Chase, initially his main base in Staffordshire. In his retirement, Lord Paget had ambitious plans for remodelling the abbey buildings into a grand manor house with the cloister garth forming a central courtyard. He clearly intended it to be one of two main residences, perhaps dividing his time between Burton and his house at West Drayton, Middlesex, conveniently close to London and high society. The work never took place. In 1563, William Paget died and was succeeded by his eldest son Henry, who was followed in 1568 by his younger brother, Thomas.

Law enforcement, poor relief and the maintenance of roads and bridges was now in the hands of three main bodies. Paget's steward acted for the lord of the manor. The two-storey Guildhall or 'High Hall' served also as the 'Leet Hall' where Paget's steward presided over the manor courts. Two constables, six assistants (or 'deciners') and a pinder were appointed annually by the Manor Court.

The parish vestry, a body made up of ratepaying male parishioners presided over by the curate, elected churchwardens and other parish officials. Repair of the highways had been a parish responsibility from 1555. Under the supervision of a locally appointed surveyor, all residents were expected to contribute a few days' labour each year to the task or to pay for others to carry out work on their behalf. A committee of 'feoffees', drawn from the leading businessmen, emerged as representatives of the town. Legislation dissolving the chantries directly affected religious guilds from 1547 and it is likely that the feoffees were reconstituted from a disbanded Burton guild. The feoffees nominated two town masters each year whose duties included collecting tolls and rents and paying the wages of constables, pinder, town cryer and others employed on official town business. It was customary for the constables to become town masters after their 12 months in office, evidence of a close working relationship between the different agencies now jointly accountable for town affairs.

The feoffees were also trustees of the Town Lands, a portfolio of charitable property endowments originally linked to various

55 *Official town documents including property deeds and parish accounts were kept in the town coffer. Made of oak and bound with iron, it once had four separate locks. Four nominated feoffees each held a key and all had to be present when the chest was opened.*

monastic chantries. Deeds, documents and official accounts were kept by the feoffees in the town coffer, a massive oak chest with four separate locks. Eventually the coffer was transferred to the church, where as the parish chest it was also used to keep the parish registers (begun on 1 November 1538) and vestry book safe.

Law and order was a community responsibility. Constables could call on members of the public for support. Under a statute passed in 1275, citizens were bound by law to respond if a 'hue and cry' (the alarm raised to apprehend a suspected criminal) were declared. The parish records for 26 November 1698 show the constables claiming 2s. expenses after sending a hue and cry in pursuit of a thief who had stolen a grey mare at Hartshorne. Around ninety acres of common land in the town kept a pinder employed rounding up stray livestock and impounding them in one of two pinfolds sited in Pinfold Lane (later Park Street) and beside Little Common (an area of land where Hawkins Lane and Horninglow Street now meet).

Burton was a poor town. Dissolution of the monastery took away the main source of poor relief for those, perhaps as much as forty per cent of the population, who survived below subsistence level and were regularly in need. Four bedesmen lost their jobs as fundraisers when the college was wound up. Church support for the poor was limited by the amount that could be raised from levying a rate on parishioners and from voluntary subscriptions. To a large extent charity depended on individual philanthropy. Lord Paget distributed food and drink on religious feast days. Lady Elizabeth Paulet, a member of the prominent Burtonian family of Blount, left property in Clerkenwell and land at Fenny Bentley to pay for almshouses to be built in the Marketstede, a small square in the centre of town. Lady Elizabeth's most famous ancestor was Sir Walter Blount, the king's standard bearer at the Battle of Shrewsbury (1403). He and other members of the family held important official posts with the Duchy of Lancaster. The Blounts owned land in Burton and, from the 15th century until it was sold

CHARITABLE BEQUESTS FOR RELIEF OF THE POOR
(16th – 20th centuries)

Date	Benefactor	Endowment
1582	Richard Caldwall	Loans for needy clothworkers.
1593	Elizabeth Paulet	Almshouse and allowances for five women (Swine Market). Bread for 12 people weekly.
1614	William Ward	Loans for needy tradespeople.
1638	Ellen Parker	Almshouse and allowances for six women (High Street).
1642	John Birchenhead	Apprenticeships for poor boys.
1647	Thomas Goodinch	Loans for five young tradespeople.
c1665	Richard Steele	Money for the poor.
c1680	Alica Almond	Bread and money for the poor annually.
1689	William Finney	Apprenticeships for poor boys.
1703	Daniel Watson	Money for the poor.
c1703	Robert Watson	Money for the poor.
c1710	Richard Hogg	Shoes for eight poor people.
c1710	Widow Morris	Money for the poor.
1713	Isaac Hawkins	Maintenance for one man.
1724	William Hawkins	Bread for the poor.
1769	Joseph Robinson	Coats for six men: Money for 20 women.
1797	Elizabeth Wilkins	Legacy for the trustees of Ellen Parker's almshouses.
c1810	Joseph Mucklestone	Almshouse for four men (Cat Street).
1863	Elizabeth Johnson	Almshouse for six women (Hawkins Lane).
1864	William Phillips	Coal, clothes, meat and bread for the poor.

56 *Dissolution of the abbey took away the main source of poor relief and left charity largely to individual philanthropy.*

57 *Lady Elizabeth Paulet, a member of the Blount family of Nether Hall, left money in her will of 1593 to provide an almshouse for five 'poor women'. When Bank Square was bulldozed to make way for Cooper's Square Shopping Centre, the doorway with the Blount coat of arms above was repositioned at the High Street entrance to the new mall.*

in 1596, lived at Nether Hall, a manor house on Wetmore Road backing on to the river. Lady Paulet's almshouses accommodated five elderly unmarried ladies, usually widows, with provision for an annual allowance of cash and clothing. Each occupant had a single room on the ground floor and there was a communal room upstairs. Above the entrance a stone tablet bore the Blount family crest.

In 1521, William Wyggeston, a Leicester wool merchant operating in Calais, then an English possession, bought a house in Horninglow and 146 acres of surrounding land to add to his endowment of a hospital founded in his home town.

Poverty was a national issue. A series of Poor Laws were passed in response to worries about the potential threat posed to public order. For the first time a distinction was drawn between the sick, old and frail 'deserving' poor and the undeserving 'sturdy beggar'. In 1572, local taxes for poor relief became compulsory. An Act of 1601 consolidated all previous Poor Laws and put parishes in charge of administration. As a result, the vestry appointed two overseers and set a poor rate to be collected from the town's landowners and business people. Goods were seized if payment were not forthcoming. Both the vestry and the feoffees sought apprenticeships for pauper children. The economic case for such decisions is demonstrated by the following entries in the vestry book:

58 *A headstone bearing the Paget family crest was rescued when the old Town Hall was taken down in 1883 and mounted in the well of the Andresey footbridge. The motto* Per il suo contrario *translates as 'By means of its reverse'.*

59 *The former* Queens' Hotel *in Bridge Street reverted in 2004 to its former name of the* Three Queens. *The current building is late 18th-century but an inn was first licensed on the site in 1531. Mary, Queen of Scots, Elizabeth I, and Adelaide, Queen Consort of William IV are all reputed to have stayed here.*

> That 9d. weekly be deducted from Grace Warrington's pay upon her John being set out an apprentice. (14 June 1716)

Illegitimacy carried no great social stigma but bastardy bonds were imposed if the father could be traced. The vestry book orders:

> That the officers use their endeavours to trace the man that got Mary Coulson with child. (14 June 1716)

Adults considered able-bodied were required to carry out road maintenance or similar work of public benefit in return for receiving assistance.

Thomas Paget (3rd Baron) succeeded his older brother as lord of the manor in 1568. He enjoyed the arts. Touring singers and players were invited to perform for the household at Burton and a piper was employed to entertain the estate workers during the long days of harvesting. Thomas wrote music himself and formed his own choir. A regular guest was a certain Mr Byrd, almost certainly the famous composer William Byrd. Byrd is known to have composed for the Latin Mass. Thomas was a Roman Catholic, a recusant, and religion may have been a motivating factor behind Paget's private choir.

Thomas was imprisoned in 1580, probably as much to force him to agree a settlement with his estranged wife Nazaret Newton, with whom the Queen sympathised, as for his religious beliefs. But these were uncertain times to profess staunch Catholicism. In the decade before his father's death the national religion had changed from Protestant to Catholic and back again. Protestantism still had only a tenuous hold. Many Catholic sympathisers saw Mary, Queen of Scots as the rightful Queen of England. Thomas's younger brother Charles played a dangerous game as a double agent. After he was implicated in the Throckmorton Plot, a plan to free Mary from captivity uncovered in 1583, Charles Paget fled abroad. Thomas was probably not involved but certain to be thought guilty by association. He had little choice but to join his brother in exile. His estate was confiscated on the orders of the Crown. Thomas Gresley, High Sheriff of Staffordshire, was given temporary charge.

Thomas undertook some restoration of the former abbey buildings in the years before circumstances forced him to abandon Burton. A considerable amount was spent on a lodge, presumably Sinai Park House. Dendrochronology tests confirm a felling date of 1572/3 for the timbers of the south wing, which ties in exactly with accounts in the Paget archives. The house was in good enough condition in 1584 for the teenage Robert Devereux, Earl of Essex to stay there and enjoy hunting in Sinai Park. Years of neglect followed by the enforced absence of Thomas Paget took their toll on the ancient buildings of the former abbey. At one point after Paget's flight abroad, it had been considered as a possible place of confinement for Mary, Queen of Scots, but was discounted as too dilapidated. Instead Mary was sent to Tutbury Castle in the care of the Earl of Shrewsbury.

In 1585, as security around her tightened, Mary was transferred to Chartley Manor, home of the Earl of Essex. A new custodian, Sir Amyas Paulet (stepson of Lady Elizabeth), was appointed and given stewardship of the confiscated Paget property in Burton. A trap was laid to obtain documentary evidence in support of a charge that Mary was actively conspiring against Elizabeth. It was crucial that Mary believed coded messages could be safely smuggled in and out of Chartley by her supporter, Anthony Babington. Watertight containers hidden inside barrels of beer supplied weekly from Burton were to be the means of conveyance. In fact the brewer involved, the lynchpin in the affair, known only and ironically by his codename 'the honest man', was party to the scheme to plant a 'smoking gun'. Letters both ways were intercepted and copied into a mounting dossier against Mary. The brewer involved could be any of around thirty licensed victuallers in the town. Most probably he was operating the confiscated former abbey brewhouse.

Mary's inevitable arrest came in August 1586. Her denials were ignored and the following month under heavy escort she set out on her final journey to Fotheringhay. Leaving Chartley by carriage in mid-morning it is almost certain that Mary would have arrived at Burton by late evening and spent the night here, either at the *Three Queens* or the *Crown*.

Thomas Paget died at Brussels in 1589. His son and heir, William, was a student at Oxford at the time of his father's exile. He had reverted to Protestantism and stayed in England. It took distinguished military service, most notably at the daring capture of Cadiz with the Earl of Essex in 1596, on his part to win back some of his inheritance. Not until the accession of James I in 1603 were all his lands and title restored.

60 *Two ancient mulberry trees on the site of the former abbey gardens beside Lichfield Street may date from 1608. James I encouraged planting to kickstart a domestic silk industry. William Paget (4th Baron) would have been keen to follow the King's lead. Unfortunately, black mulberry trees were imported and not the white variety on which silk worms feed.*

61 *The figure of a cross-legged knight at St Werburgh's Church, Hanbury is believed to be Sir John Hanbury. The armour has been dated to c.1303 and the monument has a claim to being the oldest alabaster effigy in the country.*

William Paget (4th Baron) never lived at Burton. His steward occupied the house now referred to as the 'Manor'. Stone and timber were robbed from one crumbling building to repair others on the former monastic site in piecemeal fashion. Bit by bit the once great abbey was turning into a ruined shell.

At the time of the abbey's dissolution the population of the parish was a little over 2,000. Burton's economy was still predominantly rural but trade was beginning to flourish. Initial investment by the Paget family had given the local clothmaking trade a boost. In addition to leasing out the fulling mill established by the abbey, known as Nether Walk Mill, Sir William Paget leased land beside the river beyond Bond End for a second, the Upper Mill, to be built. Thomas Paget added a third alongside in 1574. A type of woollen cloth known as 'kersey' was the main product. A large proportion of townspeople were involved in associated work (mercers, clothiers, weavers, dyers and finishers) underlining the importance of textiles to the local economy.

Brewing in the early 17th century was still a domestic, small-scale business but the introduction of hops into the brewing process during the 16th century had extended the keeping properties of ale. Beer could now be transported further. The abundance of gypsum, a rock slightly soluble in water, in the geological substructure of the area gave local well water exceptional brewing qualities and word was beginning to spread. But it was carving of alabaster, a type of gypsum with translucent qualities and natural flesh tones that made it an ideal medium for producing lifelike monuments, that was beginning to make Burton nationally known.

An effigy in St Werburgh's Church at Hanbury is thought to be of Sir John de Hanbury. With an estimated date of 1303 it is widely recognised as the oldest alabaster effigy in England. As the 14th century progressed, alabaster began to take over from oak, brass, bronze and marble as the material of choice for monumental effigies and tombs.

From around 1480, the work of Henry Harpur and Thomas Moorecock was attracting attention. By 1520, Burton had become the leading centre for alabaster sculpture. Through the middle years of the 16th century the leading exponents were Richard Parker and the Royley family. Parker had a shop in Bristol and was almost certainly exporting his work from the port there to European destinations. In the

1590s, Jasper Hollemans, a master carver from the Netherlands, set up his business in the town. Among other commissions, Hollemans was responsible for the Spencer family tomb at Great Brington, Northamptonshire. Much of the local output was unsigned and few receipts or orders survived. Enough is known to attribute satisfactorily over a hundred of the finest monumental effigies in the country to the Burton carvers.

But tastes change. The Renaissance brought new ideas. Italian marble became popular. When Hollemans stopped work in 1638, the boom was already effectively over. A Puritan backlash against elaborate memorials completed the process.

Religion continued to be a cause of controversy. It took time for Protestantism to gain a popular hold. Many ordinary people clung to traditional beliefs. Robert Sutton, son of a Burton carpenter baptised in the parish church and ordained as a Church of England minister, converted to Catholicism. His preaching led to exile in 1585. He returned illegally and was recognised while visiting prisoners in Stafford Gaol. Arrested and subsequently convicted of treason, he was hung, drawn and quartered near Stafford on 27 July 1587.

Signs of religious extremism surfaced in 1588 when a local preacher, Peter Eccleshall, was indicted for refusing to use the Book of Common Prayer. As a radical Puritan he felt the Reformation had not gone far enough and objected to references to the Trinity contained in the new liturgy. With two like-minded ministers, Arthur Hildersham of Ashby and William Bradshaw of Stapenhill, Eccleshall held evangelical-style services to promote his views.

Eager for a chance to embarrass the established Church, members of the group took up the case of 13-year-old Thomas Darling, an alleged occurrence of demonic possession. So skilfully presented was the case of 'The Boy of Burton', as it became known that it attracted national attention. A superstitious public lapped up the tale of witchcraft and occult practices that had apparently left

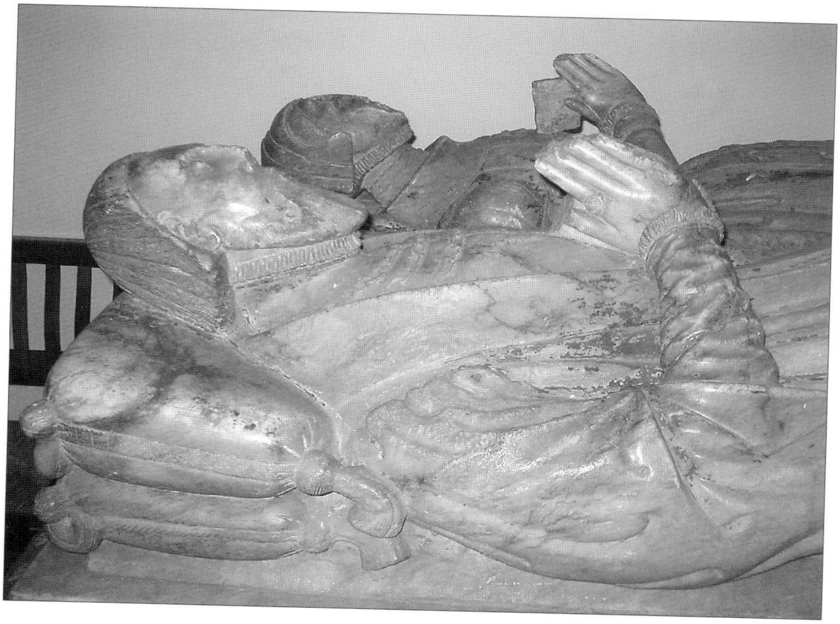

62 *Much of the work carried out by the Burton alabaster carvers was unsigned and few orders or receipts survive. This 1565 monument to Humphrey Welles and his wife Mary, of Hoar Cross, is thought to be a product of the Royley brothers' workshop.*

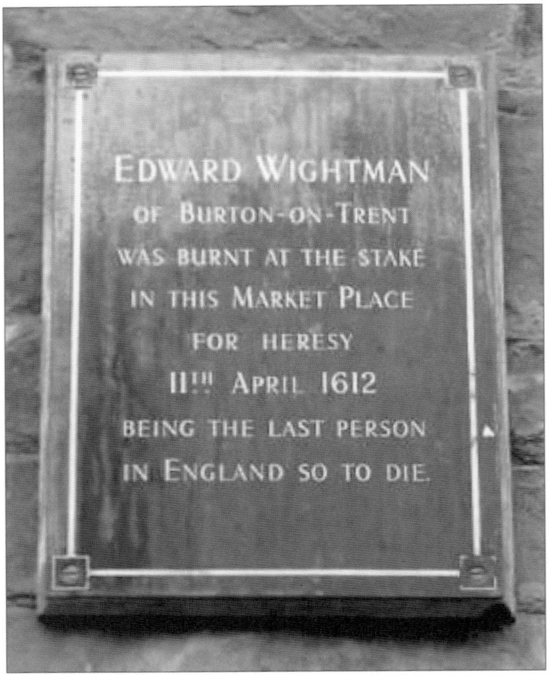

63 *The death of Burtonian Edward Wightman, the last person burnt at the stake for heresy in England, is marked by a plaque at the scene of his execution in Lichfield Market Place.*

Thomas Darling suffering fits in which he vomited and hallucinated about ghostly green apparitions. Much of the information came from the reports of Edward Wightman, a local draper and alehouse keeper who documented the boy's fits. The aim of the radicals was to show that the Church of England was ignoring the danger posed by evil in the everyday world and to demonstrate that the rite of exorcism was not the exclusive preserve of the Roman Catholic Church. Two leading members of the local Puritan activists, John Darrell and Arthur Hildersham, conducted an exorcism after which Thomas Darling was apparently restored to normality.

Unable to ignore the publicity generated, the Church responded with a judicial enquiry headed by the uncompromising Archbishop of Canterbury, John Whitgift. The whole affair was declared nothing but a fraudulent stunt. Darrell was jailed, Eccleshall and Hildersham were banned from leading religious services.

Wightman continued to publicly challenge the scriptural authority of the Church and to campaign for further reform. Among his demands was an end to infant baptism. A letter to King James led to his arrest on charges of heresy. From the public platform of the Bishop of Lichfield's court he sealed his fate by claiming divine inspiration and was sentenced to death. Since 1401, the penalty for heresy was to be burnt at the stake. Edward Wightman was executed on 11 April 1612 in Lichfield Market Place, the last heretic to die at the stake in England.

Thomas Darling grew up with extreme religious beliefs and suffered the indignity of having his ears cropped and receiving a whipping for expressing his views as a student at Oxford.

Religious differences would provide fuel for the coming armed conflict. England was on the brink of civil war and Burton would be caught in the middle.

SIX

Conflict and Resolution:
Civil War, Welfare and the Workhouse

William Paget (5th Baron) supports constitutional attempts to limit the power of the monarch. As economic and religious differences between Parliament and King Charles I escalate, both sides drift towards armed conflict. Paget argues Parliament's case and urges Charles to settle. But in 1642, when war is announced and loyalties are put to the test, he declares for the King.

With only local militia to call on, both sides needed to raise forces quickly.

Paget was assigned to form a regiment of foot. He wrote to all his contacts in the gentry, men such as Richard Bagot of Blithfield Hall, offering commissions as captains in return for recruiting a company to join his regiment. Estate workers were persuaded to sign up. Wages for a basic foot soldier or a musketeer of between 4s. and 6s. a week made it an attractive proposition for a farm labourer. Paget did not intend to lead his men in person. He appointed experienced soldier Richard Bolle to command, a man capable of training raw recruits in how to load and fire a musket or deploy a pike against cavalry attack.

Sir George Gresley of Drakelow Hall declared for Parliament and raised a troop of horse. Sir John Gell, Parliament's commander in Derbyshire, made Derby his stronghold. Philip Stanhope, Earl of Chesterfield fortified Bretby Hall on behalf of the King and set about raising a force to attack Derby. Fellow Royalist Henry Hastings, Lord Loughborough garrisoned Ashby de la Zouch and with help from Sir Edward Mosley of Rolleston, installed a force at Tutbury Castle. Locally, the battle lines were drawn and allegiances declared.

In December 1642, a division of Gell's forces led by Major Couradus Molanus besieged Bretby Hall. Stanhope was forced to abandon his house and fled to Lichfield, a Royalist stronghold. Burton, with its important crossing of the River Trent, became a strategic pawn, coveted equally by two evenly matched opponents.

By January 1643 the Royalists had reasserted control in Burton but only temporarily. In April, Gell's forces regained the upper hand and left 260 men under Captain Thomas Sanders of Lullington to guard the bridge. Three months later, Queen Henrietta Maria, at the head of a force accompanying a convoy of arms destined for the Royalist headquarters at Oxford, diverted from her march south to attack Burton. With his Queen watching,

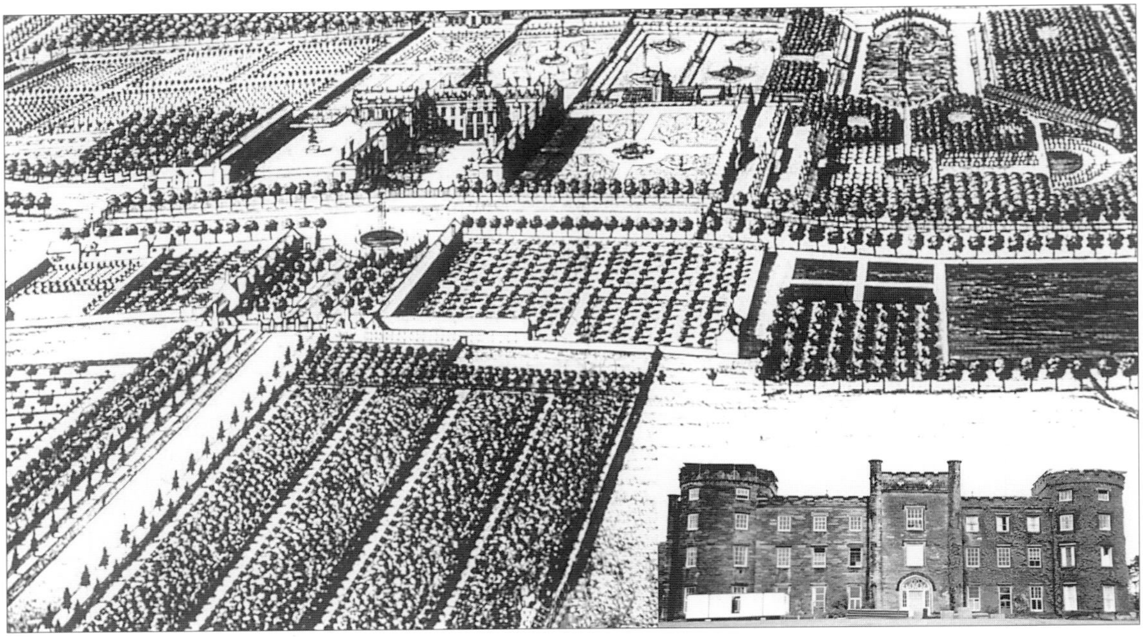

64 *Staunch Royalist Philip Stanhope, 1st Earl of Chesterfield, lost possession of his grand mansion at Bretby, designed by Inigo Jones, to Parliamentary forces during the Civil War. The 5th Earl of Chesterfield replaced the house in the early 19th century.*

cavalry officer Thomas Tyldesley earned himself a knighthood taking the bridge by storm. What happened next depends on whose propaganda you believe. According to the Royalist account, 'her majesty's goodness and clemency was so exemplary ... that she forbad any violence to be offered to the town'. Parliamentarian Sir Samuel Luke recorded a rather different version of events. In his journal he wrote that the Queen's forces:

> fell upon the townsmen and drove thirty of them into the church who defended themselves bravely and killed many of the Cavaliers but at last were glad to demand quarter. But they refused to grant it but came in the night and cut all their throats, doing great spoil in the town, ravishing the women, forcing many of them to take to the river, where they drowned insomuch that above twenty were found and taken up dead this week, and they daily find more.

Sir John Harpur of Swarkestone Hall was left in charge at Burton. Again it was a fleeting occupation. In January 1644, Major Molanus was back to rout Harpur and his forces. Lord Loughborough promptly retook the town only to lose it in a counter-attack by Thomas Sanders, now promoted to major. Sir John Gell noted that Sanders 'tooke most of the officers prisoners, and soe most miserably plundered and destroyed the towne'.

Possession of Burton Bridge by the Parliamentarians denied Lord Loughborough easy access between the Tutbury and Ashby garrisons. On 31 March 1644, there was a skirmish on a stretch of heath near Egginton. Forced to retreat, some of the Royalist forces drowned attempting to cross the River Trent by an ancient ford at Newton Solney. An incident on the same day reflects the summary justice of the times. Philip Greensmith, a Parliamentarian recruit, was found guilty of desertion and hanged from a tree at Coton-in-the-Elms.

Although the final act, the trial and execution of King Charles, was still some way off, the Battle of Naseby in 1645 effectively marked the end of the Royalist cause. Paget's regiment was destroyed in the clash and Richard Bolle killed.

Damage caused to the town by the Civil War was both physical and economic. Burton changed hands no less than eight times as power see-sawed. In 1643, two barrels of gunpowder stored in the parish church had detonated, blowing out the windows and ripping a hole in the roof. Many minor domestic tragedies went unrecorded. One that was documented relates how ropemaker Richard Shipley and his family were made homeless, turned out of their rented premises after the Queen's forces burned down their landlord Henry Watson's house following the storming of the bridge in 1643.

Trade suffered. Fairs and markets were temporarily abandoned. Horses were commandeered and provisions requisitioned. Soldiers were billeted on householders and a weekly tax imposed. Writing in the 1650s, Uttoxeter attorney and High Sheriff of Derby Sir Simon Degge reported:

> It was before the last wars a town much given to clothing, their kersies being in great esteem in this country, but since the war has declined in trade, having suffered much by the plunder, it being held out against the king.

When a national Hearth Tax (2s. per hearth) was introduced in 1666, of 480 residents assessed almost two hundred were judged to be too poor to pay and given exemption.

Public health was poor. Disease was prevalent. An open drain ran down the middle of High Street into which every type of waste was tipped. According to a contemporary rhyme, after heavy rain:

> Sweepings from butchers' stalls, dung, guts and blood,
> Drowned puppies, stinging sprats, all drenched in mud,
> Dead cats and turnip tops,
> Came tumbling down the flood.

Poverty was widespread after the end of the Civil War and Burton's economy in a particularly depressed state, but for those with resources to invest it was a time of opportunity. Generations of the Watson family had owned

65 *Burton Bridge became a strategic military target in the Civil War. In 1643, Queen Henrietta Maria watched as dashing cavalry officer Thomas Tyldesley led a charge across the bridge, successfully driving back the Parliamentarian defenders.*

land in Burton, both as tenants of the abbey and later of successive Paget lords of the manor. Henry Watson, owner of a tanning business, renovated Bond End Grange on Pinfold Lane, originally one of the abbey's farmhouses. His son Daniel, a London lawyer who had become a captain in Cromwell's New Model Army, acquired Nether Hall, former home of the Blount family. Daniel Watson's daughter married Shropshire lawyer Isaac Hawkins. Members of both families made a number of charitable bequests to the town and Daniel erected a cross at the junction of High Street, Horninglow Street and Anderstaff Lane. The legal practice begun by Daniel Watson in 1650 became Talbot and Company in the 1890s.

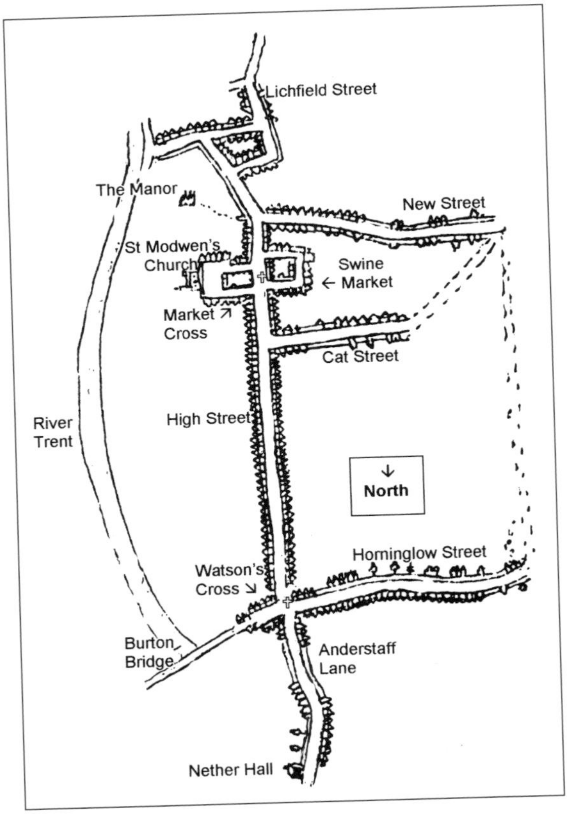

66 *Early map of Burton redrawn from an original (probably by the father of pioneering economic statistician and social analyst Gregory King) showing individual properties and a cross erected by Daniel Watson, member of a prominent Burton family and a former captain in Cromwell's New Model Army. The population at the time was around two thousand and the economy predominantly rural.*

Parish responsibility for welfare had always been targeted at taking care of its own. The Act of Settlement (1662) required everyone to have a parish of legal settlement. Anyone who did not qualify as a resident and was deemed likely to become a burden on the parish was classed as a 'vagrant' and faced eviction. Entries in the vestry book record many such orders to the overseers of the poor:

> ... that Howlett and his wife and family some time this week be sent to the place of his last abode as not having a proper certificate to gain a settlement here. (7 September 1700) ... take proper direction for prosecuting James Flaningham an Irishman for endeavouring to get settlement in this town contrary to law. (27 October 1713)

The parish found it worthwhile to allocate £5 a year to pay someone to drive out 'beggars by day and by night'.

One way in which individuals could acquire residency was to be employed by a legally settled inhabitant for a continuous period of 365 days. To avoid this happening, servants and labourers hired at the annual Statutes Fair, held at Michaelmas, started work after the celebrations and had their employment terminated the following Michaelmas Eve.

Issue of settlement certificates to Burtonians moving elsewhere, essentially a form of indemnity agreeing to cover the cost of return should it prove necessary, was not a formality. Parish officials had to consider the potential expense involved. A number of approvals appear in vestry records. All are for moves nearby where liability for the cost of

67 *The annual Statutes Fair beginning on the Monday after Michaelmas Day (29 September) appears to have developed from the festivities that followed the great court held by the abbot. Until recent times it was an occasion for farm labourers and domestic servants to meet and agree terms with prospective employers.*

repatriation, should it prove necessary, would be minimal. For example:

> Allowed a certificate to Newton Solney for Gilbert Canhill his wife and four children. (14 June 1716)

From 1697, all those 'on the parish' (i.e. in receipt of poor relief) were required to wear a pauper's badge on their sleeve. Shame was seen as a deterrent to claiming and an incentive to do so for as short a time as possible. Failure to display the badge prominently led to withdrawal of allowances, as did non-attendance at church. Most pews in the parish church were rented but some seats in the south aisle were set aside for those too poor to pay.

Poverty and its implications for the parish were a major concern. The vestry book records an order:

> That the churchwardens and overseers of the poor do stay at the church upon every 2nd Sunday in every month after evening prayer to consider further of fitting means for the better relief of the poor. (11 June 1699)

Those in receipt of allowances were subject to regular scrutiny. Beneath the above entry is added:

> ... ordered that the persons underwritten being able to work that work be provided for them (if they do not set themselves to work) and have their pay abated or taken off for ye future as is thought requisite and convenient.

On 24 June 1716, the overseers recorded a decision to:

> enquire into Joseph Budworth's circumstances they being informed that he has a house of his own.

Worries about encouraging idleness led to an Act of Parliament that made poor relief conditional upon entering a workhouse. A barn in Anderstaff Lane (now Wetmore Road) was bought and converted for the purpose. It opened in 1729. An assistant overseer was appointed as supervisor by the vestry. Those forced to enter the workhouse, fit, disabled, young and old alike, faced a harsh regime. Children from the age of five years were

68 *Until 1962 most pews in the parish church were rented, although a few seats in the south aisle were set aside for the poor. The door to pew 59 has been retained to make an interesting cupboard door in the south porch of St Modwen's Church.*

expected to work, spinning or knitting, from 5 a.m. to 9 p.m. The aim was to run the workhouse at a profit.

After the restoration of the monarchy in 1660, attempts were made to reassert the control of the Church of England following a decade of Puritan domination. From the appointments as curates at Burton of Robert Campion in 1649 and Philip Sharpe in 1651, both men with Puritan opinions, we may safely assume Lord Paget (5th Baron) sympathised with their stance. Interest in nonconformism had grown in the local area. Baptist meetings were well attended. Thomas Bakewell, rector of Rolleston, and his fellow clerics Henry Bee at Hanbury and Richard Swynfen of Mavesyn Ridware all lost their posts for professing dissenting views. Bakewell, who served ten weeks in Stafford Gaol for unauthorised preaching, found support at Burton. He was appointed to preach the weekly Boylston Lecture at St Modwen's Church, a sermon endowed in 1648 by Thomas Boylston, a London member of the Worshipful Company of Clothworkers and probably the son of Anslow farmer John Boylston.

The Toleration Act (1689) allowed a limited amount of freedom of worship. A nonconformist meeting house was registered in the town by William Tunley and Job Kinton in 1697, and a second in 1707 by John Prettie. Quakers were meeting in the 1690s but it was not until toleration was extended by an Act of 1723 that premises were officially registered. Presbyterians continued to gather. Bakewell's house in High Street was used for meetings from 1662. It was formally registered for worship in 1708 and the house next door acquired for a minister.

Despite legislative action by Parliament aimed at increasing toleration, religious differences continued to arouse strong feelings. In 1715, rioters forced their way into the Presbyterian chapel and set fire to the pews. When it re-opened an attempt was made to drive a bull through the doors with shouts of 'High Church and cheveril, Low Church and the Devil' ('cheveril' or kid glove leather used here presumably in the metaphorical sense of accommodating a wide range of views from the elasticity of the material). Maddened by

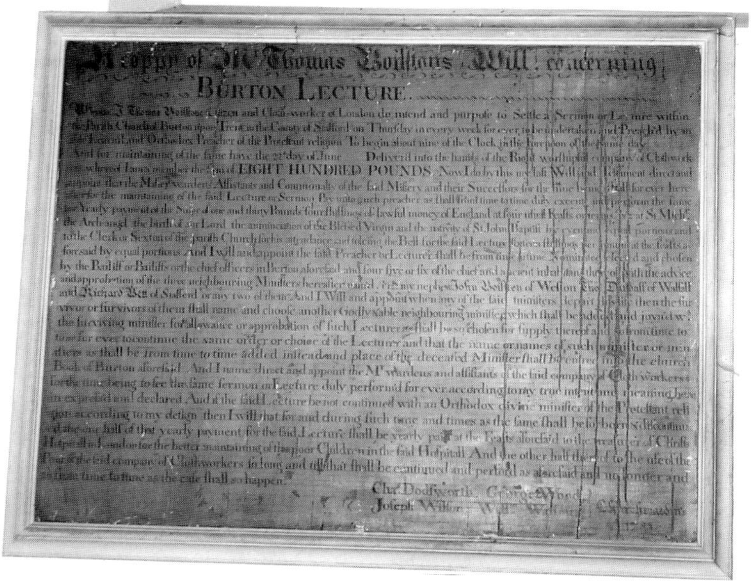

69 *In 1648, Thomas Boylston left a sum of money in his will to endow a weekly sermon in the parish church. One of the early lecturers was excluded cleric Thomas Bakewell. This extract from Boylston's will hangs in the north porch of St Modwen's Church.*

having its ears and tail cropped, the bull broke away. Pursued by the mob it ran down High Street and burst into the parish church where a large congregation was gathered for Sunday worship. There were many casualties. Possibly the animal had been taken from outside the *Bear Inn* in Horninglow Street. Baiting of bulls with dogs took place here and later at a bullring in New Street until the 'sport' was banned in 1835.

Time and conflict had taken their toll of the abbey church. The nave continued to be patched up for use as the parish church but repairs were soaking up an increasing proportion of the money raised by church rates. In 1718, with the roof underpinned by props, the doors of the south aisle nailed shut for safety reasons and the spire in imminent danger of collapse, a decision was taken to close the building.

Specialist church builders, brothers William and Richard Smith of Tettenhall, were called in to refurbish High Hall as a temporary place of worship while options were considered.

70 *George Fox, founder of the Society of Friends, preached at Anslow in 1651. A few Quakers were active in Burton but failed to establish themselves permanently. This former brewery office in Abbey Street became a meeting house in 1930. It closed in 1973 and the building was demolished the following year.*

71 *Now the Riverside Church, the Congregational Chapel built in 1842 occupies the site of Rector Thomas Bakewell's house in High Street where nonconformists met from 1662 and a Presbyterian meeting house was registered in 1708.*

An official decision to demolish the remains of the old abbey church and raise money by a levy on parishioners for a replacement was formally taken in 1719. Work began almost immediately. By 1723 a new parish church was holding the first services within its red sandstone walls, and though both the Smiths died during the contract (William in 1724 and Richard in 1726) the work was completed by younger brother Francis in 1728.

If a designer was involved his name has been lost. William Smith probably worked from plans drawn up by John Barker for a similar church built by the brothers at Whitchurch in Shropshire. A combination of clean simple lines, neat proportions and large round-headed windows is an adaptation of classic Roman style popular at the time. Inside, unfluted Tuscan columns support the nave arcades. An elegant chandelier suspended in the centre of the nave lit the interior.

72 *A fine collection of the communion plate – for security no longer kept at St Modwen's Church – includes a silver chalice and paten inscribed 'Burton upon Trent 1662' and the initials of the then curate William Middleton.*

73 *St Modwen's Church c.1847. The parish church was built between 1719-26 in classical style by the Smith brothers of Tettenhall.*

Five old bells were recast as six by the Gloucester firm of Abraham Rudham and two other bells added to make a peal of eight for the new square tower. The chimes were not universally popular. Enthusiastic amateurs had to be banned from the tower and a curfew of 10 p.m. imposed on the official ringers.

Stone from the demolition was saved for a wall between the churchyard and Market Place. When the time came much of it had disappeared, but in a small town the culprits were soon identified and the material recovered. Wrought iron railings were added above the low wall possibly from the workshop of celebrated ironsmith, Robert Bakewell of Derby. Bakewell undertook work for the Smith Brothers elsewhere and had business dealings with William Gilks, who managed the project as the parishioners' representative.

A national postal monopoly had begun in 1635 when Charles I opened up his personal letter network in order to raise money. By 1699 Burton had a postmaster who was probably also a publican. The *Three Queens* (Bridge Street), the *George* (High Street) and the *Crown* (High Street) all acted as collection houses. Post boys on horseback carried letters, a hazardous occupation on poor roads with highway robbery a constant danger. The Burton letter bag was stolen in 1742 and again in 1746.

Opportunities for education were limited but demand was growing. The Grammar School taught the 'classic' subjects of Latin, Greek and English, and some form of private preparatory tuition must have been available to feed the intake. Richard Allsopp, a local mercer who died in 1728, left money in his

74 *The interior of St Modwen's Church decked out for harvest festival c.1870. The pew doors are still in place as is the original three-decker pulpit.*

75 *Rules were introduced to curb over-enthusiastic ringers at the parish church. A qualified ringer had to be present at all times, no ringing was allowed after 10p.m., and for most purposes the ringers were restricted to 'sally height' – the limit of the woolly grip section of the bell rope.*

will to found a school offering more basic, functional literacy and numeracy for 30 boys. Education for girls was largely considered a waste of time. Schooling for all was a long way off.

The larger publican brewers, Anne Walker of the *Blue Stoops* (High Street), William Wilders at the *Three Queens*, John Wilders of the *Lamb* (Horninglow Street), and Gervas Littlefere of the *Vine* (Horninglow Street), were soon expanding the brewing side of their business. Casks of ale and small quantities of bottled beer were shipped via Derby and Hull to London on a regular basis. An overland carriage service to London operated from the middle of the 17th century and was running weekly by 1681. Transport costs made Burton beer expensive in the capital but consistent quality and a growing reputation ensured a market.

The first person to specialise as a 'common' brewer (concentrating solely on brewing for

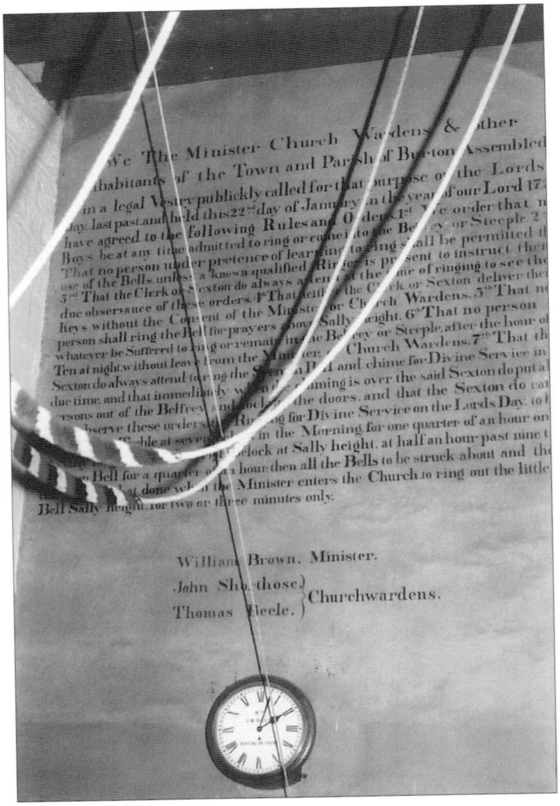

76 *Inns acted as postal collection points before post boxes were introduced in the 1850s. A Victorian wall box in Scalpcliffe Road is still in use.*

others rather than primarily for an attached inn) was Benjamin Printon, who came to Burton from Wapping, London probably around 1708 when he married local girl Maria Bannister. His brewhouse was in Bridge Street, close to the *Three Queens*. Printon became a leading citizen and served as overseer of the poor, churchwarden and town master. Hill and Sherratt in Abbey Street and Joseph Smith in High Street followed in Printon's footsteps.

But Burton was still a provincial backwater. The town's relative isolation restricted the development of trade and industry. Rural roads were so poor that three or four times the numbers of draught animals strictly necessary were required to haul waggons. To bring about countrywide improvements, turnpikes administered by trusts were authorised by an Act of Parliament in 1663. Instead of the old system of parochial responsibility, trusts were allowed to levy tolls on travellers in order to pay for highway maintenance. Charges varied according to the type and size of vehicle, the goods carried or animals herded. The road from Burton to Lichfield was turnpiked in 1729. A tollgate was put up at Branston. Main roads elsewhere remained little more than rutted, muddy tracks. Travel in winter, the brewing season, was particularly slow and difficult. The River Trent, a natural highway, offered a possible solution.

River transport was equally slow but it had the advantages of bulk carriage, it was cheap and it was safer. From the east coast ports, notably Hull, there was a thriving domestic traffic with London and regular trade links across the North Sea with the Baltic States and eastern Europe. During the 16th century the River Trent had been made navigable as far as Nottingham. In the middle of the 17th century the navigation was extended to Wilden Ferry near Shardlow where a thriving inland port had grown up under the direction of the Fosbrook family.

Sir William Paget (1st Baron) had investigated the idea of a port at Burton when he first acquired the abbey estates. Now the idea was revived by his successor William Paget (6th Baron). A survey was carried out. Plans were drawn up outlining the necessary work, including alterations to the river's natural course, straightening certain stretches to improve the flow and dredging shallows.

77 *The name of Hill and Sons is remembered in the stonework surrounding a doorway into the grounds of the* Punch Bowl Hotel *from the Dingle at Stapenhill. Hill and Sherratt began brewing in Abbey Street in 1740, became Hill and Sons in 1830, then briefly Hill and Company before becoming part of Marston and Thompson.*

Agreement was reached with all the major landowners involved and a Bill put before Parliament in 1698 was passed the following year. Authority to proceed was dependent on Lord Paget paying half the costs and the rest being raised by the town masters. Progress was slow. Leonard Fosbrook, worried about the threat to his trade monopoly, did all he could to scupper plans.

It was 1711 before any real headway was made. Under pressure for action, Paget leased the rights to Derbyshire businessman George Hayne along with property in the former abbey grounds. Hayne completed the preparatory work and negotiated a mutually beneficial deal with Fosbrook and the Trent Navigation Company opened for business in 1712. Alongside the Fleet, a long stone wharf and warehouses were built on the adjacent 'Soho', a name that suggests the area was once used for hare coursing. Shallow draught river ketches made the return trip to Gainsborough in 12 days. Boats were poled along and at certain points teams of 'halers' were employed to haul on ropes from the

78 *In 1712, a stone wharf was built alongside the Fleet for loading and unloading river barges. The area, formerly known as 'Soho', is now occupied by Burton College. A short stretch of stonework in the bank is all that remains of a once thriving inland port.*

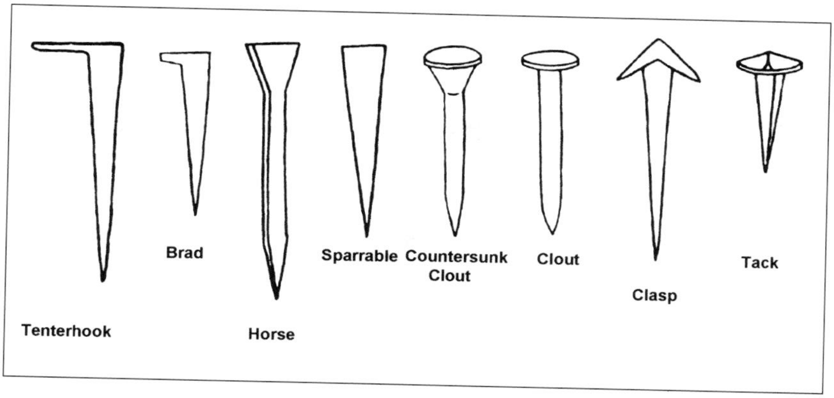

79 *Domestic nailmakers worked in outhouses using small forges. A variety of nails, each with a different use, were hammered and filed to shape. Tenterhooks were used in the textile industry to stretch newly woven cloth above a 'tenter' or frame.*

bank. Muscle power was supplemented by a single square sail. Shallow stretches of the river channel limited cargoes to less than the 40 tons capacity of each boat. A fulling mill had been built by the second half of the 17th century on an island close to the corn mill at Winshill. An agreement was reached to build a lock and allow the mill sluices to release water enabling boats to pass without grounding. In 1721, Hayne increased his control of the river upstream of the port by adding the leases of the Upper Mills and the Drakelow weir that supplied the water to power their wheels.

The port drew business from a wide area. Ale, cheese, salt, coal and metal goods from Birmingham were shipped down river. Returning boats carried pig iron, timber, hemp and flax for distribution across the Midlands. Seven thousand tons were being shipped annually by 1750 and 200 boats regularly passed through the town.

Ships sailed from Hull and Gainsborough to load timber and iron in Russia and Poland. Keen to find outward cargoes, Hull merchants helped promote a trade in ale to the Baltic. Imports stimulated other local businesses. Ironworking, hat making and ropemaking all became established. Nether Walk Mill was converted for smelting iron in 1721. In the 1730s, Sampson Lloyd, a Birmingham Quaker and ironmaster, bought the fulling mill at Winshill for use as a forge. Thomas and Francis Thornewill established a business in New Street manufacturing spades and other tools. In 1755, they leased the corn mill at Clay Mills to convert as ironworks. A domestic nailmaking industry began. Whole families worked in cramped outhouses, hammering and filing nails from iron rods supplied by the rolling mills, which then collected and sold the finished product.

Hats made of felt and of beaver fur imported at first from North America and then, when transatlantic stocks became depleted, the Baltic States were regularly sent to London. Hemp was spun into yarn to make sacks or to be woven into rope in long, narrow, open-air ropewalks.

After decades of decline triggered by the Civil War, Burton is poised for growth.

SEVEN

Industrialisation:
Transport, Turnpikes and Textiles

Burton in the mid-18th century clusters around the same core of streets that made up the medieval borough with Horninglow, Branston, Stretton, Stapenhill and Winshill forming separate small villages. But with the population at a little over 4,000 and growing, change is inevitable.

A toll-free fair for horses and cattle was launched in 1771. It was held annually each October over five days. According to the *Universal Directory*, by the 1790s it had become the biggest event of its type in the area.

In 1772, the Earl of Uxbridge paid for High Hall in the Market Place to be replaced by a Town Hall. Designed by local architect James Wyatt, it had a headstone emblazoned with the Paget coat of arms (heraldic tigers supporting a shield of eagles and lions). Social events such as balls and dances were held at the new hall as well as meetings to discuss town business. An Act of Parliament led to the formation of a new civic body in 1779. The town commissioners with the feoffees and manor steward took over much of the power formerly exercised by the vestry and set about municipal improvements.

From 1780 parishes had been ordered to replace stocks (a legal obligation from 1405) with secure places to hold prisoners requiring overnight confinement. A tiny subterranean cell known as the 'black hole' near the workhouse in Anderstaff Lane (Wetmore Road) was used. Rooms and cellars in public houses provided alternative lock-ups. A sale notice in the *Derby Mercury* for the *Old Bowling Green Inn* in the south-east corner of the Market Place advertised in 1735 'inn including profits of the gaol'. At an average of one shilling a prisoner per night, it was useful extra income. The *Wheat Sheaf* (High Street) and *Royal Oak* (Market Place) may have been used for the same purpose.

A parish fire engine bought by the vestry in 1791 to replace human bucket chains was sold to the town commissioners in 1841. A paid night watch was formed in 1793.

In 1753, Turnpike Trusts took over responsibility for the roads from Burton to Derby, Ashby and Tutbury. Tollgates were erected at Stretton, Bearwood Hill and Horninglow. The Earl of Uxbridge was allocated £20 a year by the Turnpike Trust towards the repair and upkeep of Burton Bridge in recognition of the extra traffic generated. Medieval St James's Chapel on Burton Bridge was demolished in

80 *A mounting block outside the former Bass Town House at 136 High Street is a reminder of the days before motorised transport.*

81 *In 1772, the Earl of Uxbridge paid for a new Town Hall to replace High Hall in the Market Place. Designed by local architect James Wyatt, it hosted social events as well as official town meetings. It was demolished in 1883. Brass angle plates set in the pavement mark the position it occupied.*

1777 and replaced with an inn, houses and shops. The old bridge gate where tolls were collected on goods brought to market, was moved to 'Bargates' corner at the Bridge End junction of High Street, Horninglow Street and Anderstaff Lane.

Road carriers, among them William Bass, were running six waggon services to London every week. Public houses including the *Nag's Head* (Bond End), *Vine* (Horninglow Street) and *White Hart* (High Street) acted as collection points. Better roads allowed lighter coaches to be used and reduced journey times. In 1764 a regular passenger service began between Birmingham and Sheffield via Derby with connections to London and Liverpool. Coaches *Defiance*, *Quicksilver*, *Standard*, *Rapid* and *Telegraph* all stopped at Burton. The *Crown*, *George* and *Three Queens* served as coaching inns, with stables attached where horses could be changed. Mail coaches, exempt from turnpike tolls, took over from mounted post boys in 1791. Mail coaches for Birmingham at 11.45 a.m. and for Sheffield at 1 p.m. left from the *Three Queens* and the *George* on alternate days. A direct daily light post service between London and Liverpool was introduced leaving the *Three Queens* for London at 8.30 p.m. and for Liverpool at 2.30 a.m. Burton was on the route from London to Liverpool taken by the *Red Rover*, a fast night coach that regularly carried 'transports', convicted criminals sentenced to be transported to the colonies.

82 *The west end of the old bridge was redeveloped as Bridge Street towards the close of the 18th century. Carnival parades, a popular feature of town life in the early 20th century, often ended their procession through the town along Bridge Street to gather on the Hay for a programme of entertainment.*

83 *Stout oak posts capped with iron at Bargates corner protect the double bay windows of 102 High Street from vehicles mounting the pavement at the busy junction. A gate, formerly on the old bridge, was moved to the Bargates junction when Bridge Street was developed in the late 18th century.*

Large areas of uncultivated open land in the town began to be enclosed and developed. Because the enclosure of common land took away long established entitlements, for example the right of 'commoners' to graze livestock, Parliamentary approval was required. Acts in 1771/2 allowed the enclosure of Fleet Green (now part of the Trent Washlands), Goose Moor (adjacent to modern Moor Street) and part of the Outwoods. Apportionment of enclosed land tended to favour existing large landowners. Only small parcels of land went to freeholders. Land allocated to compensate commoners was sold and most of the capital invested to fund poor relief. Acts followed in the 1820s to enclose Horninglow Moor (an area bounded today by Casey Lane, Shobnall Street, Dallow Street and Princess Street) and Little Common (off modern Hawkins Lane). Enclosure of common land at the Outwoods was most contentious. As urbanisation increased, common land had become important for recreational as much as agricultural purposes. A part of Outwoods Common was used for horse racing and objectors took direct action and pulled down the first fences. Race meetings did not begin again until 1811. Burton Meadow was the new venue and a stone grandstand was added in 1822.

Between 1770 and 1830 the face of the surrounding countryside changed. Village greens disappeared. Needwood Forest was enclosed. Trees were felled, hedges planted and new straight roads laid out with milestones at regular intervals. In 1809 the opportunity was taken to sideline Pinfold Lane in favour of a turnpike along New Street and Moor Street via Henhurst Hill to Abbots Bromley. Tollgates were erected at Wellington Road and Rough Hay.

In 1771, public subscriptions raised enough to purchase a new organ for St Modwen's Church from the most famous maker of the day, John Snetzler of London. An elegant wooden case designed by James Wyatt was commissioned to house the console in a strengthened west gallery. Leading musician Anthony Greatorex of Riber Hall, Matlock was attracted as organist, a post he held for 43 years. On his death in 1814, his son Thomas took over, but high-profile duties elsewhere limited the time he could spend here. Thomas Greatorex was an internationally renowned teacher and composer. He was organist at Carlisle Cathedral before leaving to study singing in Italy, where the exiled 'Pretender' Charles Edward Stuart befriended him. After the Prince's death in 1788, Thomas returned to England to pursue a distinguished career that included a professorship at the Royal Academy of Music and the post of organist at Westminster Abbey. In 1789, he came to Burton to play the Snetzler organ and conduct the choir at a music festival. An afternoon recital in St Modwen's Church was followed by an evening concert and dancing in the new Town Hall.

A new clock for the parish church was installed in 1785. Made by John Whitehurst of Derby, one of the best clockmakers in the country, it had a carillon mechanism that played a different tune on the church bells each day. At the same time, a Whitehurst sundial was commissioned, useful to reset the clock should it ever prove necessary to do so.

84 *The* White Hart *in High Street was one of a number of local inns that acted as a depot and collection point for horse-drawn carrier services in the 18th century.*

Thomas Hanby, a follower of John Wesley, the founding father of Methodism, met with some opposition when he preached in the town in 1754. Nevertheless, a Methodist Society registered a chapel in Horninglow Street (where the police station now stands) in 1765. Membership was given impetus by visits from John Wesley himself in 1766, 1770 and 1772. A Primitive Methodist chapel was built in Cat Street in 1829.

85 *After the enclosure of Needwood Forest in 1801, new turnpike roads were laid out with milestones at regular intervals. A new road from Abbots Bromley linked into the town centre via Henhurst Hill, Moor Street and New Street, effectively sidelining the former route along Pinfold Lane (Park Street).*

86 *An organ by the internationally renowned London firm of John Snetzler was purchased for the parish church in 1771. Leading musician Anthony Greatorex was appointed organist. An elegant case designed to house the Snetzler-built instrument was widened to accommodate a replacement in 1900.*

Richard Thomson, a Lancashire textile worker who moved to take a job in the Burton mills of Robert Peel, revived the Baptist movement locally. Baptist chapels opened in Station Street (1803), Union Street (1823) and Fleet Street (1825).

In 1818, legislative changes removed the need for an Act of Parliament to authorise new churches. The executors of lawyer Isaac Hawkins had spent almost 20 years considering how to spend his estate. A church with a large number of free seats to counter falling congregations and rising support for nonconformism had been suggested soon after Hawkins's death in 1800. Progress was frustrated by objections from the diocesan bishop at Lichfield. Now, changes introduced by the Church Building Acts meant plans could go ahead. Holy Trinity Church opened in Horninglow Street in 1824. Thomas Greatorex's son, Thomas junior, was appointed organist. A subdivision of the parish allocated Horninglow, Stretton and Winshill to the new church. Peter French, the first curate, occupied the house converted from the former abbey infirmary until the *Vine Inn* in Horninglow Street was acquired and converted into a vicarage in 1839.

By the 1780s, the occasional girl attended Allsopp's Charity School, founded over 50 years earlier with places for 30 boys. The first Sunday school opened in 1787, sponsored by the Earl of Uxbridge. Within a decade there were 11 in the town offering basic education as well as religious instruction to 450 boys and girls. A National School in Horninglow Street, connected to Holy Trinity Church, opened for both boys and girls in 1827. National Schools were based on the mutual instruction principles devised by Andrew Bell in which the most able pupils taught others. Education concentrated on the three 'R's of Reading, wRiting and aRithmetic plus sewing and cookery for girls.

The lucrative Baltic trade controlled by the Trent Navigation Company and an increasing reputation for excellent ale attracted new business to the town. John Musgrave bought Benjamin Printon's brewhouse in 1729 and expanded capacity. Samuel Sketchley moved from Newark in 1740 to open a brewery in Horninglow Street and grew by buying out part of Musgrave's operation in 1761. Benjamin Wilson, a Derby ropemaker, married Hannah Walker of the *Blue Stoops* and acquired the premises when his mother-in-law died in 1742. Joseph Clay of Derby bought the *Lamb and Flag Inn* (Horninglow Street) primarily for its brewhouse in 1751. Charles Leeson, a chandler, purchased a brewhouse formerly belonging to the *Three Queens* in 1753. Henry Evans moved from Derby to establish a brewery in High Street in 1754. William Worthington, a cooper working for Joseph Smith, bought his employer's High Street brewery in 1760. Worthington's sons, William and Thomas, both married daughters of Henry Evans. Benjamin Wilson's three sons all became

87 *A clock with a finely engineered mechanism by John Whitehurst was installed in the parish church in 1785. The mechanism engages a series of levers and bell cranks to sound a different melody for each day of the week. The musical chimes were recorded and broadcast by the BBC in 1937.*

88 *A sundial by master clockmaker John Whitehurst of Derby, calibrated exactly for its position on the south wall of the parish church, was fitted at the same time as a new clock in 1785 – useful to reset the clock if the mechanism stopped.*

89 *Clay House with its elegant doorway defined by Tuscan columns was built c.1792 by Joseph Clay junior on the site of the former* Lamb and Flag Inn. *The premises were designed for use as a bank and have a strongroom on the ground floor.*

90 *One of the challenges facing engineer James Brindley in building the Grand Trunk Canal was crossing the River Dove at Clay Mills. It was achieved with an aqueduct 1¼ miles in length. Twelve arches span the river and a further 11 are built into the embankments on either side.*

brewers. The most successful was Benjamin junior, who bought out Sketchley in 1790. Thomas Salt, an experienced brewer and maltster who had worked for Benjamin Wilson, leased Joseph Clay's business in the early 1800s.

Lack of experience was no bar to becoming a brewer for those with the necessary drive, ambition and capital. After his brother John Davies Greaves died in 1784, younger brother Robert included the following passage in an advertisement in the *Derby Mercury*, offering the family business (formerly part of John Musgrave's operation) for sale or to let:

> There is a person on the premises, who for a consideration would assist the purchaser in the Brewery, and give him insight into the Russia Trade, which is partly connected with the Brewery. The centrical situation of the Town of Burton, having communication with every capital Sea Port in the Kingdom, makes it a most eligible situation for the disposal of all importable goods.

Cool temperatures necessary to control fermentation and malting processes restricted brewing from October to April. As a result, most brewers ran diverse business operations. Payment in kind frequently formed part of the arrangement with the Baltic merchants. Benjamin Wilson Junior dealt

91 *Bridge number 1, formerly the entrance to the Bond End Canal, cut as a link from the river wharf to the Trent and Mersey Canal, now leads to Shobnall Marina.*

in timber, tallow, wheat, hemp, flax and iron. In 1800 he acquired a share in a cotton mill at Alrewas, opened in 1784 by Thomas and Francis Dicken (brewers at the *Angel Inn*). Benjamin's brother, John Walker Wilson, was the leading timber merchant in the area and formed the Burton Bank in partnership with a local solicitor, Daniel Dalrymple. Joseph Clay junior and his son Henry moved into commercial banking. Clay House was built on the site of the former *Lamb and Flag Inn* around 1792, with a strongroom on the ground floor.

Burton's port was thriving when the lease of the navigation rights became due for renewal in 1762. John Hayne, George's nephew, was now in charge of the family business. The Burton Boat Company, a powerful partnership of influential local businessmen involving Henry Evans, Isaac Hawkins, Sampson Lloyd, Joseph and John Wilkes, Robert Palmer and Uxbridge's agent William Wyatt, outbid him. The new operators extended the wharf and increased the warehouse space, but river transport was still subject to delays caused by adverse weather. Plans were being put forward for a more reliable cross-country canal.

92 *William Bass bought a brewhouse at 136 High Street in 1777. Grandson Michael Thomas (1799-1884) took charge aged 28, in 1827. In partnership with Samuel Ratcliff and John Gretton he built the family business into the biggest brewery in the world.*

93 *Tool manufacturer and foundry owner Robert Thornewill entered into partnership with engineer John Robson Warham in 1849. Together they built a worldwide reputation as manufacturers of pumping engines, locomotives and structural ironwork. Thornewill and Warham built Andresey footbridge leading to the Cherry Orchard in 1884.*

The 'Grand Trunk' was envisaged as the first step in a waterway network linking Hull, Liverpool, Manchester, London and Bristol. Chief sponsor was Josiah Wedgwood, an enterprising Burslem potter and one of a new breed of industrialists seeking improved access to markets. Gifted engineer James Brindley was put in charge of the venture and work began in 1766. Following the contours of the Trent Valley for 93 miles from Preston Brook on the River Weaver to the River Trent at Wilden Ferry, the Trent and Mersey Canal as it became known was a major undertaking. Seventy-six locks, 213 road bridges and 160 aqueducts were necessary, the largest aqueduct crossing the River Dove at Clay Mills. With a tight budget and demanding timescale, the project required all of the innovative James Brindley's outstanding skills.

Anticipating competition, Burton Boat Company added a wharf at Bond End and suggested Brindley terminate his canal there and use the river navigation from Burton to the east coast ports. When Brindley rejected the idea, the Boat Company cut a channel from their Bond End wharf to meet the new canal at Shobnall. The Burton stretch of the Grand Trunk opened in 1770 but permission to connect the Bond End Canal was refused. Boats had to be loaded and unloaded across a 40m. 'bar'. The decision was partly about rivalry: to protect their investment the directors of the Grand Trunk had ensured the canal was wide enough to take broad-beamed river craft from Wilden Ferry as far as Horninglow, beyond which point the size of the locks restricted passage to narrowboats. There was also a practical reason. A drop of over a metre to the River Trent would have drained the Grand Trunk. A connection was finally allowed in 1795 after locks had been added to equalise water levels.

Direct access to large timber yards at Bond End made Shobnall wharf a busy depot. A popular public house on the site, the *Mount Pleasant*, better known in later years as *Bessie Bull's* after a characterful landlady, did brisk business with bargees. According to tradition it replaced an inn that predated the canals known as the *Gateway to Sinai*. The main warehousing for the Grand Trunk was built at Horninglow around a large basin. To ensure tolls were not avoided the Turnpike Trust added an additional gate in Horninglow Road.

The Grand Trunk Canal opened fully in 1777. It was soon linked via the Coventry Canal and the Oxford Canal to the Thames and London. Burton was now at the centre of an efficient distribution network.

William Bass was quick to recognise that canal traffic posed a threat to his waggon trade while offering scope for new enterprise. He bought a brewhouse at 136 High Street in the year that the Grand Trunk opened. His sons Michael and William inherited in 1787. Michael was in sole charge by 1795 and with partners John Ratcliff and John Gretton laid the foundations of a great brewery empire.

Problems with the Baltic trade began to emerge in the 1790s. Russia increased import tariffs in an effort to promote a domestic brewing industry and war with France left ports blockaded. If the Napoleonic Wars caused problems for exporting brewers, Burton's hat trade temporarily prospered. Well established in the 18th century, it was given a boost by the demand for military headgear. John Port, whose Soho Hat Factory opened alongside the river wharf around 1800, was prominent among a number of hatmakers in the town.

Attempts by Burton's brewers to revive trade through the Baltic ports after war ended in 1815 looked briefly promising until Russia's increasingly protectionist stance resulted in a ban on imported beer. In 1822 the market collapsed. A period of consolidation followed. The number of big breweries in the town was reduced to five. Samuel Allsopp was now in control of his Uncle Benjamin Wilson's business. William Worthington had taken over the premises of Henry Evans. The other three were Thomas Salt, John Sherratt, and Bass and Ratcliff. In 1827, 28-year-old Michael Thomas Bass took charge of the family business. At Horninglow, still considered a separate village, John Marston was running a small brewery that had begun as Coats and Company around 1800.

The search for a new market focused on India. There was demand from British servicemen, administrators and their families for an ale able to withstand the long voyage and suitable for a hot climate. An emerging market was monopolised by Mark Hodgson, a London brewer who had developed a light coloured, hoppy, slightly sparkling ale. Burton's leading breweries undertook trials and a consignment of what was to become known as India Pale Ale left Allsopp's for Calcutta in 1822. Bass and Ratcliff and Thomas Salt both began exporting large quantities the following year.

94 *To celebrate victory over Napoleon at Waterloo, trees were planted on a high point east of the town. Waterloo Mount, or 'clump' as it was soon dubbed, became an even more distinctive landmark when South Staffordshire Water Company added a water tower to improve and equalise the pressure of domestic supplies.*

In 1807, Thomas Thornewill junior bought the forge leased by his father and uncle at Clay Mills along with Dove Cliff House and seven acres of surrounding land. As the foundry business developed Thornewill began casting components for steam engines. In 1849, Robert Thornewill entered into partnership with John Robson Warham, an engineer from the north east of England. Together they acquired a worldwide reputation as manufacturers of pumping machines, winding engines and locomotives. By the middle of the 19th century Thornewill and Warham were branching out into constructional engineering.

95 *Abraham Hoskins built a castellated folly on Bladon Hill overlooking Burton. Bladon House was added behind the façade. In the 19th century it became the home of brewer John Gretton.*

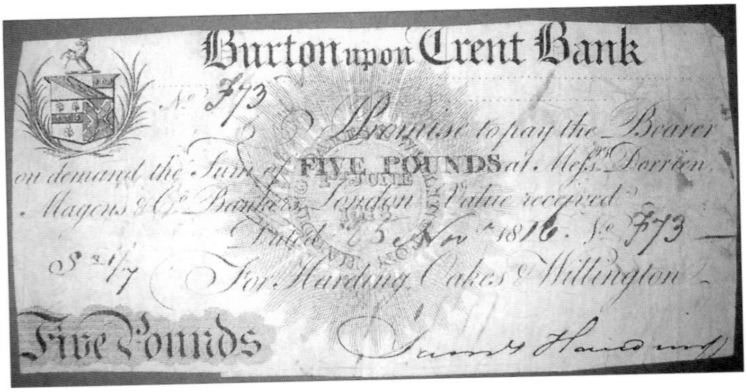

96 *Commercial banks issued their own notes, each individually numbered and signed by the cashier. Before the Bank Charter Act (1844) banking was a risky business. There was no limit to the amount of notes that could be issued. Harding, Oakes and Willington of Lichfield Street was one of many casualties, becoming bankrupt in 1819.*

Although an absentee landlord, Henry Paget (7th Baron and, from 1743, Earl of Uxbridge) remained a major influence in the town. The 8th Baron and 2nd Earl died a bachelor in 1769 and the titles passed to Henry, son of a distant cousin Caroline Paget and her husband Sir Nicholas Bayly.

Day-to-day administration of the Paget interests was left to an agent, now living at Sinai Park House. Estate management was firmly rooted in the medieval manorial system. Property leases were commonly for the term of a life, even for modern businesses such as commercial banks. Farm tenancies were let on a year-to-year basis.

Henry Paget, a distinguished soldier and diplomat, succeeded his father as Earl of Uxbridge in 1812 and commanded the cavalry at the Battle of Waterloo. With one of the last shots of the battle he was wounded in the knee. His leg was amputated in a makeshift field hospital. Created a marquess, he took the title 'of Anglesey', now the family's main home. Trees were planted in a 'Waterloo Clump' on a high ridge east of the town to commemorate victory against Napoleon.

97 *When Robert 'Parsley' Peel moved his cotton spinning operation to Burton in 1780, there was a ready-made site with weirs and sluices in place on an artificial island next to the flour mill at Winshill.*

A few years earlier, Abraham Hoskins, solicitor, businessman and high bailiff of Burton, had made a rather more ostentatious attempt to dominate the skyline. After building an impressive hall in landscaped parkland at Newton Solney, he added a folly along the summit of Bladon Hill overlooking Burton. A brick wall with battlements gave the impression of a castle. It proved so unpopular that Hoskins added a central block of rooms and two flanking towers and moved in to deflect criticism, an extra cost that proved financially ruinous.

Part of Burton Boat Company's response to the opening of the Grand Trunk was a new multi-storey warehouse on the north side of Burton Bridge serving the brewery businesses clustered around the east end of Horninglow Street. Despite efforts to remain competitive, the river navigation closed in 1805. By then the Boat Company's lease of water rights and mill sites was proving an important concession.

Cotton, as colourful as silk but a fraction of the price, had overtaken worsted woollen cloth as the material of choice for everyday wear and demand was huge. In Lancashire, Robert Peel had discovered the secret of using iron acetate to fix patterns permanently in linen. One of his designs, a single parsley leaf repeated in diagonal lines, was so successful he was nicknamed 'Parsley' Peel. He began mass production at a mill near Blackburn using racks of spinning jennies invented by his friend and neighbour James Hargreaves. Angry hand spinners threatened with the loss of their livelihoods had rioted and smashed the machines. Now Peel was looking for a new location distant enough to avoid a repetition.

Burton offered a number of advantages. It was close to the East Midlands hosiery manufacturers who formed a significant customer base. The Grand Trunk Canal gave access to raw cotton imported through Liverpool, and offered efficient distribution of finished products. Importantly, Peel's son, Robert junior, was already involved in commercial ventures with Joseph Wilkes, a farmer from Overseal. Wilkes had made a fortune from a variety of successful investments including banking. Robert Peel junior and Joseph Wilkes almost certainly opened the first commercial bank in Burton in conjunction with partners Thomas and William Pyecroft.

98 *The Peel family bought and refurbished this large Georgian townhouse in Lichfield Street, close to their Bond End textile mills.*

As a director of the Burton Boat Company, Wilkes was in a position to offer leases for mill sites. At Newton Road, Winshill the site was ready-made: weirs and sluices were in place. In 1780, a new purpose-built cotton spinning mill was built beside the existing corn mill. Peel's Lancashire venture had employed the spinning jenny but technology had already overtaken this innovation and it is most likely that Richard Arkwight's newly patented water frames were installed.

Within a few years water was being drawn from the Drakelow weir supplying the Upper Mills, along a specially dug channel known as Peel's Cut, to power a second mill at Bond End. Robert Peel bought and refurbished a large Georgian townhouse in Lichfield Street, close to his Bond End works. In 1792, he retired and returned to Lancashire leaving younger members of the family in charge. Robert junior had by then struck out on his own, again in partnership with Wilkes, and was on his way to making a fortune in Tamworth.

Business boomed. A third mill was built at Burton on the Upper Mills site. By the early 1790s another had followed at Bond End. In 1814, the Peels converted Sampson Lloyd's iron forge at Winshill for cotton production. For around forty years the textile industry provided the main source of employment in the town. Keeping looms supplied with thread and loading spindles was noisy, repetitive and boring. Children carried out much of the work. Many parishes took the opportunity to off-load pauper children as apprentices. Long working days typically began at 6 a.m. and ended at 9 p.m. It was 1819 before the Factories Act banning the employment of children below nine years of age was passed.

When it was ordered in 1792, a 26 horse-power Boulton and Watt steam engine for the new Bond End Mill was the first in Staffordshire. But it was the only one to be installed. Failure to keep pace with technology made the Burton mills uncompetitive and Lancashire's re-emergence as the main textile centre left them geographically isolated. By the 1830s the burst of growth was effectively over in the local area.

In the early years of the 19th century a number of ambitious plans were put forward to extend the local canal system. Two proposals receiving support were a link through the South Derbyshire coalfields to the Ashby Canal and another to join the Caldon Canal at Uttoxeter. Neither progressed beyond the drawing board. The next transport revolution was about to arrive.

EIGHT

Brewing Capital of the World:
Beer, Benefactors and a Municipal Coming of Age

In 1839 the first train steams full through Burton. Five years later, Cat Street, widened, extended and renamed Station Street, links a railway station to the town centre. The population has grown steadily but slowly and is now a little over 6,500.

In 1859, George Hudson, go-ahead chairman of the Midland Railway Company, obtained an Act of Parliament authorising a replacement for Burton's narrow medieval bridge that would be capable of carrying rail traffic. In return for being relieved of all future maintenance liabilities, the Marquess of Anglesey paid a third of the construction costs and surrendered his entitlement to a share of the turnpike tolls. Burton's new bridge was opened with a fanfare of publicity in 1864. A few years later the old bridge was demolished. All tolls were removed from local roads in 1873 and the Turnpike Trusts were wound up.

In 1860, proposals for private brewery railways connected to the main network were approved by Parliament. At its peak in the 1890s, the system comprised 87 miles of track with 80 separate sidings. Thirty-two level-crossing gates controlled the movement of freight across public roads.

99 *The railway arrived in Burton in 1839. Cat Street was widened and became Station Street in 1844. In 1971, a small concrete ticket office replaced a spacious timber passenger hall added in 1883 with stairs leading to an island platform.*

INNS, TAVERNS and BEERHOUSES: *c.*1830

Anchor	New Street (James Cox)
Angel	Swine Market (Bank Square) (Thomas Whitehead)
Barley Mow	Pinfold Street (Park Street) Thomas Stenson
Bear	Horninglow Street (John Thompson)
Bell	Horninglow Street (Thomas Swift)
Blue Posts	High Street (John Yeomans)
Boat House	Little Burton (Thomas Leck)
Boot	High Street (Thomas Blood)
Bowling Green	Market Place (Joseph Bladon)
Bull's Head	New Street (Thomas Rice)
Carpenters' Arms	New Street (William Wright)
Coach & Horses	High Street (William Baldwin)
Cross Keys	High Street (William Barratt)
Dog	Lichfield Street (Joseph Bracey)
Dragoon	Anderstaff Lane (Wetmore Road) (Catherine Cornell)
Dusty Miller	High Street (Philip Tyzack)
Falcon	Bond End (James Turner)
Fox & Goose	Bridge Street (Margaret Hall)
George	High Street (Benjamin Baldwin)
King of Prussia	New Street (Elizabeth Baldwin)
Lamb	High Street (William Simnett)
Lord Nelson	Lichfield Street (Mary Creswell)
Malt Shovel	Anderstaff Lane (Wetmore Road) (John Stone)
Man in the Moon	Market Place (George Lee)
Marquis of Anglesey	Burton Extra (John Ward)
Mason's Arms	High Street (Joseph Harrison)
Nag's Head	Burton Extra (Thomas Bell)
Old Crown	High Street (George Goodwin)
Old Peacock	Anderstaff Lane (Wetmore Road) (Samuel Morris)
Old Queen's Head	New Street (William Shorthose)
Old Spread Eagle	Lichfield Street (James Turner)
Punch Bowl	Burton Extra (Thomas Roe)
Rising Sun	Horninglow Street (Sarah Morris)
Roe Buck	Horninglow Street (John Tarratt Titterton)
Rose & Crown	Bridge Street (William Chambers)
Royal Oak	Market Place (Samuel Preston)
Royal Oak	Burton Mill (Newton Road) (John Gaunt)
Saracen's Head	Bridge Street (William Davison)
Ship	Bridge Street (Thomas Clark)
Shoulder of Mutton	Anderstaff Lane (Wetmore Road) (John Evans)
Spread Eagle	New Street (Henry Bagnall)
Star	High Street (Robert Measom)
Swan	Anderstaff Lane (Wetmore Road) (Samuel Talbot)
Talbot	Horninglow Street (Joseph Rhodes)
Three Queens	Bridge Street (John Lees)
Vine	Horninglow Street (John Whitehurst)
Wheat Sheaf	High Street (Richard Roe junior)
White Hart	High Street (Thomas Newbold)
White Horse	High Street (Thomas Woolley)
White Lion	Burton Extra (Francis Robinson)

100 *Fifty licensed premises in Burton and Burton Extra served a population of approximately 6,500 in 1830. Many licensees combined running a public house with other business. John Thompson was also a baker, Joseph Bracey a shoemaker, John Evans a butcher, and Richard Roe blacksmith and town constable.*

101 *This new crossing built of Derbyshire millstone grit replaced the narrow medieval bridge in 1864.*

102 *The Bass fleet of eight steam locomotives in 1919. Private brewery rail systems grew into an extensive network when a government ban on engines crossing the public highway was lifted in 1865. Many of the locomotives were built locally by Thornewill and Warham, and later by E.E. Baguley.*

Scientific and technological advances revolutionised brewing in the 19th century. Mechanisation using steam power allowed large quantities of beer to be produced cheaply. Better understanding of chemical processes led to consistent quality control. The development of the 'Burton Union' system, in which ale was fermented in sets of casks and excess yeast expelled for re-use before the beer was 'racked' in barrels for despatch, was soon adopted as the industry standard. Improved cooling methods enabled brewing to take place all year round. With the railways now offering a fast and efficient distribution network at a quarter the cost of canal transport and less vulnerable to pilferage (a major problem with barge traffic), the breweries were poised for expansion.

103 *Bass, Ratcliff and Gretton pursued an innovative, marketing-led sales approach based on a reputation for quality.*

Bass's and Allsopp's led the way. By 1879, when it became a limited company, Bass and Company was the biggest brewery in the world. A deliberate policy of acquisition resulted in a property portfolio of hundreds of 'tied houses' (inns contractually bound to a single brewery) across the United Kingdom. A network of agents promoted the company at home and abroad. Bass ales were on sale in 58 countries. Success was largely due to an innovative, marketing-led approach. In a shrewdly calculated gamble, Michael Thomas Bass expanded production ahead of demand. His 'red triangle' was the first trademark to be registered and Bass was the first businessman to establish and exploit a brand image in the modern commercial sense. Humorous advertising caught the popular imagination but the company's reputation was primarily founded on quality.

Brewing made the name of Burton famous around the globe. As business boomed, other major national brewers opened branches in the town. Ind Coope were first to arrive from the London area in 1856. They were followed by Charrington's, who took over Meakin's Abbey Street premises in 1872 and built the *Leopard Inn* around the corner in Lichfield Street. Truman, Hanbury and Buxton opened the Eagle Brewery, Derby Street in 1873. In 1874, Crossman, Mann and Paulin began work on a 'model village' site centred around their Albion Brewery on Shobnall Road. Later arrivals included Peter Walker from Warrington in 1880 and Everard Son and Welldon of Leicester in 1886.

The growth in trade was so meteoric there were labour shortages, particularly during the malting season. Brewing was now a year round activity but malting was still carried out in the winter months when the arrested germination

BURTON BREWERS IN 1869

Samuel Allsopp and Sons	High Street and Station Street. Trademark: Open Hand
Bass, Ratcliff and Gretton	High Street, Guild Street, Station Street. Trademark: Red Triangle
John Bell	Lichfield Street. Trademark: Bell
Joseph Bowler	New Street. Trademark: Anchor
Burton Brewery	High Street. Trademark: French Eagle
Carter and Scattergood	Victoria Street
Clements and Berry	High Street. Trademark: Star
Thomas Cooper	Victoria Crescent. Trademark: Crescent
James Eadie	Cross Street. Trademark: St Andrew's Cross
Sydney Evershed	Bank Square. Trademark: SE
Charles Hill and Son	Lichfield Street. Trademark: HS
Ind Coope	Station Street. Trademark: Britannia
William Measom	High Street. Trademark: Star
Nichols and Stone	Moor Street. Trademark: Spread Eagle
Joseph Nunneley	Bridge Street.
Phillips Brothers	Derby Street.
Thomas Robinson	Union Street. Trademark: R
Thomas Salt	High Street. Trademark: Maltese Cross
John Thompson	Horninglow Street and Horninglow Road. Trademark: TS
Henry Whitehead	Old Bridge.
William Worthington	High Street. Trademark: Shield and Dagger
John Yeomans	High Street.
NON-OPERATIONAL BREWERIES	
Green Man	New Street.
London and Colonial	Victoria Crescent.
Meakin	Abbey Street (taken over by Charrington's in 1872).

Source: W. Molyneux (1869)

104 *Although Ind Coope had arrived by 1869 most of the town's breweries were 'home grown'. Burton's reputation for beer soon attracted other leading brewers, including Charrington's from London, who took over Meakin's Abbey Street brewery in 1872.*

critical to controlling the process could be achieved. To resolve the situation, agricultural labourers from East Anglia were hired, mostly single men laid off after harvest time. Known locally as 'Norkies' or 'Suffolk Jims', they arrived in large numbers each autumn and lodged in the town until the following Whitsuntide. Malting was hard, laborious and uncomfortably hot. Temperatures frequently rose to 215° Fahrenheit. Dehydration was a potential problem and maltsters were kept supplied with large quantities of ale.

As the breweries grew, so did the town. By 1870, the population was approaching 25,000. To meet the demand for housing from brewery and railway employees, streets of terraced brick cottages were laid out in neat grid patterns on the former town commons of Goose Moor and Horninglow Moor, forming the Uxbridge and Victoria areas.

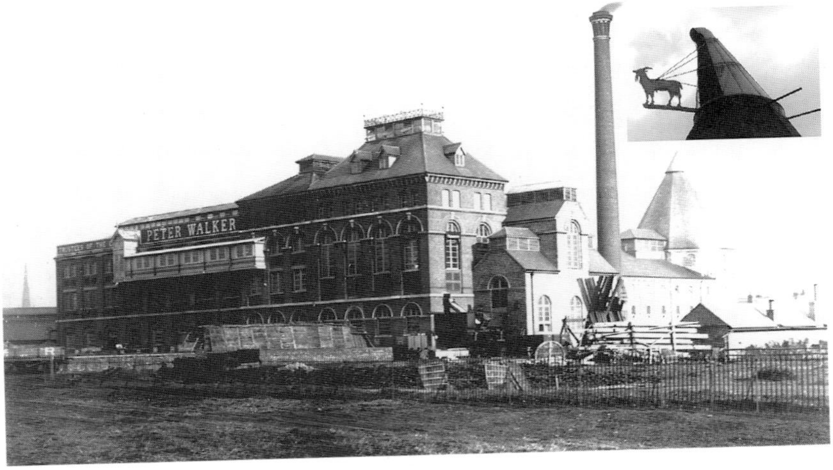

105 *Warrington brewer Peter Walker moved to Burton in 1880 and built the Goat Maltings in Clarence Street with its distinctive weather vane. The brewery closed in 1927. The maltings were taken over by Yeomans, Cherry and Curtis and remained in use until 1967.*

For many years older properties shared a water pump and continued to use backyard 'privies', the contents of which were collected at intervals by a 'night-soil' dealer for sale as fertiliser. The South Staffordshire Water Company provided a piped water supply from 1864. Mains pressure remained inconsistent until a water tower was built on top of Waterloo Mount in 1904 using gravity to assist equalisation. New houses were built with a cold water tap and often an outside water closet. Outfalls drained directly into local waterways. The open drain running down the middle of High Street had been covered as a priority under the improvements begun by the town commissioners after 1779. In 1843/4 it was properly culverted when the roadway was macadamised. Linking sewers were connected to the Bond End Canal, an arrangement that flushed the system every time the lock was used. Trade effluent in the growing industrial town was a considerable problem. Typhus and diphtheria were not uncommon and there were serious outbreaks of cholera in 1832 and 1849. Amid increasing concern about pollution and the adverse effects on public health, an inspector of nuisances was appointed by the commissioners in 1866 to monitor waste. Work began in the same year on a plant at Clay Mills where settling tanks allowed basic filtration before waste was expelled into the river downstream of the town. In 1880, plans were approved for a more efficient sewage treatment 'farm' at Egginton. Engines were installed at Clay Mills to pump effluent the additional two miles.

New streets had shops on every corner. A thriving outdoor market was expanded with the building of a Market Hall in 1883. To make room, the *Old Bowling Green Inn* and a house built by solicitor James Drewry in 1834 known as the Priory were demolished. In 1890, a Co-operative Society was launched and grew rapidly to dominate retail trade in the town. Large central offices for the Society opened in Byrkley Street just a decade later with shops below and a large hall on the upper floor.

Facilities everywhere were expanding to meet the demands of a rising population. Privately owned gas works opened on the corner of Union Street and Station Street in 1832. Gas lamps were introduced in town centre streets. Ownership of the gas works

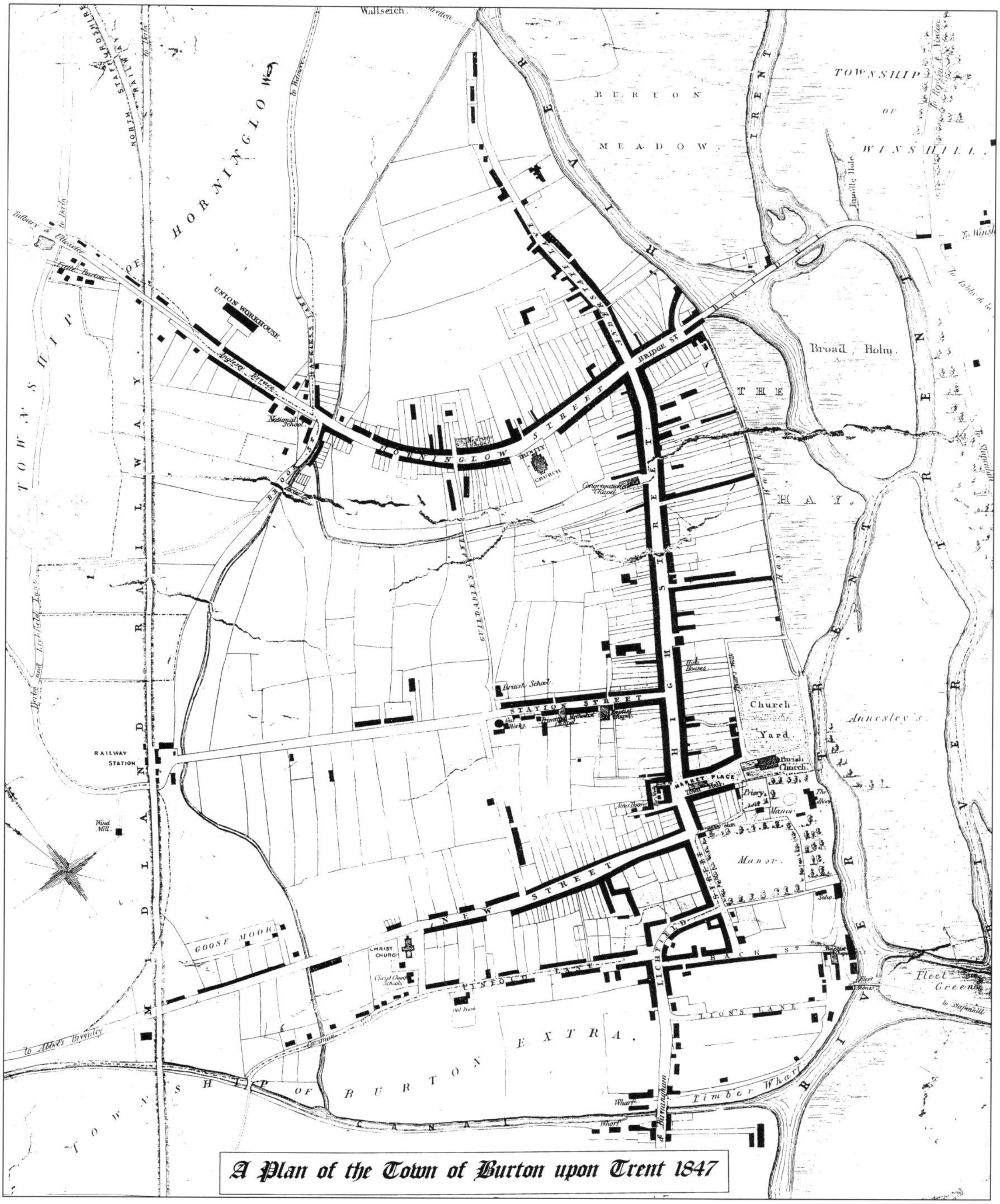

106 *The medieval borough layout is still recognisable in this map of 1847 by W. Wesley. Growth fuelled by a boom in brewing transformed the town in the second half of the 18th century. Vast brewhouses, maltings, cooperages, stores and spacious offices filled the town centre. Streets of terraced cottages were laid out on the former town commons.*

107 *Burton Co-operative Society's central offices in Byrkley Street, built by Thomas Lowe in 1899. Horse-drawn vans delivered bread from the Co-operative Bakery until the late 1950s.*

108 *A privately owned gas works on the corner of Station Street and Union Street, established in 1832, was transferred in 1853 to the Town Commissioners, who moved production to Wetmore Road. Penny in the slot meters were introduced into homes for domestic supplies.*

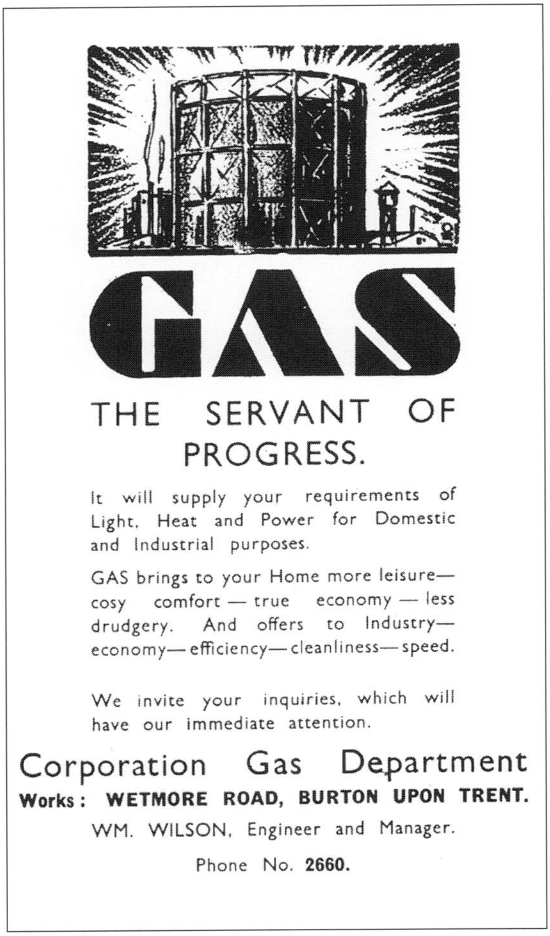
GAS
THE SERVANT OF PROGRESS.
It will supply your requirements of Light, Heat and Power for Domestic and Industrial purposes.
GAS brings to your Home more leisure—cosy comfort — true economy — less drudgery. And offers to Industry—economy—efficiency—cleanliness—speed.
We invite your inquiries, which will have our immediate attention.
Corporation Gas Department
Works: WETMORE ROAD, BURTON UPON TRENT.
WM. WILSON, Engineer and Manager.
Phone No. 2660.

was transferred to the town commissioners in 1853 and production moved to Anderstaff Lane (Wetmore Road). It proved a profitable exercise for the municipal borough authorities. Electricity generating works in nearby Electric Street were added in 1894.

Churchyards filled up as the population grew. Pressed by the vestry, the town commissioners established a Burial Board in 1864. Land was purchased at Stapenhill from the Marquess of Anglesey and a municipal cemetery consecrated in 1866.

The National Telephone Company began a local service in 1895. Trunk calls were available three years later through the Post Office. Burton 1 was allocated to the Fire Brigade and the police station number was Burton 42.

A weekly livestock market was held on Mondays behind the *Station Hotel*. A cattle sales yard known as the Smithfield opened in Derby Street in 1874.

Holy Trinity became a separate ecclesiastical district in 1842. Peter French, the minister, had been an outspoken critic of horse-racing on Burton Meadow. Meetings were frequently accompanied by disorderly behaviour. Popular

Electrically Cooked Food
Retains all its Flavour
and Nourishment.
The food in an electric oven is cooked in pure air, free from fumes that spoil the flavour.
Mrs Modern says.-
"I'm thankful
I live in an age
of electricity"
COOK BY
ELECTRICITY
Electric cooking keeps the best in and gets the best out of all kinds of food.
Its pure radiant heat preserves the most delicate flavours, conserves all the nourishing juices, and makes the plainest food appetising.
FOR NOURISHMENT, TASTE AND HEALTH
ELECTRIC COOKING IS BEST,
Cookers may be had on hire at 5/- per quarter, suitable for three to five persons. Wiring and Fixing free (up to 30ft. of cable).
CORPORATION
ELECTRICITY SHOWROOMS,
STATION STREET, BURTON UPON TRENT.

109 *Corporation electric works opened in Electric Street in 1894. By 1924, 150 houses in the town had electric cookers and 40 people were on a waiting list for connection.*

support for his views ensured that racing stopped in 1841. The following year the grandstand was taken down and the stone recycled in a new frontage for the Congregational Chapel in High Street.

Further parish districts emerged centred around Stretton and the new churches of Christ Church, Moor Street (1844), St Saviour's, Branston (1864), St John's, Horninglow (1864-6) and St Mark's, Winshill (1867-9). Stapenhill became an independent parish in 1864. St Peter's, with a foundation dating back to Anglo-Saxon times, was totally rebuilt in 1834 and again in 1884. The ecclesiastical districts of Christ Church and St Saviour's were reorganised into three districts in 1898 with a separate All Saints parish, for which the Bass family promised a new church. Plans were put on hold after the death of Lord Burton's brother Hamar Bass later that year.

As lord of the manor, the Marquess of Anglesey appointed the vicar of St Modwen's. When a vacancy occurred in 1870, an offer was made to leave the decision with the churchwardens and congregation. The Reverend Charles Thornewill, eldest son of local businessman Robert Thornewill, was subsequently appointed. In 1884 he raised £500 to purchase the right of presentation and transferred it to the Bishop of Lichfield.

Roman Catholics celebrated mass at a malthouse and in private houses before land was acquired for a school and chapel in Guild Street in 1851. The Church of St Mary and St Modwen followed on the site in 1879.

Protestant nonconformism continued to flourish and several additional chapels were built in the town. The Salvation Army established a centre in Wetmore Road in 1886 and moved to a citadel in Brook Street (off Horninglow Street) three years later. A destructive fire in 1946 forced relocation and a former Primitive Methodist chapel in Mosley Street was chosen.

A National School attached to Christ Church opened in 1844 and was soon sharing its premises with Allsopp's Charity School. Holy Trinity Church added an infants school in Anderstaff Lane (Wetmore Road) in 1847 and new premises in Hawkins Lane in 1862. National schools had close links with the established church. The British and Foreign

110 *A band was formed soon after the Salvation Army established a centre in Wetmore Road in 1886.*

School Society, formed in 1814, took a more liberal approach. A school based on the British System was built on Guildables Lane (Guild Street) in 1843. In addition to formal establishments there were a number of private or 'Dame' schools run by individuals, often in their own homes. The Education Act of 1870 made schooling compulsory for all children from the ages of five to 13 years. The formation of Burton School Board in 1873 put the town commissioners in control of education. The British School transferred to the new Board, who built their offices next door. An ambitious building programme followed, with new schools in 1875 (Victoria Road, Bond Street), in 1876 (Anderstaff Lane, Grange Street, Uxbridge Street and Wellington Street), and 1887/8 (Broadway).

The Grammar School moved from Friars' Walk to a new building in Bond Street in 1877. St Modwen's Church purchased the old premises for a Sunday school. After the establishment of the School Board, Allsopp's Charity School moved to premises between Waterloo Street and Princess Street. When the boys' section was absorbed by the Grammar School in 1884 it became the Girls High School.

The Victorian concept of morality and self-improvement through education and 'rational recreation' led to improved opportunities for adults. A Mechanics Institute offering evening classes began in 1867. A School of Science and a School of Art were launched shortly afterwards. Together with the town's Literary Society they joined forces as Burton Institute in 1876 and moved to shared premises in Union Street three years later. Literacy levels rose. Bookseller, George Scott, started a small subscription library in the early 19th century which was followed by William Darley's library at 35 High Street in 1826. Darley initially specialised in printing beer-bottle labels, possibly the first company to do so in the country. Before the introduction of labels, glassmakers marked bottles. St Modwen's Church made a small collection of books available for loan in 1829. Burton Institute's collection was transferred to the Borough Council in 1894 to form the basis of a town library.

Local newspapers appeared. The earliest, a *Monthly Advertiser* in 1842, managed only a few editions. Several weekly papers also proved short-lived. By far the most successful were the *Burton Chronicle*, first published by J. Tresise in 1860, and the *Burton Evening Gazette*. The weekly *Burton Observer* and daily *Burton Mail* first appeared in 1898.

A self-supporting dispensary opened in the Market Place in 1830 and moved to Duke Street when an infirmary with three wards and facilities for 24 in-patients was built in 1869. Land for the infirmary between Duke Street and New Street was donated by the Marquess of Anglesey. Both hospital and dispensary relied on subscriptions and donations. Weekly collections were taken in the town. In 1899 the infirmary was extended to provide 72 beds. A separate 'fever' hospital for treating infectious diseases was built at Outwoods in 1895.

Brewery employees benefited from company sponsored sports clubs and organised social events. All the leading breweries ran excursions. From the first small outing to Liverpool in 1865, annual day trips run by Bass grew into enormous events arranged with military precision. Only the largest resorts could cope with the sudden influx of around ten thousand visitors. Four main destinations were visited in rotation: Liverpool, Blackpool, Great Yarmouth and Scarborough. Up to 17 trains ran at ten-minute intervals from as early as 3.45 a.m. with the last return not arriving until 2.30 a.m. the following day.

From the middle of the 19th century the town centre was rebuilt as brewery output rocketed. Large-scale brewhouses, spacious offices, vast maltings, cooperages and stores filled the town centre. Well-designed and functional, many of the buildings were of considerable architectural merit. Brickmaking had been part of the local industrial scene since

111 *W.B. Darley's library at 35 High Street opened in 1827. The bookshop closed in 1960.*

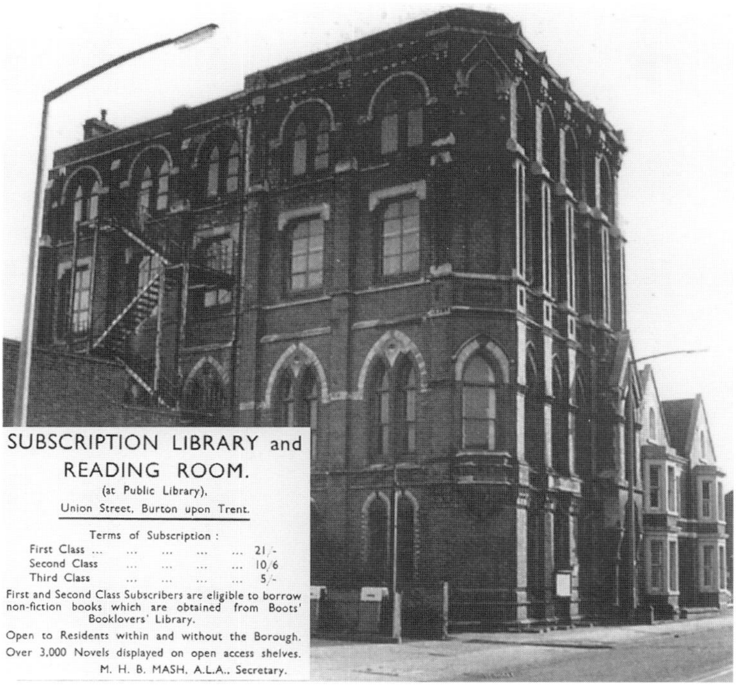

SUBSCRIPTION LIBRARY and READING ROOM.
(at Public Library),
Union Street, Burton upon Trent.
Terms of Subscription :
First Class 21/-
Second Class 10/6
Third Class 5/-
First and Second Class Subscribers are eligible to borrow non-fiction books which are obtained from Boots' Booklovers' Library.
Open to Residents within and without the Borough.
Over 3,000 Novels displayed on open access shelves.
M. H. B. MASH, A.L.A., Secretary.

112 *A collection of books at Burton Institute in Union Street formed the basis of a town library in 1894. A new Public Library opened on the Riverside site formerly occupied by redundant maltings in 1976. The Union Street building was demolished a year later.*

113 *The General Infirmary closed in 1993 and houses were built on the site. This view along Duke Street in 1962 shows the large glass windows of the Solarium at the end of the hospital wards. Beyond the brewery buildings on the left-hand side of Duke Street was the Violet Evershed wing opposite St Modwen's, a private ward.*

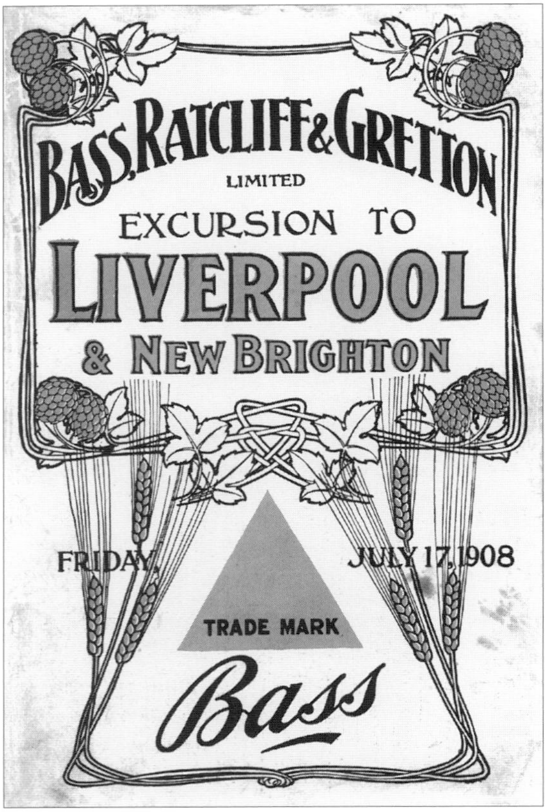

114 *Bass's annual railway trips began with an excursion to Liverpool in 1865 and grew into huge events involving up to 17 trains. Only the largest venues could cope. Liverpool, Blackpool, Scarborough and Great Yarmouth were visited in rotation. Annual trips ended with the outbreak of the First World War. One last 'special' was organised to the British Empire Exhibition in 1924.*

the Middle Ages. Brickyards at Shobnall, Stapenhill and Winshill supplied the materials for the expansion of the town in the 18th and early 19th centuries. The local yards of Lowe and Sons, Chamberlain and Lowe, Hodges and Co., and Smith and Co. were unable to keep pace with the demand that arose from the 1850s and large quantities of bricks had to be brought in from further afield. Much of the construction work was carried out by Thomas Lowe and Sons and by engineers Thornewill and Warham.

Thomas Lowe served an apprenticeship as a bricklayer before starting his own business in Moor Street at the age of 21. Generations earlier, the Lowe family had been prominent in the town's textile business. The companies of Thomas Lowe, George Hodges and (from 1877 until 1956 when it was taken over and eventually absorbed into Bovis Ltd) Richard Kershaw were the leading builders in the town.

Typically, the brewing families had lived 'over the shop' in elegant Georgian town-houses that fronted malthouses, breweries and offices. Now they began to move into country mansions. Michael Thomas Bass moved from 136 High Street to Byrkley Lodge while Rangemore Hall was built. Henry Allsopp (later Lord Hindlip) transferred to Foremark Hall and then to Doveridge Hall. John Gretton moved from 65 High Street to Bladon House before leasing Drakelow

Hall. The Ratcliffs occupied Newton Park, George Allsopp went to Foston Hall, Cecil Salt to Willington Hall and James Eadie to Barrow Hall.

Of the town's older substantial properties, the Marquess of Anglesey's agent now occupied the Manor House, while at the former abbey infirmary Peter French, minister of Holy Trinity, was followed by members of the Thornewill family and brewer John Allen Bindley, who carried out substantial rebuilding. Sinai Park House was leased to a tenant farmer. By the 1860s old Nether Hall was part of the Town Lands portfolio and in the hands of the feoffees. It was now in a poor state of repair and a decision was taken to demolish. The land was leased and a cooperage built on the site.

115 *Allsopp's Brewery in High Street occupied the site of the Blue Stoops and Benjamin Wilson's brewery. Part of the site became Eatough's shoe factory in the 1920s. The remaining brewery buildings were demolished in 1937, the shoe factory following when the east side of High Street was redeveloped in the late 1970s.*

116 *Ind Coope's spacious offices in Station Street. In 1856, Ind Coope became the first of many national brewers to move to Burton.*

117 *Rangemore Hall, country house of the Bass family from the 1860s. Michael Arthur Bass was a friend of Edward VIII, who was a regular guest.*

118 *Michael Arthur Bass presented the Liberal Club and St Paul's Institute built by his father to the town to serve as municipal offices. He added an elaborate oak-panelled council chamber with a decorated ceiling and handsome raised chair for the mayor and seats and desks for the aldermen, councillors and officials.*

The influence of the brewing magnates extended to all aspects of civic, social and economic life. Michael Thomas Bass was an active Member of Parliament for Derby and played a significant role in improving conditions for rail workers. Samuel Allsopp was MP for Worcestershire, Henry Wardle, director of Salt and Co., represented the South Derbyshire constituency. Until secret ballots were introduced in 1872 voters' names were recorded in a poll book. Burton was part of a larger County Division. Few local people bothered journeying to Stafford to register their vote. Michael Arthur Bass, Michael Thomas's son, was elected to represent Staffordshire East in 1868, and defeated Gerald Hardy to be the first MP for a newly created Burton Division in 1885.

Brewers served as town masters, feoffees, commissioners and, after incorporation, as members of the town council. Principled, benevolent paternalism was a hallmark of the times. St John's Church, Horninglow (John Marston), St Mark's Church, Winshill (John Gretton), and St Paul's Church, Rangemore Street (Michael Thomas Bass) were all partly or wholly paid for by leading brewers. Michael Thomas Bass footed the bill for St Paul's Institute, intended as a venue for 'scholastic, recreational and intellectual pursuits'. Michael Arthur Bass built a replacement and gave the original, with the addition of an elaborate council chamber, as a Town Hall in 1894.

Richard and Robert Ratcliff donated public swimming baths on the Hay alongside the new Burton Bridge in 1875. A team from the town won the first English water polo championships held in 1888 and followed up their success with two further national titles in the next three years.

Rowing was popular on the River Trent. Burton Leander (1847) and Burton Anglesey (1848) were the first clubs. Burton Rowing Club and Trent Rowing Club followed in the 1860s. Burton Cricket Club first played around 1827, probably started by Abraham Bass, younger brother of Michael Thomas. Burton Football Club was founded in 1870, initially combining both disciplines before deciding to concentrate on rugby. Burton and District Football Association was formed in 1871 with a core membership made up of church and works teams. In the 1880s Burton

119 *Richard and Robert Ratcliff donated public swimming baths on the Hay alongside the new Burton Bridge in 1875.*

OPENING

OF THE

FERRY BRIDGE

PRESENTATIONS TO LORD AND LADY BURTON.

ENTHUSIASTIC DEMONSTRATION.

At last the long-looked-for bridge over the river Trent at the ferry is a reality, and its creation is accompanied by the decease and sepulture of the venerable and patriarchal ferry. "The ferry's dead: long last the bridge" may now be sung, and thousands of voices will acclaim the praises of Lord Burton, through whose spontaneous and large-hearted munificence the decease of the one and the birth of the other has been accomplished. But an old friend has departed, and before we chronicle a record of the enthusiastic proceedings attendant upon the inauguration of the latest arrival, we must give, as far as we can, an obituary notice of "the departed." The compilation of it has entailed a vast amount of inquiry and trouble, but we considered it was only due to the memory of "our ancient friend" that something should be written about it.

YE ANTIENT HISTORIE OF YE FERRIE.

Across ye Trent to Stapenhill,
And back to Burton town,
A penny fee will carry me,
Though well 'tis worth a crown.

So wrote a local rhymester many years ago, when no one had even the audacity to dream that Stapenhill would ever be in "Burton town," or that the river Trent would be spanned at the ferry by as handsome and noble-looking a bridge as can be found in the country. From that day—and for many a day anterior—to this the penny fee has been demanded, but the formal opening of the bridge, which has been so generously built by Lord Burton, strikes, we venture to think, the warning bell for the abolition of the toll. An old institution is the ferry, and we suppose it has a history, but, as far as we can learn, no one has attempted to write it in detail, and we shall not set the example. Its origin, like Topsy's progenitors, is lost in mystery, but we "specta" that the monopoly or right to charge the penny fee "growed, like other" feudal excrescences, until no one could dispute its strict legality.

120 *Lord Burton (centre) next to his daughter Nellie (wearing a hat), Mayor Charles Harrison and his wife with Lady Burton (holding a bouquet of flowers) head the dignitaries gathered for the official opening of the Ferry Bridge on 4 April 1889. The* Burton Chronicle *reported in detail, devoting nine broadsheet columns to the event.*

Wanderers and Burton Swifts both played in Division 2 of the English league. Burton Golf Club began in 1894 with a nine-hole course off Woods Lane, Stapenhill and the *Grove* public house standing in as a clubroom. The club moved to Branston in 1897 before settling at Bretby in 1907.

Burton Meadow was the main sporting venue. From 1841, the Hay was also made available by the Marquess of Anglesey after a petition was presented complaining about lack of facilities following the enclosure of common land. Gardens and a riverside walk at Stapenhill began development in 1865 on land leased from the Anglesey Estate. The Oxhay and St Modwen's Orchard were leased in 1884 and Andresey Bridge built by Thornewill and Warham to link the island with the town centre. Outwoods recreation ground was laid out in 1884.

Despite industrialisation the pace of life was still largely dictated by that of a horse. The railway was fast and efficient but a rural population still had to get to the station. Gentry had their carriages, farmers a horse and trap. Horses could be hired by the day. Water troughs were handily placed around the town on Horninglow Road North, at the junction of Ashby Road and Stapenhill Road, outside the *Branstone Arms*, Branston Road, and at the corner of Moor Street and Wellington Street. Public transport in the town began with a horse-drawn omnibus service from the *Three Queens* to the railway station in

121 *William Henry Worthington (1826-94) was chosen as the town's first mayor when Burton became a Municipal Borough in 1878.*

1851. A service from the *White Hart* started in 1876 and William Marriott began carrying passengers from Stapenhill in 1880. Marriot charged a fare of four pence compared with a halfpenny for using the ferry. Many public houses on the rural fringes offered stabling and cab services to attract customers. In 1896, the Borough Council found it necessary to pass bylaws restricting the proliferation of horse-drawn taxis.

From the Middle Ages a ferry at Stapenhill had saved pedestrians a long detour. By 1864, two flat-bottomed punts were carrying over five thousand passengers between Stapenhill and Burton each week. The ferry operated under licence from the Marquess of Anglesey, who still owned shipping rights on the river. In 1865, the Marquess obtained an Act of Parliament authorising a bridge but took no action. Numbers using the ferry rose to 12,000 in the mid-1880s. Michael Arthur Bass, 1st Baron Burton from 1886, offered to finance construction of a bridge if the Borough Council purchased the rights. The 75m. wrought-iron latticework Ferry Bridge of three spans, carried on the suspension principle and engineered by Thornewill and Warham, opened in 1889. Thomas Lowe and Sons built the supporting piers on foundations sunk deep into the bedrock below the river. Lord and Lady Burton (Harriet Bass was a member of the Thornewill family) caught the last ferry to attend the official opening ceremony before adjourning to St Paul's Institute for a lavish celebratory banquet. Within a year a new cast-iron viaduct replaced a plank walkway that led over the flood-prone washlands between the bridge and the town. The cost of acquiring the rights was to be recouped by a toll and the bridge was closed overnight from 11 p.m., but in 1898 Lord Burton again came to the aid of the town and paid off the outstanding balance.

A series of local government reforms began in 1853. The Burton upon Trent Act extended the authority of the town commissioners and ended shared control with the feoffees. Burton Extra and Horninglow were brought into the borough. Administration of the town was now in the hands of 18 elected commissioners with offices on the corner of Guild Street and Horninglow Street and, by virtue of his office, the high bailiff. New powers allowed the compulsory purchase of land for civic improvements, control of fairs and markets, and regulation of the town constables. Growth demanded more far-reaching changes. A petition raised by the townspeople persuaded the commissioners to seek municipal borough status. In 1878, the borough was enlarged to include Stapenhill and Winshill. Later that year a Charter of Incorporation was granted and the first town council was elected with six councillors representing each of four wards in the new borough. William Worthington was chosen as the first mayor, and six of his fellow aldermen – Samuel Allsopp, Michael Arthur Bass, Sydney Evershed and Henry Wardle – were also brewers. Thomas Lowe and Henry Mason filled the remaining two posts.

The town's first police station was built on Station Street, near the junction with Guild Street, in 1848, anticipating legislation passed in 1856 requiring every county and every town to provide a police force. Long-serving town constable Richard Roe was promoted to inspector with two constables of the Staffordshire District in support. A nightly curfew that had applied from the Middle Ages was officially discontinued in 1867. By 1896, with the population fast approaching 50,000, Superintendent James Gilbride was in charge of three sergeants and 24 constables.

Major reform of the Poor Laws after 1834 led to the grouping of individual parishes into 600 Poor Law unions. Burton was the centre for a coalition of 53 parishes, 13 in

122 *Thomas Lowe built the town's first police station on Station Street near the corner with Guild Street in 1848.*

Staffordshire and 40 in Derbyshire. A new workhouse in Hawkins Lane opened in 1839 with room for 300 occupants and provision for a school. Application of a workhouse test enabled those considered unable to work through no fault of their own to qualify for relief in their own homes – if they possessed one. A board of guardians, the Union Board, was elected locally to oversee administration. Inmates continued to face a rigorous regime. Able-bodied men were given manual work similar to the hard labour set for convicted prisoners. Tasks included breaking stone, repairing roads and unpicking old hemp rope for recycling as oakum, a caulking material mixed with pine tar and used to seal joints in wooden boats. Workhouse accommodation improved with the opening of the Andressey on Belvedere Road in 1884. Separate wings allowed segregation of men and women.

New almshouses built on Wellington Street in the early 1870s provided accommodation for 21 individuals and brought all the almswomen of the town under one roof. A smaller unit for men was added in York Street a few years later. The former Paulet almshouse was taken over by the Borough Council who used it for storage and later as an office for weights-and-measures officials. Almshouse properties in High Street and Hawkins Lane were sold. In 1875, charity administration was re-organised under a board of trustees, with separate administrative units responsible for almshouses, the Town Lands, and help for those in need.

Most of the various civil functions of the manor court became obsolete or were superseded. Probate jurisdiction vanished with the Court of Probate Act of 1858. A courthouse was added to the police station in 1862 and sittings moved from the *Angel Inn* in Bank Square. Petty sessions convened every Tuesday and a county court met monthly. In 1894, a parish council took over the remaining secular responsibilities of the vestry.

Brewery employees were relatively well paid and Burtonians enjoyed increasing leisure time. St George's Hall, built in 1867 on the corner of George Street and Guild Street, was converted 20 years later as the Opera House and staged a variety of live shows. A music hall occupied a room behind the *Staffordshire Knot* public house in Station Street and there

123 *Richard 'Dick' Roe (c.1779-1853) regularly served as town constable, doubling as blacksmith and landlord of the* Wheat Sheaf *in High Street. When a police force was formed and a station built in 1848 he became the first Inspector. A memorial obelisk was moved to the perimeter along with other markers when the Gardens of Remembrance were laid out.*

124 *The new County Borough was granted a coat of arms by Norroy, King of Arms at the College of Arms.* Honor alit artes *(honour nourishes the arts) is a quotation from Roman statesman and orator Cicero. Blue and white lines on the shield (barry wavy of six argent and azure on a chief gules) represent the rivers Trent and Dove.*

was more variety on offer at the Queen's Theatre, Wetmore Road. From 1901, regular shows took place at the Anglesey Palace, a hall attached to a new Young Men's Christian Association building off High Street. A number of local bands played at bandstands in Stapenhill gardens and Outwoods recreation ground. Circuses made annual visits. In 1878, Thomas Batty's Great London Circus closed their season here and overwintered. Regular concerts and dances were held at the Town Hall and in the Co-operative Hall.

Estimates in 1898 suggested the population of the town had already passed the 50,000 point at which Burton could become a County Borough, able to organise its own affairs free of county council control. The Burton upon Trent Corporation Act passed in 1901 marked a municipal coming of age. A tide of optimism would carry the town through a confident decade. But in many ways it was a turning point. The rate of growth was unsustainable. Economic change and world conflict would impose austerity.

NINE

Into the Twentieth Century: *Triumphs and Tribulations*

Throughout the spring of 1903 there is disruption as tracks, kerbside standards and cables prepare the streets for a public tramway system. On 3 August Mayor Arthur Roberts pays a penny fare and becomes the first customer.

A fleet of 24 double-decker trams, 16 covered and eight open-topped, supplied by the Electric Railway and Tramway Car Works Company of Preston, ran from the Town Hall to Horninglow, Stapenhill and Winshill. Different coloured signals indicated routes. Cars carried up to 20 passengers 'inside' and a further 23 upstairs. Businesses on the routes were soon advertising 'trams run by our door'. Not all trams ran by every door. When the privately owned Burton and Ashby Light Railway began operations in 1906, influential householders on Ashby Road forced a route alteration along High Bank Road and Bearwood Hill. Burton and Ashby trams were allowed to use corporation lines but were diverted along Horninglow Street and Guild Street to leave corporation trams a monopoly in the town centre.

A new fire station (1903), head post office (1905) and showpiece magistrates court and police station (1910), all built by Richard Kershaw, reflected the town's new County Borough status.

Sir William, Hamar Bass's son, ensured the completion of All Saints Church in 1905. Lord Burton died in 1909. Public subscriptions paid for a commemorative statue in King Edward Place, surrounded by the complex of elegant

125 *A corporation tramway system began operating in 1903. All the electric tramcars had been phased out in favour of motor buses by 1930.*

126 *A new police station and magistrates court opened in 1910, its Baroque styling echoing London's 'Old Bailey', not least in number one court (inset). The site cut across the entrance to the tram depot and the building had to be angled to allow access. The tram leaving here is decorated for the coronation of George V in 1911.*

127 *St Chad's Church, Hunter Street (a separate parish from 1905) was completed in 1910, a final gift to the town from Lord Burton. A masterpiece of creative design by G.F. Bodley, it is arguably the finest building in Burton. The main entrance is beneath a separate tower connected to the main body of the church by a vaulted corridor.*

buildings bestowed on the town by Bass and his father. St Chad's Church, Hunter Street, a final gift from Lord Burton and arguably the finest building in Burton, held its first services in 1910.

Louis Bleriot flew across the English Channel and into history in 1909. The following year Burton gave the Midlands a glimpse of the future, hosting a display by French aviation aces on Burton Meadow. Thirty thousand spectators attended the event. A chain for the mayoress with an aeroplane incorporated in the design was bought out of the profits.

It was an assured start to the 20th century but problems were looming. In retrospect the warning signals were apparent a decade earlier. Beer sales were being eroded by a combination of licensing restrictions, rising excise duties and a powerful temperance lobby. Faced with intense competition, many smaller breweries amalgamated to achieve efficiencies. Marston, Thompson and Evershed began their partnership in 1905, taking over the Albion Brewery of Crossman, Mann and Paulin. Others became the subjects of acquisition by ambitious rivals. Often the aim was to secure tied houses rather than production capacity and brewing operations were closed down. Thomas Salt and Company were forced to re-capitalise in 1906.

128 *A display by French aviators on Burton Meadow in 1910 attracted 30,000 spectators. The proceeds paid for an 18-carat gold chain for the mayoress on which the event was celebrated by incorporating a small medallion of a biplane.*

129 *Marston, Thompson and Evershed's Albion Brewery on Shobnall Road was originally designed as part of a model village by London brewers Crossman, Mann and Paulin.*

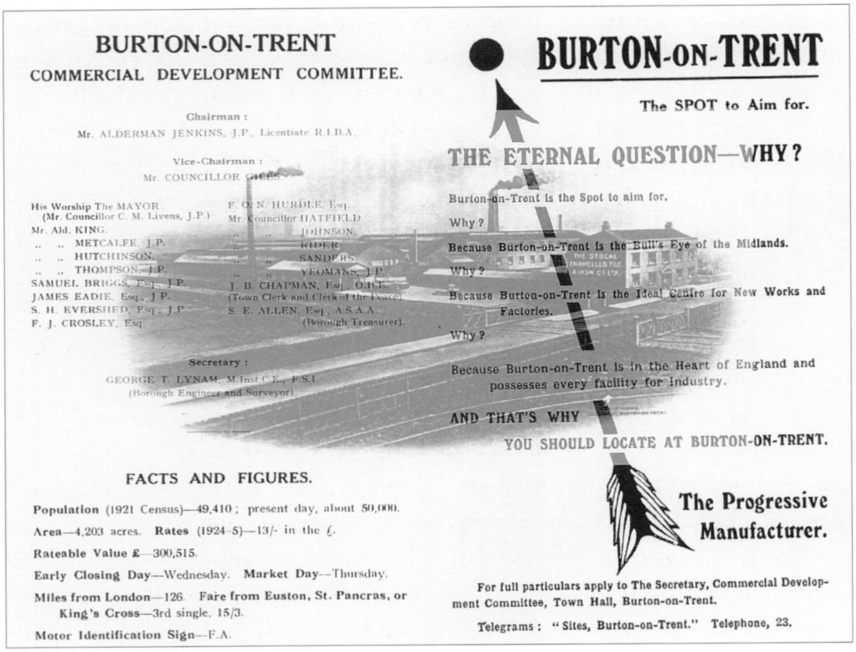

BURTON-ON-TRENT
COMMERCIAL DEVELOPMENT COMMITTEE.
Chairman :
Mr. ALDERMAN JENKINS, J.P., Licentiate R.I.B.A.
Vice-Chairman :
Mr. COUNCILLOR
His Worship The MAYOR (Mr. Councillor C. M. Livens, J.P.)
Mr. Ald. KING.
„ „ METCALFE, J.P.
„ „ HUTCHINSON.
„ „ THOMPSON, J.P.
SAMUEL BRIGGS, Esq., J.P.
JAMES EADIE, Esq., J.P.
S. H. EVERSHED, Esq., J.P.
F. J. CROSLEY, Esq.
F. O. N. HURDLE, Esq.
Mr. Councillor HATFIELD.
„ „ JOHNSON.
„ „ RIDER.
„ „ SANDERS.
„ „ YEOMANS, J.P.
J. B. CHAPMAN, Esq., O.B.E. (Town Clerk and Clerk of the Peace).
S. E. ALLEN, Esq., A.S.A.A. (Borough Treasurer).
Secretary :
GEORGE T. LYNAM, M.Inst.C.E., F.S.I. (Borough Engineer and Surveyor).
FACTS AND FIGURES.
Population (1921 Census)—49,410 ; present day, about 50,000.
Area—4,203 acres. Rates (1924-5)—13/- in the £.
Rateable Value £—300,515.
Early Closing Day—Wednesday. Market Day—Thursday.
Miles from London—126. Fare from Euston, St. Pancras, or King's Cross—3rd single, 15/3.
Motor Identification Sign—F.A.
BURTON-ON-TRENT
The SPOT to Aim for.
THE ETERNAL QUESTION—WHY?
Burton-on-Trent is the Spot to aim for.
Why?
Because Burton-on-Trent is the Bull's Eye of the Midlands.
Why?
Because Burton-on-Trent is the Ideal Centre for New Works and Factories.
Why?
Because Burton-on-Trent is in the Heart of England and possesses every facility for Industry.
AND THAT'S WHY
YOU SHOULD LOCATE AT BURTON-ON-TRENT.
The Progressive Manufacturer.
For full particulars apply to The Secretary, Commercial Development Committee, Town Hall, Burton-on-Trent.
Telegrams : "Sites, Burton-on-Trent." Telephone, 23.

130 *A Commercial Development Committee set up by the Corporation in 1909 aimed to attract new industry to the town. One of the early successes was Stocal Enamels, who moved from Lancaster in 1913. Stocal made enamel advertising signs and iron tiles until the 1950s, when the site between Horninglow Road and Dallow Street was taken over by Renold Chains.*

131 *Ryknield Engine Company (Ryknield Motor Company from 1905) manufactured internal combustion and steam-driven cars, vans and buses at their pioneering factory in Shobnall Road from 1903 until bankruptcy forced the works to close in 1911.*

Recognising that economic dependence on brewing left the town vulnerable, the Corporation established a Commercial Development Committee in 1909 to try to attract new industry. Werneth Rubber Company (1911), Stocal Enamels (1913), Burton Constructional Engineering (1914), Burton Foundry (1916), India Rubber and Gutta Percha (along with Werneth, later absorbed by British Tyre and Rubber, 1916), Cyclops Engineering (1918), Eatoughs Shoes (1921), and Pirelli (1929) were among the bigger names attracted.

A promising motor industry began in 1903 with the Ryknield Engine Company manufacturing cars, vans and buses on a site between Wellington Street and Shobnall Road. Despite the latest production line efficiencies imported from the United States, bankruptcy forced closure in 1911. Managing Director Major Ernest Baguley went on to form Baguley Cars. Works manager Percy Salmon also branched out to start his own company in Lichfield Street. Both ventures were short-lived, although Baguley successfully switched to manufacturing locomotives.

A difficult business climate worsened with the First World War. Scarcity of grain and shortage of labour were compounded by restrictions imposed on brewing. The Bass railway trips ended at the outbreak of war and never restarted. One last 'special' was organised as part of a town event to visit the British Empire Exhibition at Wembley in 1924. In place of the annual outing, employees were given an additional half-day holiday.

Builders Thomas Lowe and Sons undertook a number of government contracts and were commissioned to build the National Machine Gun Factory in Burton Road, Branston. German prisoners-of-war, housed in converted maltings on Anglesey Road, worked as labourers on the project, helping to build a high perimeter wall in decorative brickwork. Other local companies also contributed to the war effort. The works of George Orton and Charles Spooner, collaborative partners since the 1890s, had a national reputation for building fairground rides and luxurious showmen's living waggons. Under the direction of the War Office their pre-fabrication expertise was applied to the production of portable hangars for the newly formed Royal Flying Corps. In Park Street, the Navarro Aircraft Company manufactured spare parts for aeroplanes. At the outbreak of war in August 1914, the Town Hall was pressed into service as a Red Cross military hospital.

Many Burtonians enlisted. Around thirteen hundred gave their lives. William 'Bill' Coltman joined 1/6 Battalion of the North Staffordshire Regiment and fought in early exchanges in France. Torn between a sense of duty and deeply held religious convictions, he volunteered to become a stretcher-bearer. For the rest of the war Coltman was on the front line, selflessly risking his life in no man's land, rescuing and treating injured comrades under enemy fire. Lance Corporal Coltman's courage was recognised by a string of citations and awards culminating in the Victoria Cross.

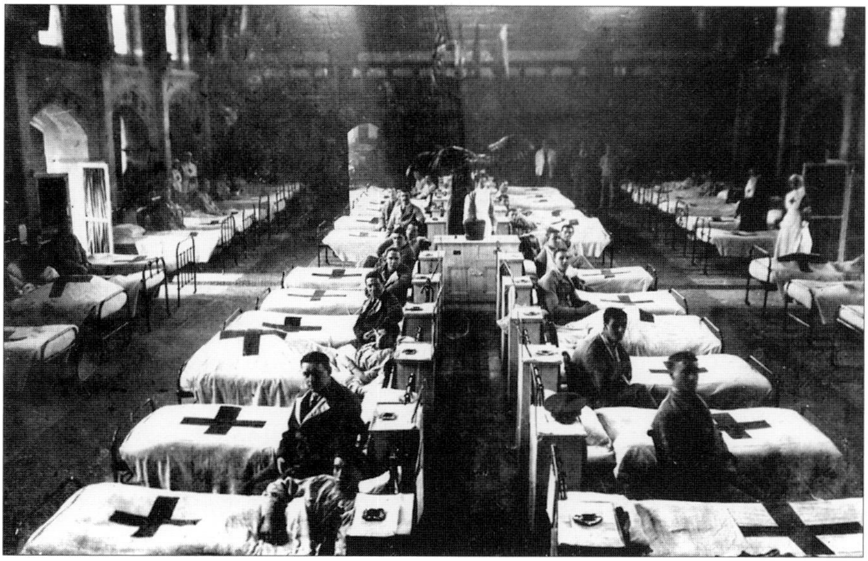

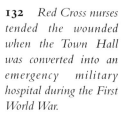

132 *Red Cross nurses tended the wounded when the Town Hall was converted into an emergency military hospital during the First World War.*

In 1916, three hydrogen-filled Zeppelin airships passed over Burton and unloaded around fifty bombs, killing 15 and injuring many more. Two of the Zeppelin commanders thought they were over Sheffield. The other may have mistaken the Trent for the Mersey and the lights of Stapenhill for Birkenhead and believed he was bombing Liverpool.

There was barely time to recondition a few firearms at the National Machine Gun Factory before war ended. Crosse and Blackwell bought the premises in 1920. Production of Branston Pickle began shortly afterwards, made to a secret recipe allegedly cooked up in the kitchen of Branstone Lodge by Caroline Graham and her daughters Evelyn and Ermentrude. Ingredients were purchased in bulk from Covent Garden and much of the firm's output went back to London for distribution, a logistical inconvenience that led the company to relocate in 1925. Branston Artificial Silk Company acquired the premises in 1927. When they went into liquidation in 1930, the receivers arranged a series of short leases.

In 1926, the imposition of new terms of employment for colliers led to the General Strike. Miners refused to accept revised contracts and were locked out. The Trades Union Congress (TUC) called out workers in key industries in support. Mayor Carey Livens set up a committee to handle the emergency and called for volunteers to maintain essential services. Corporation transport stopped as employees came out in sympathy. Elsewhere the response was patchy. Most companies continued to work normally. Despite appeals not to hoard supplies the Co-operative coal depot, the largest domestic supplier in the town, had soon sold out. Coal was rationed nationally.

A local strike committee was formed and met in the Co-operative Society Hall. Burton Trades Council set up a distress fund. Food vouchers were distributed at the newly established Working Men's Club in Shaftesbury House on the corner of New Street and Orchard Street. The Union Board at the workhouse agreed to pay strikers' wives 10s. a week plus 4s. for each child up to a maximum of 25s. Around a thousand strikers attended a special service in the parish church on Sunday 9 May. Print workers went on strike. Managers at the *Burton Daily Mail* continued to put out a free single sheet bulletin. An editorial denounced the withdrawal of labour as 'deplorable'. Burton Town Football Club organised matches for strikers. Whist drives were arranged for wet days.

Proposals for a national wages board and a minimum wage guarantee were accepted by the TUC and the General Strike was called off after two weeks. The miners, who had not been consulted, continued the dispute alone. Police reservists were called up as strong feelings led to tension. Many miners and their families suffered severe hardship. A gradual drift back to work effectively brought the dispute to a close by the end of the year.

Economic depression in the 1920s led to further rationalisation in the brewing industry. Peter Walker ended their association with the town in 1925. Charrington's closed its Abbey Street brewery in 1926. Bass and Worthington merged in 1927, swallowing up Salt's in the same year and adding James Eadie in 1933. Ind Coope bought out Bindley's, Burton Brewery and Robinson's before merging with Allsopp's in 1934. Economies of scale delivered increased efficiency but there was a cost in jobs.

Charles, 6th Marquess of Anglesey, possibly responding to criticism of being an absentee landlord, served a term as mayor in 1911/12. In the aftermath of war, Paget links with the town were loosened. A full inventory and survey of the Marquess of Anglesey's local estate was carried out in 1918. Large holdings were sold over the following years. Various local companies bought the freehold to the land they occupied. Importantly, the sale allowed the Corporation to purchase land for development at a crucial time.

The first of a series of Housing and Town Planning Acts in 1919 asked local authorities to review housing stocks and draw up proposals for improvement. Government subsidies were available to help finance approved work. The Corporation had already built a few houses in Watson Street and Richmond Street. Now there was an opportunity for large-scale projects. By 1939 over a thousand council houses had been built, most of them on estates at Horninglow, Stapenhill and Winshill.

In 1927, redevelopment of High Street began with the demolition of buildings on the foundations of the abbey gatehouse along with an adjacent row of old shops. In the 1930s, the Abbey Arcade was built in the latest Art Deco style.

Motor buses were introduced on some corporation routes in 1924. Tramlines still threaded through cobbled streets but the tram era was all but over. The Burton and Ashby Light Railway closed in 1926. There had been two serious accidents: in 1919, a Burton and Ashby car ran back on Bearwood Hill and overturned, killing two and injuring 16; in 1924, a broken axle derailed a corporation tram in Station Street injuring 28 passengers.

By 1930 all the trams had been phased out and replaced with a fleet of single-decker Guy motor buses. Corporation buses ran a parcel service from an office at 181 Station Street. Packages were charged by weight. Regular users could obtain a discount by buying a book of prepaid tickets.

133 *Charles, 6th Marquess of Anglesey served a term in office as mayor in 1911/12 before marrying Lady Marjorie Manners.*

The rapid adoption of motorised transport spelled the end for the town's horse fair, held annually since 1771. Trade declined and sales were held for the last time on 22 October 1924.

Large crowds gathered for the annual Statutes Fair, held on the Monday and Tuesday following Michaelmas Day. The fair appears to have developed from the traditional festivities following the great court held by the abbots rather than one of the charter fairs. Until 1905 and the introduction of a Labour Exchange it was still an occasion for farm labourers and domestic servants to agree terms with prospective employers before spending their hiring-on fee enjoying the various attractions on offer. To show that they had found a job, individuals displayed a red, white and blue ribbon in their hat.

Many Burtonians had their first taste of 'moving pictures', projected from a bioscope on to a canvas screen, at the Statutes Fair. Occasional shows were also held in venues such as the Town Hall and Anglesey Hall. A room above shops in Station Street was the Cosy Corner Picture Palace until regulations introduced by the Cinematograph Act (1910) imposed safety standards it was unable to meet. Films were also shown at Curzon Hall, an iron and brick roller-skating rink in Curzon Street. A dedicated cinema, part of the national Electric Theatre chain, opened in High Street in 1910. It later became the Gaumont. Curzon Hall turned over fully to films as the Picturedrome in 1913. It was completely rebuilt in 1931 and became the Odeon in 1956. A pianist or occasionally a small orchestra vamped a soundtrack to accompany the early silent movies. In 1920, the Picturedrome acquired a second-hand organ from a London church.

The Derby Turn Palace opened in 1920 and was renamed the Regent Cinema in 1932. During the Second World War it acted as a munitions store. For many years after the war it was used as a warehouse before being turned into a venue for bingo. Film was taking over from live theatre. The Opera House closed in 1932 to open two years later fully refitted as the Ritz Cinema. The Queen's Theatre closed around the same time and the premises were put to various business uses, including a spell as a temporary postal sorting office, before demolition in 1988.

134 *Two died, including the conductress, and 15 passengers were taken to hospital when car 19 of the Burton and Ashby Light Railway lost traction and ran back down Bearwood Hill in 1919. Twenty-eight passengers were injured when a corporation tram broke an axle and overturned in Station Street in 1924 (inset).*

Just as cinema replaced live theatre it was in turn supplanted by television. Audiences began to dwindle from the mid-1950s. When the Gaumont closed in 1956 the Ritz adopted the name. Conversion of the Curzon Street Odeon into a bingo club in 1965 left it Burton's only cinema. Three years later it became the Odeon.

135 *Live shows at the Opera House in George Street ended when it closed in 1932 and was converted into the Ritz Cinema.*

The town's fascination with aviation continued with a visit by Alan Cobham's Flying Circus in 1933. Sir Alan had earlier surveyed a landing strip on Henhurst Hill prepared for the display and lent his support to proposals for an airport on the site. Air Ministry approval had already been secured but the idea failed to materialise. The Royal Air Force (RAF) used the landing strip as part of a pilot training school during the Second World War. Afterwards plans for the aerodrome were abandoned in favour of a housing project and the site was developed as Aviation Lane.

In 1933, a telephone exchange was built in Fleet Street. There were still only 800 subscribers in the town, but the number was growing. A new larger exchange proved necessary in 1957.

War was declared in 1939. Large numbers of Burtonians enlisted in the armed forces. Some three hundred and fifty never returned. On the domestic front individuals volunteered for civil defence duties either in what evolved into the 'Home Guard' or as firewatchers and wardens with the Air Raid Precaution Service. The War Office had bought back the former National Machine Gun Factory at Branston as an ordnance store. An aerial reconnaissance photograph taken by the Luftwaffe shows the depot as an identified target. Bombs fell on the Uxbridge and Broadway areas in August 1940 killing six. Calais Road and Carlton Street were hit in 1941. A clutch of practice bombs, fortunately lightly charged, was accidentally dropped during an RAF training flight in 1944. Overall, the town escaped relatively lightly with no sustained raids.

Disaster struck unexpectedly on 27 November 1944. A lethal arsenal of bombs stored in the underground chambers of former gypsum workings at 21 Maintenance Unit RAF Fauld detonated. It was the biggest non-nuclear blast of the war, setting up a seismic shockwave that was recorded as far away as Switzerland. A million tons of debris hurled into the air left an enormous crater. Seventy people were killed including a number of Italian prisoners-of-war. Nineteen bodies were never recovered. Upper Castle Hayes farm at Hanbury disappeared. Twenty-seven

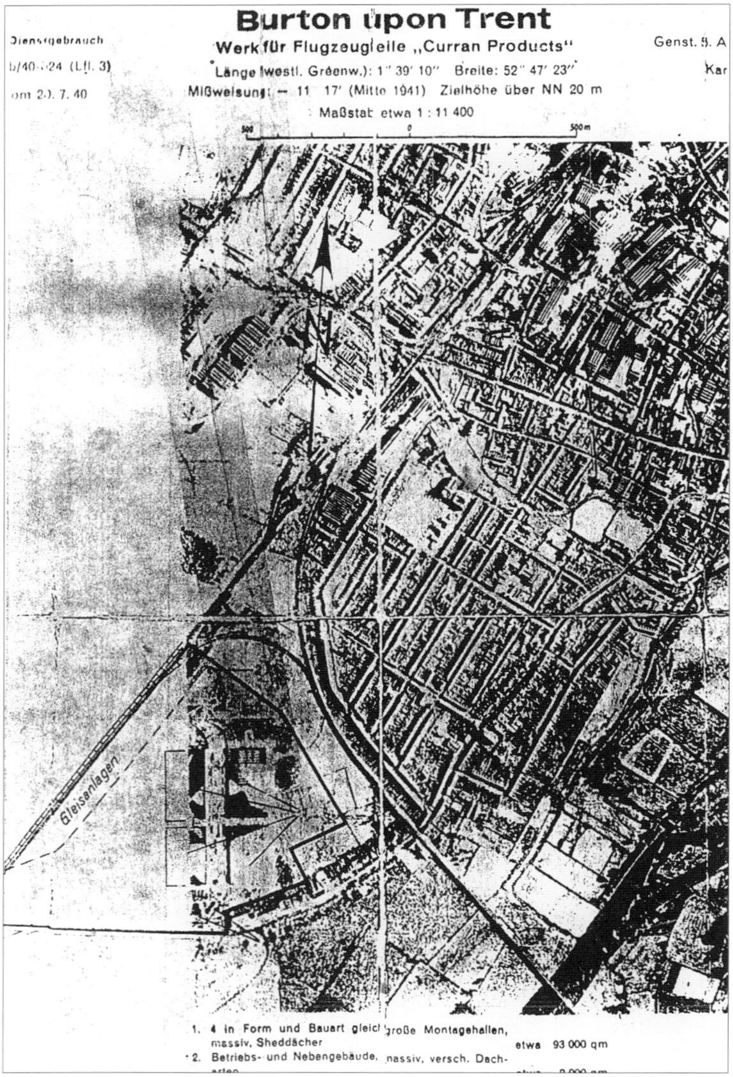

136 *An aerial reconnaissance photograph taken by the German* Luftwaffe *during the Second World War shows the ordnance depot at Branston as a potential target. Additional information gives the scale, precise location co-ordinates and a description of the roof sizes, railway junction and surrounding fields seen from target height. It also suggests that the depot was assembling parts for aeroplanes ('flugzeug').*

of those who died lost their lives when a reservoir burst, sending an avalanche of sludge sweeping downhill and swamping a farmhouse and nearby plaster works. Pockets of trapped gas and unexploded bombs hampered rescue work. The spire of Christ Church cracked and had to be demolished. A satisfactory explanation for the disaster has proved elusive. Theories of sabotage have been proposed. An accident, a spark from a hammer, perhaps the result of working under pressure, is the most likely cause. Huge quantities of bombs were being handled daily to keep Bomber Command supplied.

There was further tragedy on 16 April 1945. An Allied aircraft apparently ran into difficulties and crash-landed on a row of seven houses in Stafford Street, killing six people including the pilot. Four of the fatalities occurred at number 55, which was demolished by the impact.

Rationing had become necessary only during the closing weeks of the First World War to guarantee supplies and combat panic buying; this time shortages were more serious. Bacon, butter and sugar were rationed in January 1940. Meat, fish, cheese, eggs, milk, butter, breakfast cereals, tea, preserves, biscuits, and tinned fruit soon followed. Clothing was rationed from 1941. A national registration scheme was introduced and identity cards were issued. These were used to apply for ration books. A 'Dig for Victory' campaign encouraged people to grow their own vegetables. For those without a garden,

Burton was well supplied with allotments dotted around the town and available for a small rent. Rationing was only gradually relaxed. Bread (1946) and potatoes (1947) were even added to the list of rationed goods after the war was over. Restrictions continued until 1954. Bananas provide one example of the shortages experienced. The first available in Burton for five years arrived in January 1946. Ration-book holders were allowed to buy just one pound. Identity cards were discontinued in 1951.

Administration of poor relief transferred from local bodies to the Ministry of Health in 1918. All 'Poor Laws' were finally abolished in 1930. The National Insurance Act (1946) made welfare provision a state responsibility. Burton Infirmary became part of the new National Health Service in 1948, funded out of central taxation and National Insurance contributions.

A Local Education Committee, set up by the new County Borough to take over from the School Board in 1903, proved innovative in the area of secondary education. In 1928, the Girls High School had moved from Waterloo Street to new premises at Winshill. The following year, all-age education began to be phased out in line with government recommendations. The School of Art expanded and moved from a floor in the Burton Institute into the now empty Waterloo Street site in 1934. Guild Street and Broadway Schools were formed in 1941 into a selective school focusing on vocationally relevant technical and commercial subjects linked to the School of Science at Burton Institute. It was partly based at the Broadway School premises between South Broadway Street and Branston Road but made use of a variety of sites. In 1946 it evolved into the Technical High School and then Dovecliff Grammar in 1965. The School of Science expanded into temporary huts at Manor Croft beside Abbey Street and developed as Burton Technical College in 1948. A new building went up on the site in 1955 and was substantially extended in 1969. A School of Speech and Drama, launched in 1946 complete with its own 'Little Theatre' in Guild Street, made Burton the only local authority in the country running specialised full-time drama courses. Another first was the introduction of remedial literacy and numeracy courses in 1947.

After peaking at the turn of the century the population had declined slightly and remained fairly static at just under 50,000, but housing shortages were acute in the immediate post-war period. Squatters, many of them demobilised ex-servicemen and their families, moved into empty huts left behind when the RAF moved from Henhurst Hill airfield. Pre-fabricated two-bedroom bungalows were erected at Weir Bank and off Harper Avenue as an emergency measure while a massive programme of council-house building was instigated.

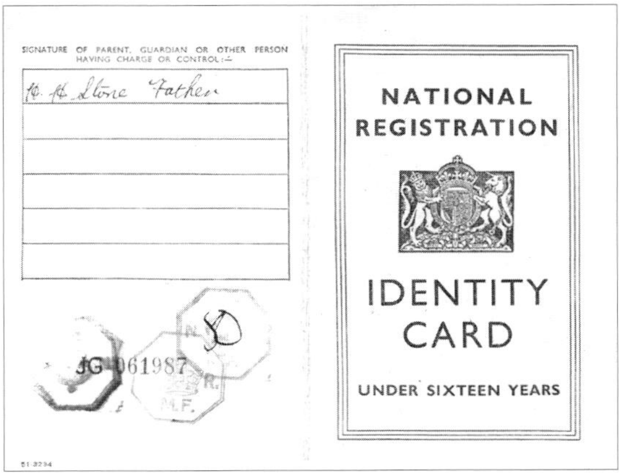

137 *Emergency measures introduced at the outbreak of the Second World War included a national registration scheme that continued until 1951. Identity cards were needed in order to apply for ration books.*

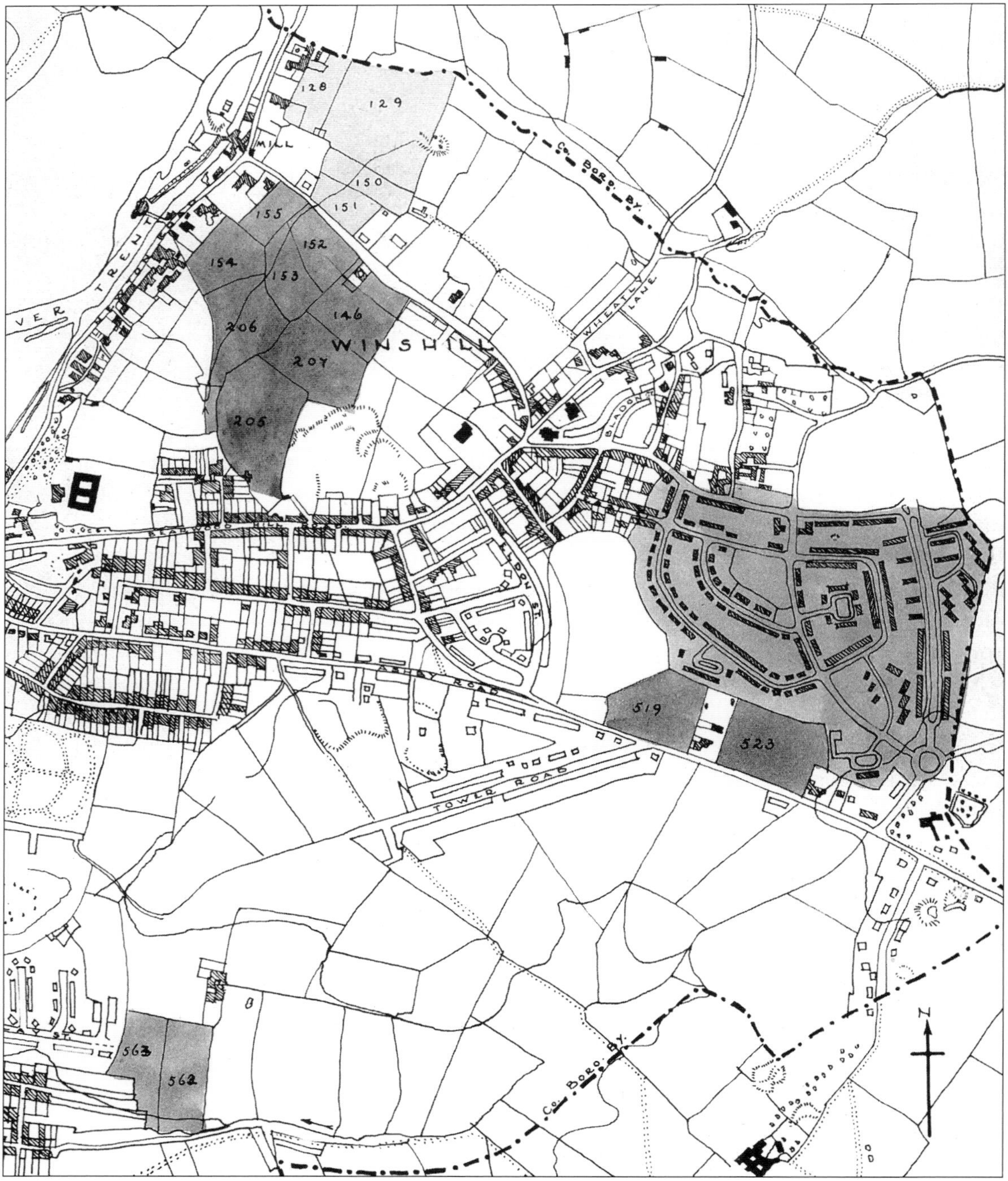

138 *Large numbers of council houses on Manners Estate between Ashby Road, Bretby Lane and Hawfield Lane were built on land purchased by the Corporation from E.J. Manners in 1945. Adjacent plots were added later. Private houses were built at Dalebrook north of Mill Hill Lane; Abbot Beyne School now occupies the land earmarked for development on the south side.*

The majority of new houses were constructed on planned estates at Waterside and Edgehill, Stapenhill, Manners Estate, Winshill, and around the Eton Road area of Horninglow. Most of the older, Victorian properties in the town had no fixed bath, no hot water tap and outside lavatories. As new houses became available the worst were cleared and others were targeted for improvement.

139 *One casualty of local branch-line closures in the 1950s and '60s was the Tutbury 'Jinnie' that made a sentimental last run on 11 June 1960. The 'Jinnie' shuttled between Burton and Tutbury via Stretton and Rolleston for 111 years, pulling the carriages outward and pushing them on the return journey.*

An Industrial Development and Expansion Committee replaced the Commercial Development Committee. Renewed efforts were made to draw in new industry. Wellington Road Extension was the key development site and attracted Lloyd's (iron castings, 1945), FNF (knitting machines, 1946), Conder (engineering, 1955), and Darley (who closed their High Street bookshop to concentrate on printing in 1960). Marmite, already established in Cross Street, expanded to new premises in 1961 and later became part of the Bovril group of companies. Renold Chains moved to Dallow Street/Horninglow Road (1957), taking over the Stocal Enamels site and building a new factory.

Burton's central location at the hub of a good distribution network was a key promotional message but rail links were already under threat. Local branch lines were axed in the 1950s and 1960s. One casualty was the much-loved Tutbury 'Jinnie' service that shuttled between Burton and Tutbury until 1960.

British Rail's push to drive down the costs involved in maintaining an extensive network of links and sidings at Burton was a major concern to the town's brewers. After a strike by railway footplatemen in 1955, alternative options were explored. The threat of further disruption, this time by train drivers in 1958 and British Rail's decision not to invest in a freight depot at Burton, combined to tip the balance in favour of road transport.

By the mid-1960s most of the level crossings had vanished from town-centre streets. Railway sidings and shunting yards lay disused and empty. Trade at the Derby Street Smithfield, where weekly cattle markets had been held since 1874, declined rapidly in the 1950s and the site was converted for use as a lorry park and transport depot.

By 1961, commercial canal traffic had effectively ceased and leisure use was minimal. With no road access *Bessie Bull's* canalside pub at Shobnall closed its doors and was demolished the following year.

A demand for lager was emerging but with beer sales declining and costs rising the local brewing industry needed to adapt. In 1961, Ind Coope merged with Tetley Walker and Ansell's to form Allied Breweries.

140 *High Street from New Street corner to Bank Square in 1962. In little more than a decade the town centre was transformed. Every building in this picture disappeared.*

Across the industry, investment in technically advanced automated processes and computerisation led to the shedding of hundreds of jobs. Old brewery buildings became redundant. Traditional crafts became obsolete. In the 19th century coopers were the best-paid tradesmen in the town, proud of their craft and jealously protective of entry to the trade. Apprenticeships often stayed within families as sons followed fathers. Coopers were the first brewery employees to organise themselves into a trade union. Considerable skill with specialised tools was required to make wooden casks by hand. From start to finish each cask was the work of a single tradesman who stamped his initials on the result. Six common sizes were produced. The largest, a butt, had a capacity of 108 gallons, followed in order of size by a hogshead (54 gallons), barrel (36 gallons), kilderkin (18 gallons), firkin (9 gallons) and the smallest, a pin (4½ gallons). Steam-powered cooperages introduced automation from 1889 and reduced coopers to repair work. Numbers dwindled and training ceased. When metal casks and canisters replaced wooden barrels, the few remaining craftsmen lost their jobs. Land used to store and weather oak staves, 25 acres at Bass alone, was now surplus to requirements.

For the first time in over a century and a half land in the town centre was available for re-development. The first target of the planners was the Bargates area of High Street. Take a good look at Burton before work begins in 1964. In a few short years the townscape will change beyond recognition.

TEN

Modern Town:
Burton Past and Present

Everything changes in the 1960s, the way we live, work and travel, even the way we shop. House ownership rises. Private housing projects replace council building programmes. New properties swell the populations of Branston and Stretton. Traffic increases. The opening of the A38 by-pass in 1966 removes some through traffic but congestion, particularly on Burton Bridge, is a problem only partly eased by the opening of a second river crossing, St Peter's Bridge, in 1985. Car-parking provision can barely keep pace with demand. The large Victorian railway station is replaced in 1971 with a small concrete ticket office and a forecourt for cars. Bargates shopping centre opens.

Familiar sights disappeared almost daily as the town renewed and reinvented itself. Closure and demolition of Eatough's shoe factory in 1975 freed more land.

The public library in 1976 was the last major local project carried out by Thomas Lowe before the company was absorbed by Tarmac plc. With the opening of Meadowside Leisure Centre (1980) the old swimming baths closed and were demolished. New Bass offices on the former Eatough's shoe factory site (1981) completed the transformation of the east side of High Street and opened up views across the river.

A modern extension added two additional courtrooms and offices to the magistrates courts in 1991. A new police station followed alongside.

Bass acquired the Carling lager brand in a merger with Charrington's in 1968 and developed it as the market leader. Two hundred years of brewing was celebrated by the opening of the Bass Museum in 1977.

Allied Breweries went through a series of mergers to become Allied-Lyons by 1981 and began a joint venture with Carlsberg. In 1994, the company turned its focus away from brewing and, as Allied Domecq, began to build the wines and spirits side of the business. The company's interest in what was now Carlsberg-Tetley was disposed of in 1996, and in 1999 its extensive pub chain was sold to Punch Taverns Group.

In 1998, Bass added Carlsberg-Tetley to become once again the largest brewery in the United Kingdom. Faced with government restrictions that precluded growth, a decision was made to concentrate on its expanding international hotel business. The Burton breweries were sold, first to Interbrew of

141 *Eatough's shoe factory, High Street, demolished in 1975 to make way for a new office block.*

142 *Bass's 1866 water tower was retained when former maltings beside the Hay were demolished as part of the development of the east side of High Street. The Public Library now occupies the site.*

Belgium in 2000 and within two years to Coors, third largest brewery in the United States. Bass Museum was renamed the Coors Visitor Centre & Museum of Brewing.

Marston, Thompson and Evershed, still brewing beer using the traditional Burton Union System, were taken over by the Wolverhampton and Dudley group in 1999.

At the other end of the scale, 'micro' breweries began to emerge. In 1980, Burton Bridge Brewery acquired the former *Fox and Goose* public house in Bridge Street. Brewing began a year later on a site almost immediately opposite the premises where Benjamin Printon set up his operation as the town's first common brewer. Tower Brewery, occupying part of Salt's former Walsitch Maltings (a name harking back to the Anglo-Saxon boundary stream now culverted beneath the building), and others have since followed.

Holy Trinity parish was reunited with St Modwen's in 1969 and Holy Trinity Church demolished in 1971. Part of the district allocated to Christ Church returned to Burton parish when the building was sold to an Elim Pentecostal group in 1983. In 1990 the former Christ Church hall was taken over by Burton Caribbean Association. Salem Baptist Chapel on Station Street, rebuilt in contemporary style in 1957, was incorporated on the fringe of town-centre development. New uses were found for chapels as many of them, affected by falling congregations, began to close or unite. The Methodist chapel on the corner of Station Street and Union Street closed in 1958 and was demolished.

A large Sunni Moslem community worshipped at a house in Byrkley Street before opening the Jamia Islamia Mosque in Princess Street in 1977, replaced by the Jamia Hanfia Ghousia building in 2000. Premises in York Street and the former Methodist chapel in Parker Street were both adapted as Islamic cultural and religious centres. Uxbridge Street School was converted as a mosque and community centre in 1994.

Cooper's Square Shopping Centre, partly open in 1970, was completed by 1974. As well as reclaiming derelict industrial land the precinct obliterated the cobbled quaintness of Bank Square and Fennel Street, sweeping away the historic commercial heart of the town and, with it, Lady Paulet's 16th-century almshouse. Worthington Walk (now Burton Place) and the Octagon Centre followed in the 1980s. Local specialist shops closed, replaced by branches of national chain stores and supermarkets.

143 *Until Holy Trinity Church opened in Horninglow Street in 1824, St Modwen's served the whole parish. The new church offered a large number of free seats and its building was in part inspired by the need to counter falling congregations. Holy Trinity was rebuilt in 1880-2 and demolished in 1971.*

Railway sidings and redundant brewery premises beside Hawkins Lane, Wetmore Road, Anglesey Road, Dale Street and elsewhere were cleared or converted for development into light industrial estates. Canals were revitalised as a leisure resource. Work begun in 1973 led to the re-opening of Shobnall Basin (where the Bond End Canal had met the Trent and Mersey) as a Marina. A modern bungalow was built on the site of *Bessie Bull's* pub.

The Victorian pumping station at Clay Mills, replaced in 1974 by a new sewage treatment plant, was saved after vigorous lobbying by the Save Claymills group. Members of the Claymills Pumping Engine Trust set up in 1993 have overseen restoration of the site, complete with working beam engines and steam-driven workshop.

At the Town Hall, a Kirkland organ, installed in the original St Paul's Institute building in the 1880s, was no longer serviceable. In 1972, it was replaced by a 'Mighty' Wurlitzer, originally made for a theatre in Ohio but since the 1930s housed in a Manchester cinema.

Burton lost its County Borough status in 1974. A shake-up of local government created an East Staffordshire District Council of Burton, Tutbury and Uttoxeter. Staffordshire County Council took over responsibility for schools. From 1975, a comprehensive system of secondary education abolished selection and re-organised Burton's senior schools into four new comprehensive units.

Burton Technical College moved with the times. Four departments in the mid-1960s (commercial, general education, engineering and building) grew and adapted in response to the demands of students and local industry. When the School of Art and the School of Speech and Drama both closed in 1984 their courses were assimilated into the college prospectus. 'Technical' was dropped from the title in 1998, reflecting the wide range of education and training now on offer at Burton College. Temporary huts, dating back to 1944, were dismantled and a new building added in 2002.

Burton Club, a male exclusive, took up residence in the former abbey infirmary building at the beginning of the 20th century, adding a billiards room in a brick-built extension. In 1975, the club occupied only an upper floor in the former infirmary chapel. The remaining rooms were converted into the *Abbey Inn*.

Phase One of a new hospital with an updated casualty department opened at Outwoods in 1971. All services were transferred to the new District Hospital Centre in 1993. It was renamed Queen's Hospital when Queen Elizabeth gave her formal consent to the change during an official visit in 1995. After closure and demolition of the New Street wards, the former infirmary site was reclaimed for housing.

The Odeon Cinema changed its name once more to become Robins before closing in 2000 when the nine-screen Cineworld opened on the new Middleway retail development. Of the Victorian newspapers, only the *Burton Mail*, first published in 1898, was still reporting as the town entered the new millennium.

Not all regeneration activity was business orientated. A number of residential projects reversed a long established trend to the suburbs and made town centre living once more fashionable. The changing shape of the town led to a review of ward structure. From 2003, along with Branston and Stretton, there were eight Burton wards: Anglesey, Brizlincote, Burton, Eton Park, Horninglow, Shobnall, Stapenhill, and Winshill.

144 *A new coat of arms was granted when the County Borough became part of East Staffordshire District Council in 1974. The District Council became a Borough Council in 1992.*

In 2001, a 10m. high sculpture by Andy Hazell, masquerading as a malt shovel, caused controversy when it was erected at a cost of £45,000 on the corner of New Street and High Street.

In common with many towns, Burton has lost much of its individuality. Despite the changes that have taken place, echoes of the past still resonate. There are many reminders of the people who lived and worked in Burton past. Early examples of urban terraces, charming, simple functional houses where large families were raised, have survived (in Wetmore Road, Horninglow Street, Moor Street and elsewhere) to be renovated as desirable cottages. Small country house-style villas are a feature of the outskirts of town: older models with bay windows flanking a central doorway, later versions semi-detached.

Sinai House is being painstakingly rescued from a state of almost terminal dereliction. Tales of an underground passage between Sinai and the abbey precinct have persisted for many years. Any such structure defies both logic and geology, but short tunnels that once connected abbey buildings may lie undiscovered beneath the Market Place and Market Hall. The cellar of the *Olde Royal Oak* contains an intriguing bricked-up doorway.

Legend, too, attaches to Abbey Cottage at 127 Horninglow Street. A monks' hospital is said to have occupied the site. A vaulted cellar used as a chantry in medieval times and by recusant worshippers in the 17th century is reputed to lie beneath the current house.

High Street and the eastern end of Horninglow Street were at the core of the early borough. Many properties still respect the original burgage plot boundaries laid out eight centuries ago. In some cases, later frontages cloak timber-framed medieval houses. Jettied upper storeys have been picked up by new brick front elevations allowing projecting joists to be cut away. Tree-ring dating of roof beams at 187 Horninglow Street revealed a felling date of 1345. Timbers in 51/52 High Street have been dated to 1388, a clear demonstration that renewal is not something new but has been a constant feature of the town.

Elegant Georgian townhouses along Horninglow Street reflect the prosperity of 18th- and 19th-century brewers and business-people. Pilasters, columns, decorative fanlights and moulded architraves emphasise doorways. Almost every house on the approach to Bargates contains some telling period detail.

The oldest surviving malthouse in the county, behind the former 18th-century Charles Leeson brewery at 6 Horninglow Street, has been converted as a private residence. Across the road, Wilson's brewery once occupied 166 and 167. Number 167 became the Allsopp family townhouse. With an adjoining malthouse the block is now

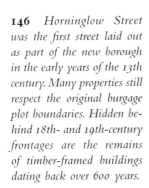

145 *One of many lost public houses, the* Roebuck *with its distinctive 27-light window closed in 1981.*

146 *Horninglow Street was the first street laid out as part of the new borough in the early years of the 13th century. Many properties still respect the original burgage plot boundaries. Hidden behind 18th- and 19th-century frontages are the remains of timber-framed buildings dating back over 600 years.*

converted into modern apartments. Samuel and William Sketchley owned numbers 179 and 180 Horninglow Street. Anson Court, restored in the 1990s, is the site occupied in turn by the breweries of John Davies Greaves and Francis Thompson. Joseph Clay ran a brewery and later his commercial bank from 5 Horninglow Street. Nunneley House, 22 Bridge Street is another example of an 18th-century townhouse that once fronted a brewery.

On the corner of Bridge Street and Wetmore Road, the *Three Queens* former posting house and coaching inn is a late 18th-century building, but an inn was first licensed on this site in 1531. Burton Boat Company probably built Trent Bridge House off Meadow Road as a warehouse. Boddingtons and later Everards brewed beer here. It was converted into flats in 1988. In cellars beneath the building is an arch of the old medieval bridge and possibly the foundations of the medieval bridge chapel demolished in 1777.

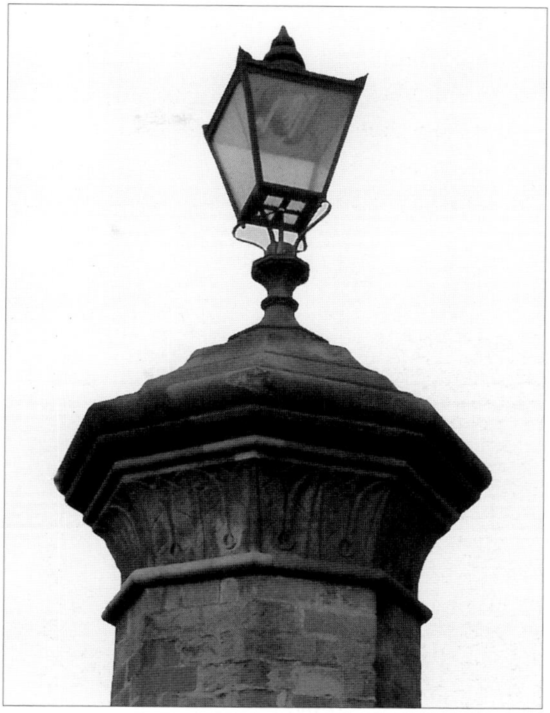

147 *Gatepost detail from Anson Court, Horninglow Street, site of the brewery run by John Davies Greaves and later occupied by Francis Thompson.*

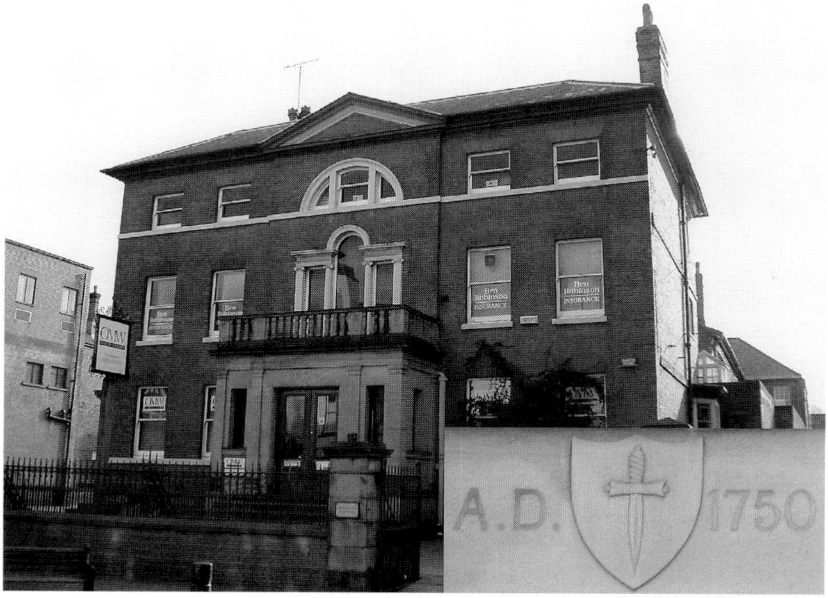

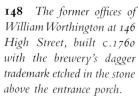

148 *The former offices of William Worthington at 146 High Street, built c.1760 with the brewery's dagger trademark etched in the stone above the entrance porch.*

149 *One of four weather vanes set at the corners of the parish church tower.*

Stout oak posts outside 102 High Street were installed to protect the property's Georgian double-bow windows from horse-drawn carriages mounting the pavement. Further along is the former Congregational Chapel, Burton's first nonconformist meeting place in 1662, rebuilt in 1762 and again in 1842 using stone from the racecourse grandstand for the front elevation. It is now reborn as the Riverside Church. The offices of Coors occupy the site of the *Blue Stoops* from where Burton Ale was sent to London in the 17th century and where Benjamin Wilson met Hannah Walker and began the first great Burton brewery. The Bass townhouse is 136 High Street. Above the porch of Worthington House (146 High Street) the former brewery's 'dagger' trademark is carved in the stonework. The Constitutional Club (150 High Street) was once the Post Office headquarters. Lord Burton and Robert Ratcliff bought the building and presented it to the club at a peppercorn rent in 1905. Number 164 High Street was the Electric Theatre, Burton's first purpose-built cinema.

150 *Among many reminders of Burton past in the parish church, an eye-catching Gothic-style memorial to brewer Thomas Fosbrooke Salt (d.1864) depicts Faith, Hope and Charity.*

A stone bearing the Paget family crest, removed when the old Town Hall was demolished, has been reset into a well beside the Andresey footbridge. The motto *Per il suo contrario* translates Delphically as 'By means of its reverse'.

The parish church on the site of the abbey church looks out over the Market Place. St Modwen's served the whole community until Holy Trinity was built in 1824. Beautifully proportioned and deceptively spacious, it is a superb example

151 *The Art Deco geometry of Abbey Arcade, built in the 1930s.*

of an untouched early Georgian church. Few changes have taken place internally beyond the removal of the pew doors, the addition of lighting, stained glass (new in 1865) and alterations to the original three-decker pulpit. The Snetzler organ was replaced in 1900 when the case front was widened to accommodate a larger console. It was rebuilt in 1971 using parts salvaged from a similar model removed from Holy Trinity Church.

Memorials decorating the walls provide a roll-call of names – Peel, Wilson, Hoskins, Hawkins, Wilders, Yeomans, Ratcliff, Gretton, Allsopp, Thornewill, Greatorex etc. – resonant of Burton past. Finely carved eye-catching monuments in Victorian Gothic style commemorate William Worthington and Thomas Salt.

At the west end of the nave is the 16th-century oak chest or town coffer. It now has a single lock but had remained unopened for many years until the key was discovered in 1929. Lifting the lid, a solid strip of oak 8cm thick, required two people. Inside was a collection of documents, indentures and accounts including property deeds dating back to 1310. In the south porch, an incised sepulchral slab rescued from the churchyard is typical of 14th-century memorials. The font also predates the church. Although difficult to date securely, the octagonal sandstone bowl is an immersion font with Perpendicular tracery, entirely consistent with late medieval style, and may be the only surviving item from inside the abbey church. The stem, a later addition, is dated 1662 and bears the initials of William Middleton, curate from 1662-5, along with TH and TW, presumably churchwardens at the time. A superb collection of communion plate (no longer kept in the church) includes a silver chalice and paten both also dated 1662. (See pp. 39 and 64.) The chandelier has been moved from its original position in the centre of the nave. When it was installed in 1725 it was the only source of light in the church. John Whitehurst's intricate control mechanism with its attachment to operate the carillon is still in working order. A 1.5m. diameter drum studded with steel pins like a giant musical box engages a system of bell cranks and striking levers as it turns. In 1937 the chimes were recorded and broadcast by BBC Radio. A notice board inside the tower sets out the rules introduced to curb enthusiastic bellringers in the early 18th century. Whitehurst's sundial is still in place on the south wall. Fire caused significant damage in 1999 but complete restoration has now taken place.

152 *The* Leopard Inn, *Lichfield Street was built by Charrington's shortly after the brewery moved to Burton in 1872. A cast-iron plaque on the wall is of the United Order of Smiths and includes a lathe and beam engine.*

A collection of buildings around the Market Place represents Georgian, Victorian, Edwardian and Art Deco building styles. Brass angle plates set in the block paving and in the tarmac of Manor Croft show where the old Town Hall and abbey gatehouse once stood. Behind 18th- and 19th-century brickwork, medieval braced roof trusses in a wing of the Manor suggest that this was the former abbot's chamber and guesthouse where royal visitors were entertained. It is described in the post-dissolution inventory compiled for Sir William Paget (1st Baron) as the 'great chamber'.

Old beams and the tracery of a lancet window are concealed in the attic behind the 19th-century façade of the *Abbey Inn*. Exterior stonework at the north end shows where a vaulted building, almost certainly Abbot William Bromley's 1320s great hall, once extended over what is now lawn. Between the garden and the rear of the Market Hall are the blocked-up entrances to the chapter house and parlour that once led to the east range of the abbey cloister.

Burton College occupies the former Soho, where Burton Boat Company wharves once despatched cargoes around the world. The Memorial Gardens are on the site of the abbey gardens. Just inside the perimeter wall are two gnarled and arthritic mulberry trees, ancient limbs propped up by trestle supports, probably planted as saplings by William Paget (4th Baron) shortly after he had restored the family fortunes and regained his inheritance. In 1608, James I began promoting the importing of mulberry trees in a bid to stimulate a domestic silk industry. Unfortunately, the trees bought from Flemish suppliers were of the black mulberry variety, as are these specimens, not the white mulberry on which silkworms feed.

Pints are still pulled at the *Leopard Inn* in Lichfield Street, built as a flagship first public house in Burton by London brewers, Charrington's. On the wall is a plaque of the United Order of Smiths, who once met in a room here. A beam engine, lathe and a journeyman smith are depicted on the cast-iron plate.

153 *A portrait of Charles, 6th Marquess of Anglesey on the sign of the* Uxbridge Arms, *Queen Street, is one of many local references to the Paget family, lords of the manor of Burton from 1546.*

Peel House, refurbished by the Peel family who came to Burton to establish their state-of-the-art textile factories in 1780, is in Lichfield Street. The fragile shell of Peel's first cotton mill in the town stands on its island in the River Trent. Next to it the former flour mill buildings on Newton Road hold one end of a thread of history that stretches back a thousand years to the foundation of the abbey and into a Dark Age beyond. Traces of the sluices and channels that once powered the mills at Bond End can still be found on the Trent Washlands.

Paget lords of the manor are commemorated in the names of streets, schools and on public-house signs. Wealthy Leicester wool merchant William Wyggeston and his cross-Channel trading connections are recalled in the names of Wyggeston Street, Calais Road and Dover Road, three of the streets that define the Wyggeston Hospital Trust land purchased in 1521.

154 *Coopers were the highest earning tradespeople in 19th-century Burton, proud of their craft and jealously protective of entry to the trade. The Burton Cooper, unveiled in 1977, has become an instantly recognisable symbol of the town.*

The great legacy of public buildings bequeathed by the Bass family is most striking in King Edward Place. More architecturally notable is St Chad's Church, Hunter Street, a masterpiece of richly inventive grand design by G.F. Bodley with sheer walls of Hollington red sandstone and a splendidly flamboyant tower rising almost independently of the main structure.

The story of Burton is not just about beer and brewing. It is the story of early settlement in the Trent Valley by our distant ancestors; of an enigmatic saint and the coming of Christianity; perilous days on a lawless border between Saxon and Dane; the founding of a great and powerful monastery; and of pioneering industrialists. But, perhaps inevitably, beer and brewing lie at the narrative core of the tales we spin of the town, central to our perception of and identity with the past. Only fitting then that the Burton Cooper, currently in Cooper's Square, a finely observed bronze statue by James Butler RA commissioned by Burton Civic Society and unveiled in 1977, has become an instantly recognisable symbol of the town, a touchstone and commemoration of our proud heritage.

Sources and Further Reading

Main Sources

Staffordshire Record Office:

Burton upon Trent Vestry Book and Vestry Order Book

Burton upon Trent Parish Registers

Papers of the Burton Feoffees

Paget MSS

Constables' Bills and Accounts

Memo of contents 'Ancient Oak Coffer'

Memo of boys put out

William Wyatt's map of Burton upon Trent in 1760

Lichfield Record Office:

Burton upon Trent Magistrates Court Records

Northamptonshire Record Office:

Papers of Gregory King

Midland History:

Insley, C., 'Politics, Conflict and Kinship in Early Eleventh-Century Mercia' (vol. xxv, 2000)

Staffordshire Studies:

Bartlett, R., 'The Miracles of Saint Modwenna of Burton' (vol. 8, 1996)

Transactions of Burton Natural History and Archeological Society (various volumes including):

Rye, H.A., 'St Modwen' (vol. iv, 1899); 'Sinai Park' (vol. vi, 1910)

Transactions of the South Staffordshire Archaeological and Historical Society:

O'Brien, C., 'Excavations at the Abbey, Burton upon Trent' (vol. xix, 1977-8)

Leahy, K., 'Anglian Cruciform Brooches from Wychnor and Brizlincote near Burton upon Trent' (vol. xix, 1977-8)

Meeson, R.A. and Kirkham, A., 'Two Medieval Buildings in Horninglow Street, Burton upon Trent' (vol. xxxiv, 1992-3)

Atherton, I., 'Burton Abbey Church: A Reconsideration of its Built Form' (vol. xxxvii, 1995-6)

Martin, A. and Allen, C., 'Two Prehistoric Ring Ditches at Tucklesholme' (vol. xxxix, 2001)

Universal British Directory (1793)
Victoria History of the County of Staffordshire (vols. i and iv, 1958)
Bridgeman, G.R.O., *The Burton Abbey Twelfth-Century Surveys* (1916)
Dugdale, W., *Monasticon Anglicanum* (editions 1661 and 1846)
Hooke, D., *The landscape of Anglo-Saxon Staffordshire: The Charter Evidence* (1983)
Kelly's *Directory of Staffordshire* (various years)
Marquess of Anglesey, *One Leg* (1961)
Molyneux, W., *Burton-on-Trent: its History, its Waters, and its Breweries* (1983)
Morris, J. (ed.), *Domesday Book, Staffordshire* (1976)
Owen, C.C., *The Development of Industry in Burton upon Trent* (1978)
Sawyer, P.H., *Charters of Burton Abbey* (1979)
Shaw, S., *The History and Antiquities of Staffordshire* (1978)
Stuart, D.G., *County Borough History of Burton upon Trent* (Part i, 1975 and Part ii, 1977)
Stuart, D.G., *An Illustrated History of Burton upon Trent to the 18th Century* (1993)
Tresise's *Directory of Burton upon Trent* (various years)
Underhill, C.H., *History of Burton-on-Trent* (1941)
Underhill, C.H., and Pitchford, H.H., *The Parish Church of Burton upon Trent* (1975)
Wain, H.J., *The Early History of Burton-on-Trent* (1968)
Wesley, W., *History and Description of the Town and Borough of Burton upon Trent* (1847)
White, W., *History, Gazetteer and Directory of Staffordshire* (1851)

Secondary Sources and Further reading

Greenslade, M.W. and Stuart, D.G., *A History of Staffordshire* (1965)
Hibbert, F., *The Dissolution of the Monasteries* (1910)
Hornsey, B., *Ninety Years of Cinema in Burton-on-Trent* (1992)
Lloyd, J.R., Burton Civic Society, *Burton upon Trent: The Years of Change 1962-1987* (1987)
Owen, C.C., *Burton upon Trent: the Illustrated History* (1994)
Parry, D., (trans.), *The Rule of St Benedict* (1984)
Polkey, A., *The Civil War in the Trent Valley* (1992)
Staffordshire County Council Education Unit, *Burton upon Trent and District in Maps Before 1850* (1977)
Stone, R.J., *Moats, Boats and other notes* (1999)
Stone, R.J., *A Stone's Throw of Burton* (2002)

Index

Numbers in **bold** refer to illustration page numbers

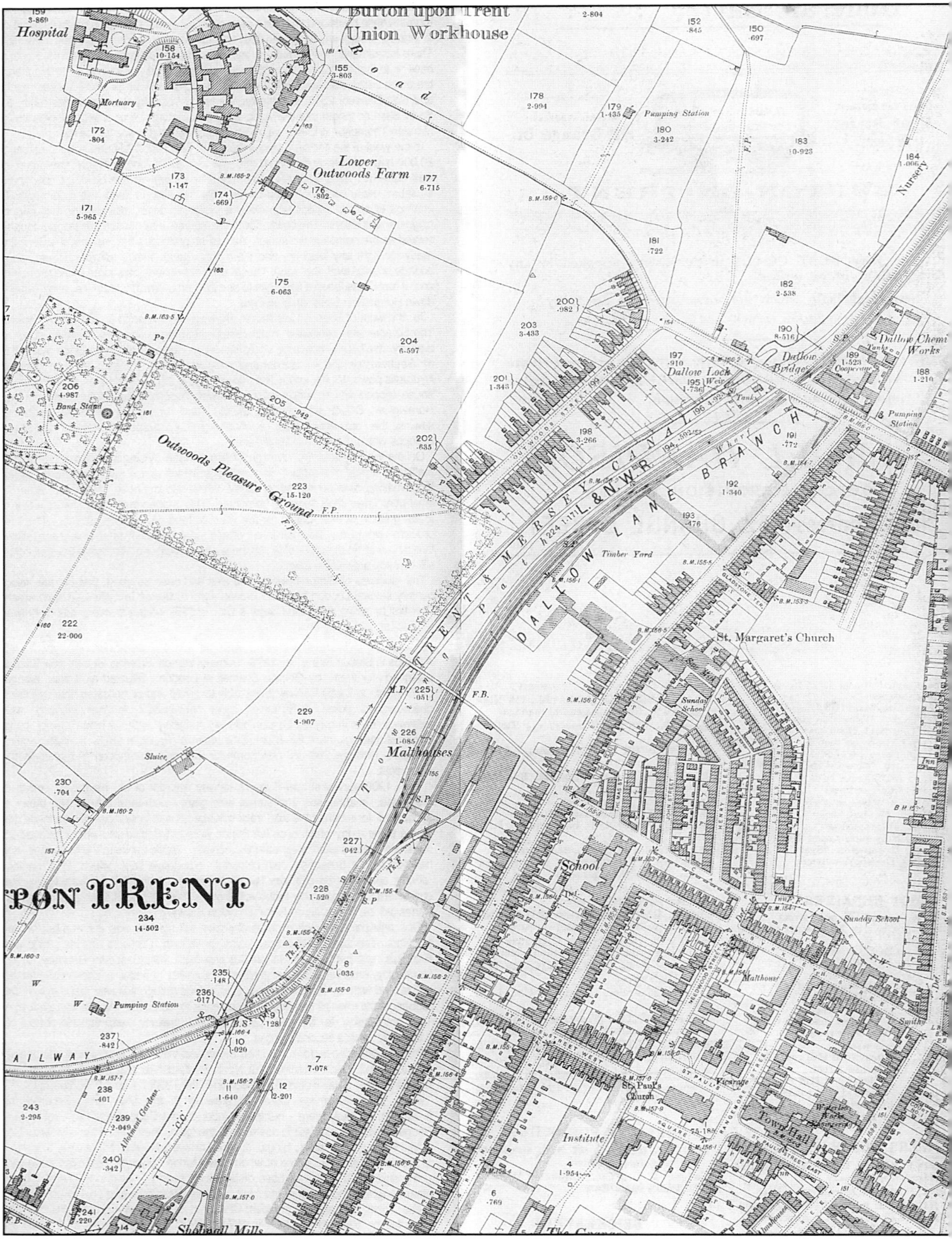

Burton upon Trent Union Workhouse
Hospital
Mortuary
Road
Lower Outwoods Farm
Pumping Station
Nursery
Outwoods Pleasure Ground
Band Stand
Dallow Lock
Weir
Dallow Bridge
Dallow Chemical Works
Cooperage
Tanks
Trent & Mersey Canal
L. & N.W.R.
Dallow Lane Branch
Wharf
Timber Yard
Outwoods Street
Gladstone Ter.
St. Margaret's Church
Sunday School
John Street
Henry Street
Charles Street
Malthouses
Sluice
Towing Path
School
Malthouse
Sunday School
Smithy
Inn
St. Paul's Street West
St. Paul's Church
Vicarage
St. Paul's Square
Rangemore Street
Institute
Town Hall
St. Paul's Street East
Waterloo Works
Allotment Gardens
Railway
Shobnall Mills
The Grange
upon TRENT

Line in the Sand

French Foreign Legion Forts and Fortifications in Morocco 1900-1926

Richard Jeynes

Helion & Company

Helion & Company Limited
Unit 8 Amherst Business Centre
Budbrooke Road
Warwick
CV34 5WE
England
Tel. 01926 499 619
Email: info@helion.co.uk
Website: www.helion.co.uk
Twitter: @helionbooks
Visit our blog at blog.helion.co.uk

Published by Helion & Company 2023
Designed and typeset by Mach 3 Solutions Ltd (www.mach3solutions.co.uk)
Cover designed by Paul Hewitt, Battlefield Design (www.battlefield-design.co.uk)

Cover: Photograph of the remains of Fort Tazougerte (Richard Jeynes)

ISBN 978-1-915113-83-2

British Library Cataloguing-in-Publication Data.
A catalogue record for this book is available from the British Library.

For details of other military history titles published by Helion & Company Limited contact the above address or visit our website: http://www.helion.co.uk.

We always welcome receiving book proposals from prospective authors.

Contents

List of Illustrations and Maps

Acknowledgements

I would like to thank my good friends Richard Parke and Ian Bell, my sons Richard, Patrick, and Douglas, and Jez Dix and the students of Worcester University Department of Archaeology for their help with the fieldwork in Morocco without which this book would not have been possible.

I am also grateful to Prof Seth Mallios of San Diego State University for allowing me to reference his work on the film set of Fort Zinderneuf. It was this film which first inspired my interest in the Foreign Legion as a child.

Preface

The remote desert outpost, manned by a handful of rugged and desperate legionnaires, surrounded by hordes of camel borne tribesmen has become something of an iconic image since P.C. Wren first published his novel *Beau Geste* in 1924. The book was an instant best seller and the story of the last stand of a beleaguered garrison resulted in many Hollywood films and books of similar genre.

Whilst the Legion has operated in many parts of the world since its formation by King Louis Phillipe of France in 1831 it is with the deserts and mountains of Morocco that it is most often associated. The romantic images of hot, sandy deserts, picturesque oases, mud brick villages, and numerous colourful tribes and cultures provided an ideal backdrop for stories of tough legionnaires with their distinctive uniforms and white kepis fighting against seemingly insurmountable odds.

However, the startling reality is that the Foreign Legion did build and garrison remote forts and outposts in challenging conditions across Morocco and last stand actions were not plots in popular novels but a harsh reality in the early part of the twentieth century.

Whilst providing a general outline of the conquest of Morocco this book concentrates on the use of forts and other fortifications built by the French Foreign Legion to secure the territory gained and pacify the areas of operation during the French conquest of Morocco.

It covers the construction of the outposts, garrison life in them during peace and war, operations in the desert and mountains and desperate last stands.

Particular emphasis is given to two sites where the author has undertaken extensive archaeological investigations over the past 10 years and advice and information is provided to encourage and assist others to undertake their own investigations.

Chapter 1

Morocco in the early twentieth century

In 1900 Morocco was a country, as recognised by the United Nations today, in name only. Whilst nominally ruled by the sultan, Moulay Abdel Aziz, from his capital in Fez, the reality was that vast tracts of the country were run by tribal chiefs and local warlords with the influence of central administration, the makhzen, considerably limited, particularly in the southeast.

Located in the northwest corner of Africa Morocco was only thirty miles from Spain, its nearest European neighbour, and yet knowledge of the country by Europeans was largely limited to the coastal region of the Straits of Gibraltar and the information provided from the few travellers who had returned from forays further inland.

Surrounded by the Atlantic Ocean and the Mediterranean Sea to the west and north and the Sahara to the east and south it is a country dominated by mountains. To the north the Rif Mountains form a formidable barrier to those seeking access from Spain whilst, further south, the Middle and High Atlas Mountains follow a roughly diagonal line from the southwest to northeast across the middle of the country effectively dividing it into two distinct zones.

To the northwest of the Atlas the land, bordered by the Atlantic Ocean, is the relatively well watered and fertile of the two zones. It is within this region that the major cities of Fez, Marrakesh, Casablanca, Rabat, and Tangiers are located and where the largest part of the population is sustained. With a climate similar to that of Southern Europe it was a region that was easily recognisable to the early European travellers to the country. Regions of the Middle Atlas in particular, supporting large areas of cedar forest and with a relatively cooler climate, became locations for idyllic hill stations where European settlers, and later administrators, could escape the intense heat of the lower plains during the height of the Summer. These days this zone provides the bulk of food production in the form of wheat, olives and citrus trees but pre 1900 the region was far less cultivated with a greater reliance placed on the herding of sheep and goats in a more nomadic lifestyle.

To the south the High Atlas Mountains rise to a height of almost 4,000 metres and they are snow covered for a large part of the year. Little grows

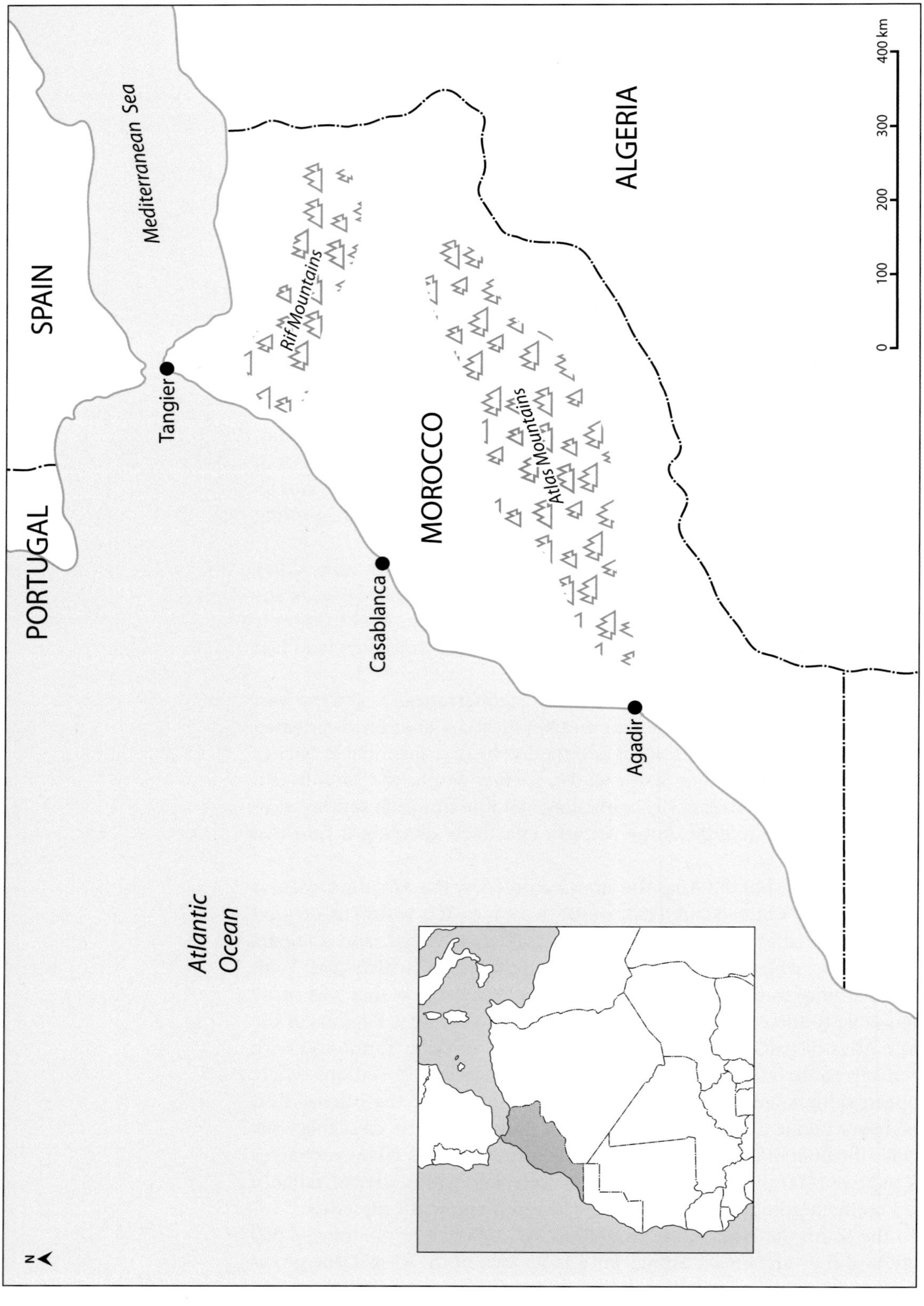

Physical map of Morocco in northwest Africa.

at height and such population as exists is located around villages of dried mud and stone buildings situated, almost invisible to the untrained eye, on precipitous rocky ledges and deep, steep sided valleys created over thousands of years by the annual rush of ice cold melt water that cascades down from the snow-capped mountains each spring.

They form a highly effective barrier and crossing to the southwest is, even today, not always easy. There are three main passes and a few other minor trails. Most of the routes across the mountains are long, winding, and tortuous as they follow ancient herding tracks round countless hairpin bends, and skirt precipitous drops. Such main roads as now exist were initially surveyed and constructed by French military engineers in the early part of the twentieth century and even these can be subject to closure during inclement weather.

Descending from the southern slopes of the High Atlas the traveller is struck by the dramatic change of landscape and climate. There is a distinct transformation from green to brown. southeast of the Atlas, in the region known as the Hammada du Guir, the land is dry and arid, and the temperatures become extremely hot in summer. With only a few inches of rain a year, and none at all at times, the population is concentrated into the only areas of guaranteed water, the river valleys of the Oued Draa, Oued Ziz and Oued Guir. At times even these become dry as the water disappears beneath the surface to continue a course south providing just enough water to sustain a network of oases and date palms that were sufficient to sustain the wandering nomads and their herds of camels and flocks of sheep and goats.

There were no major cities in this region but, perhaps surprisingly, it did sustain a population of some 200,000 in the late nineteenth and early twentieth century. The static population built large, fortified structures called a ksar. Built of mud brick some of these were extensive housing a community of several hundred people and they were designed to provide protection from both the climate and raiding neighbours. These castle-like structures would play a central role in local affairs, and some would become surrounded by similar, but much smaller, structures. Individual buildings would be scattered throughout the landscape, but location was always dictated by the availability of water. A significant proportion of the population followed a nomadic existence following their animals from one water hole to the next. However, not all of these lived in tents all of the time with some groups living in fixed houses surrounded by small tracts of cultivated land for at least part of the year.

Because a large proportion of the population followed a nomadic or semi nomadic existence there was no concept of political borders. The borders to the east and south were simply lines on a map and maps, of any accuracy, were almost non-existent. There was nothing physical on the ground and the nomadic tribes simply moved at will wherever their needs took them. The concept of belonging to a unified country controlled by a central ruler who would set rules and demand taxes was a totally alien concept and not one in which they were much interested!

The mountains also created cultural division with the population split between Arab and Berber. The Berber were the original people of North

Africa who had been gradually moved west by Arab invasions. From the eleventh century onward the Berber from the Moroccan lowlands were gradually merged with the Arab invaders but those in the highlands fiercely maintained their culture, religion, and language and became much feared and loathed by the tribes on the plains. The most important Berber tribes in the southeast of Morocco were the Ait Seghrushin, the Ait Atta and the Ait Izdig. Their first language was Tamazight although many spoke Arabic, for trading purposes, as well.

With few roads of any quality, very poor communications, religious and ethnic diversity, and the challenges created by climate and geography there is little wonder that the sultan would struggle to develop strong, unified control over the territory he claimed to rule. As things stood in 1900 Morocco was divided not just geographically but politically into two parts – the fertile north-western region containing the major cities and under the direct, albeit weak, control of the Sultan has been described as the 'zone of government'. The south-eastern region of mountains, desert and nomadic tribes was the 'zone of dissent'. It was a confused situation fraught with difficulties and ideal for exploitation by any colonial power.

During the great nineteenth century 'Scramble for Africa' by the European powers, all competing to develop their colonial influence, Morocco had been largely overlooked. It's very proximity to Europe was, ironically, to save it from colonial conquest until long after the rest of Africa had been divided up. Britain, France, Spain, Italy, Germany, even Russia, all recognised the strategic importance of the territory controlling, as it did, the southern shore of the Straits of Gibraltar and the access to the Mediterranean from the north Atlantic. However, none was prepared to make an overt move on the country for fear of provoking a reaction from the others.

Of all the European powers the two major contenders for Morocco were Britain and France and in 1904 the signing by them of the Entente Cordiale formalised an agreement acknowledging that France could have freedom of action in Morocco providing that Spain's interests in the north were taken into consideration. Not made public at the time, and kept secret for many years, was an agreement that Britain would agree to France annexing the whole of Morocco, less areas of Spanish control, should the Sultan be unable to exercise full control of his subjects. As this had never been achieved the French were happy to accept that they had full permission to act whenever it suited. The Treaty resulted in an immediate rise in tension with Germany and in March 1905 Kaiser Wilhelm went to Tangier, declared his support for an independent Morocco, and actively encouraged the Sultan to break his agreements with the French. This dangerous situation could not be allowed to escalate and in 1906, in an attempt to finally resolve the issue, all the interested European powers plus the United States and a delegation from Morocco met in Spain at the Conference of Algeciras. With the concluding treaty it was agreed to open Morocco to international trade whilst administration was formally granted to Spain and France.

Of the two France was without doubt the most dominant partner. She already had a strong colonial presence in Algeria and Tunisia and, with Italy's interests in Libya and Britain's control of Egypt, a move into Morocco was seen by many in France as not only a natural extension of their influence in North Africa but an essential one. In addition, tentative links had already been established and the Sultan was already in heavy financial debt to France so that, by the early part of the twentieth century, the French were simply looking for any excuse to extend their influence west from Algeria into Morocco.

The uncontrolled nature of the 10 or so distinct tribes in southeast Morocco gave the French the very excuse they were looking for. These tribes were largely tent dwelling nomads ranging in size from around 4,000 to around 20,000 whose seasonal movement would range far across the Moroccan/ Algerian 'border'. Some, such as the Ait Izdig tribe who occupied a region to the west of Boudenib were more sedentary and peaceful whilst others, most notably the 50,000 strong Ait Atta, were considerably more warlike and controlled extensive areas covering both Morocco and Algeria. Conquest and looting of other more sedentary tribes was second nature and they were constantly looking for opportunities for expansion. However, despite religious and cultural differences when the situation required tribes could unite and work together so it would not always be easy to predict who was friend and who was foe.

Essential for life in the region were the oases. Regardless of size these pockets of irrigated, fertile land were areas of intense cultivation producing the food so essential to the inhabitants. Vegetables, date palms, wheat, and animal feed were grown in every square inch of available land and often in between an extensive network of mud brick houses and fortified ksar. Individual fields would be irrigated by a network of small irrigation canals with the supply of water controlled by a series of sluice gates.

Whilst essential for food production the oases were also critical centres for trade and commerce as well as being locations for tribal gatherings, religious ceremonies, and meetings. By far and away the most important oasis was Figuig. Used by numerous tribes as a central meeting and trading place it is situated very close to what the French regarded as the border with Algeria. The oasis sustained around 16,000 permanent residents based in seven completely independent ksars. Over a 100,000 date palms grew in the flat area surrounded by small hills irrigated by a constant supply of water delivered via underground springs and a complex system of tunnels and irrigation canals access to which was a continuous source of local conflict.

Significantly its location placed it in very close proximity to French army units based in the area of southwest Algeria known as South Oranais. Whilst it was the stated policy of the French government not to make any move into Morocco, at this location the tribes of the area simply regarded the French military units as legitimate targets for raiding with impunity whenever the opportunity arose.

There had already been numerous incidents involving marauding parties from Morocco and units of the French army in Algeria all along the border but particularly in South Oranais. The area was open to dispute for, as far back as 1845, the French had advised the Sultan that the only defined border was the 480 or so kilometre straight line from Port Say on the Mediterranean coast south to the oasis at Figuig. south of Figuig there would be no defined border whilst the one declared by the French was treated in a very ambiguous way by Moroccan tribes whose raiding parties and herders crossed at will and the French military who drifted further west using the pursuit of 'Moroccan Rebels' as a convenient excuse.

The oasis at Figuig became a constant flash point. In 1900 the French established a small garrison a few miles southeast of the oasis at Beni Ounif in, according to the French interpretation of the border, Algeria. Attacks on the supply columns for this outpost were frequent and profitable and over the next three years the French lost over 50 men and numerous animals and supplies to raiders operating out of Figuig.

In May 1903 there was a more serious incident when the newly appointed governor general of Algeria, Celestine Jonnart, was fired upon during a visit to the oasis with the French military commander for South Oranais, General O'Connor. Their escort of soldiers, heavily outnumbered by the attackers, returned fire but wisely resisted the urge to enter the oasis which, with its maze of walls, irrigation canals and buildings, would likely lead to heavy casualties. The attackers maintained heavy, if somewhat inaccurate, fire on the governor's party who began a fighting withdrawal back to the comparative safety of the camp at Beni Ounif. They sustained a number of casualties and one fatality. The governor had had a narrow escape, but the experience was all that was needed to justify a more forceful response. The popular press back in France declared the attack as a major humiliation and demanded action and it became a situation the government could no longer ignore.

The problem however remained that, even though it was agreed something needed to be done, the situation in Europe (pre The Entente Cordiale and The Conference of Algeciras) and the views of many in the French Parliament required that any response needed to be carefully handled by an expert in such matters. The man selected for the task was Col Hubert Lyautey, who Jonnart had met back in France shortly after his unfortunate experience at Figuig.

Lyautey was something of an enigma. At first glance more suited to a life in academia or politics he had never been comfortable in the regular, metropolitan army based in France. He had little interest in the petty rules, regulations, and routine of garrison life and he was generally unhappy and bored. His transformation came with a posting to the staff of General Gallieni in Tonkin followed by a posting, also with Gallieni, to Madagascar where he had been given a substantial part of the island to subdue. Life in the colonial army was challenging, exciting and full of action. Largely viewed with disdain by the career officers back in France, many of whom had never heard a shot fired in anger, the colonial army was a place where Lyautey could thrive and when offered the chance of a posting to Morocco he grasped it with enthusiasm. However, he was not without self-doubt and after some early setbacks he wrote to his mentor Gallieni, whose methods of operating had so impressed him: 'Gallieni and only Gallieni is needed here. I need your touch and I do not have it'.[1]

---

1 Louis H. Lyautey, *Vers le Maroc: Lettres du Sud-Oranis,1903–1906* (Paris: Armand Colin, 1937), p.14.

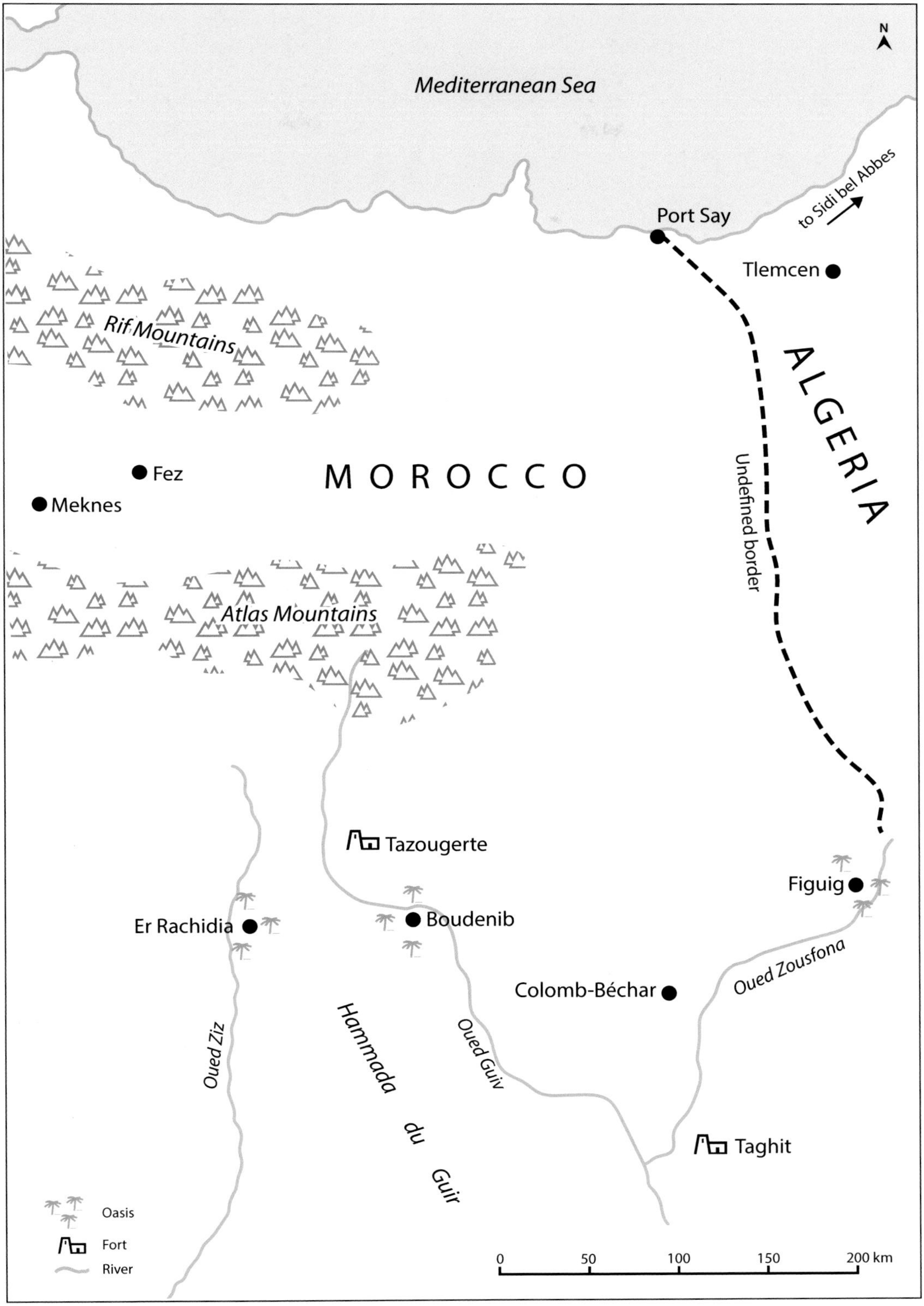

Southeast Morocco/ southwest Algeria – Frontier Region. There was no defined border between the two countries.

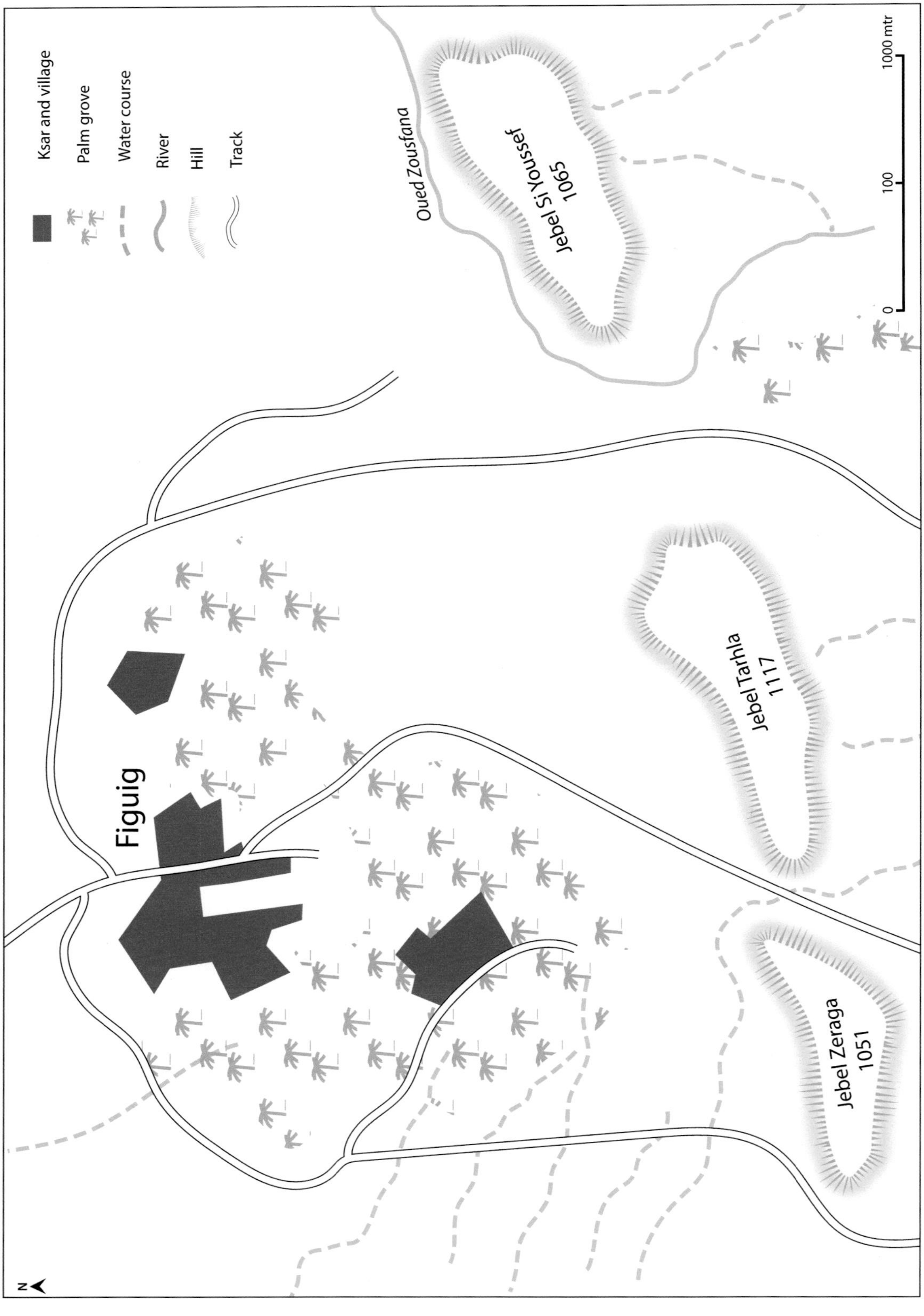

The oasis and kasbas of Figuig in southeast Morocco.

In October 1903, when still only 48, Colonel Lyautey was promoted to the rank of Brigadier General. Unprecedented freedom of action to carry out such actions as he thought necessary was granted to him by Governor General Jonnart, to whom he was to report directly thereby bypassing his superior officer in Algeria, General O'Connor with whom Jonnart had become less impressed.

From the outset it was clear that his initial focus should be on the south of Morocco and, in particular, the region around the oasis and ksars at Figuig where the most trouble was concentrated. By pacifying and controlling this area, future moves into Morocco further north would, Lyautey believed, be protected by a secure flank. To achieve this, he would need to act with care because there were still a substantial number in the French government who did not want an aggressive approach to Morocco or any actions that could be perceived as openly hostile by the Sultan or other European powers.

His method for achieving this was based very much on the lessons he had learned in the Far East and Madagascar where he had witnessed the so-called 'Gallieni method' at close quarters. What had worked so well before was, he felt, sure to work again in the challenging Moroccan environment. Under his direction Morocco would be 'absorbed' rather than invaded.

Lyautey's approach was based around a number of essential requirements. Carefully selected officers able to operate on their own initiative, leading well trained and motivated troops, would be given freedom to operate within specified areas which they were expected to know in detail. Speed of movement was critical and yet, what might be conceived by local tribes as aggressive military action, was not. His plan involved military and political aims at the same time. Working from oasis to oasis, ksar to ksar, tribe to tribe, he hoped that a show of force would prevent the use of force. It was a laudable plan, and one not unfamiliar to those involved in more recent operations in Afghanistan and Iraq. It was however essential that whilst trying to avoid a fight his ability to do so would never be in doubt. The tribes of the region respected military strength and, unless they fully believed in the fighting prowess of the French, the plan would fail.

Lyautey's plan would require mobile forces able to react quickly to any situation and able to move from location to location at speed. These units would need a series of outposts built in carefully selected locations that would not only become tactical military bases but also, in due time, act as more strategic centres for trade and administration thus demonstrating the advantages to local communities of working with the French rather than against them. Later, as areas became more pacified a network of road and rail would be established to support the resupply and movement of troops. Crucial to the success of the plan were the legionaries of the French Foreign Legion for whom Lyautey, who had seen them in action in Vietnam and Madagascar, had a great regard.

Chapter 2

The Legion in Morocco

At the start of the twentieth century French military forces in North Africa, known as the Armee d'Afrique, consisted of a range of troop types and was a mixture of conscripted and volunteer units. From the French settlers in Algeria, it had been possible to raise four, white European, zouave regiments using short service conscription. Arab volunteers were used to create four tirailleur regiments led by French officers whilst other tirailleur units were made up from men recruited in another French province Senegal.

French civilian and military criminals could serve out their sentences in one of four battalions of light infantry known as the Bats d'Af. Finally, two regiments of the all-volunteer Legion Etranger (Foreign Legion) made up the largest proportion of the overall army.

Whilst the Foreign Legion has a long and illustrious history dating back to its formation by King Louis-Philippe of France in 1831 it is probably for its service in Morocco in the early part of the twentieth century that it is most well-known. The remote desert outpost, manned by rugged and desperate legionnaires in blue overcoats and white kepis, surrounded by hordes of mounted tribesmen has become an iconic image ever since P.C. Wren first published Beau Geste in 1925. The original story was an immediate bestseller and resulted in several Hollywood films and numerous other books and films of a similar genre.

Whilst Wren's own claims to have served in the French Foreign Legion are difficult to verify it is generally accepted that his research was thorough and that much of what he describes in his stories are quite accurate. The Legion had been used in desert campaigns across North Africa since its formation. They did indeed fight, often heavily outnumbered, skirmishes and battles and they did build and garrison isolated forts and blockhouses that did, at times, become the focal point of military actions beyond even the imagination of novel writers. Outposts being defended to the last man were not plots in popular novels but frequent occurrences in Morocco during the early part of the twentieth century.

The Legion's reputation for resolution under fire was already well established but incidents such as an ambush in July 1900 near the outpost at Taghit served to enhance the image. For just over five hours a mounted company of 2nd R.E. (Regiment Etranger) held off repeated attacks from a force of around 900 Doui Menia tribesmen, many of whom were mounted, sustaining the loss of eight legionnaires and many more wounded.

A couple of years later a half company from the same regiment was again in action against overwhelming odds. Ordered to escort a resupply convoy of some 600 camels, the force of around one 120 Legionnaires and two officers was ambushed near El Moungar by a war party of almost 2,000 warriors from the Chaambas tribe. With no rations, no water and very low on ammunition the legionnaires fought a running battle for almost eight hours under the hot desert sun before a relief party finally arrived to help and the war party withdrew. By then the legion had 33 dead, including both officers, and taken a further 40 casualties.

Given the extreme conditions in which they fought and the tough life that they endured it is perhaps surprising that anyone would wish to join the Legion at all. Only a small number would survive a full 15-year term of service to qualify for a small pension and many would end their service abruptly in an unmarked grave somewhere in North Africa. Five years' service would gain a recruit French citizenship but, for many, unemployment and poverty were the prime motivators. Contrary to popular belief the Legion was not a place for hardened criminals to disappear and, certainly by the start of the twentieth century, the vetting process was quite efficient at preventing the enlistment of the more undesirable elements. That is not to say that all recruits enlisted under their real names or nationalities. French citizens were originally barred from joining but, from 1881, they were allowed to do so provided they had already completed their national service in the regular army based in France. Garrison life in France would have little appeal for those seeking travel and action so it is unsurprising that re-enlistment in the Legion had a real appeal for those who enjoyed military life but, even so, many chose to describe themselves and Belgian or Swiss to avoid too many questions. For those with more petty crimes to their name, five years in the legion could, sometimes, be an alternative to time in prison.

For some the legion would offer prospects beyond that which they could hope to achieve in civilian life. A literate recruit who was physically fit and hardworking could gain rapid promotion to NCO status and those with a good command of the French language could gain entrance to the Saint-Maxent officer training academy. There is even record of ex-regular army officers from a number of countries enlisting in the ranks and working up through the system to regain previous rank.

Enlistment was open to any healthy man between the ages of 18 and 40 but there is no doubt that many preferred to be somewhat vague about their ages and a legion unit may have recruits of any age between late teenage and early 50s. By the early twentieth century records show that the vast majority of those serving were in their mid-30s and that many had previous military service in either the French metropolitan army or the armies of other countries. The maturity and previous experience of the legionnaires was in stark contrast with the young age and complete immaturity of similar sized, largely conscripted, units of the regular French metropolitan army and goes a long way to accounting for their resilience and combat effectiveness in the harshest conditions.

In addition to previous military experience the Legion could also count within its ranks men with numerous trade skills. Builders, carpenters, bakers, butchers, blacksmiths, and numerous other useful trades could be found within the ranks of the Legion. As such the Legion could be regarded as largely self-sufficient but also perfectly suited to deployment onto civil engineering and other construction projects that were so critical to the Lyautey vision of colonial expansion. From the building of large garrison towns such as the legion's 'home' at Sidi-bel-Abbes to the smallest blockhouse, from roads and railways to tunnels and bridges the trade skills and manpower required could be provided by the Legion and many legionnaires could expect to spend a larger proportion of their service working on such projects than in actual combat.

Despite its title as a 'Foreign' Legion by 1900 around 45 percent of recruits were French. From the start a large number had come from Germany or German occupied Alsace-Lorraine but rigorous attempts to deter Germans from joining the Legion by the German government, was having some success and numbers dropped dramatically only to see a rise again after Germany's defeat in the First World War. Belgians and Swiss appeared to make up a large percentage, but this may simply be because, as French speaking countries, a Frenchman could enlist under an assumed nationality. Of course, there were recruits from all over the world. Those from Britain were a tiny minority and were not generally highly regarded.

Training for new recruits took place in the Oran province of Algeria at either Sidi-bel-Abbes, the spiritual home of the legion and HQ of 1st Regiment Etranger (1RE) or at Saida, the HQ of 2nd Regiment Etranger (2RE). Instruction was largely carried out by NCOs and covered everything from bed making, cleaning and maintaining clothing and equipment through to shooting, route marches and tactics.

The standard daily routine would be:

Table 1

0530	Reveille
0545	First Parade (Fall In)
0630–0800	Training
0800–0930	General Administration
0930	Breakfast (soupe)
1000	Second Parade (Report)
1030–1600	Training
1630	Evening Meal (soupe)
1700–2045	Personal Administration and Free time
2045	Retreat sounded
2100	Parade (Roll Call)
2200	Light Out

The ability to cover vast distances across the desert and fight a battle at the end of it was a particular requirement of the Legion so great emphasis was placed upon it during training. Route marches took place every week with recruits starting on 20 km routes in relatively light equipment gradually building up to 45 km distances in full campaign gear which could be as heavy as 36.3 kg in total.

Shooting skill was also essential with considerable emphasis being placed upon marksmanship. Badges for marksmanship were highly prized and many subunit commanders would run competitions on a regular basis and offer prizes for their men.

Tactical training would cover skirmishing, fire and movement, bayonet fighting, formation of defensive squares and movement in large formations. During long route marches the recruits were taught how to create defended campsites when they stopped each evening. Where possible an overnight camp would be positioned close to a water supply so that, in the event of a prolonged attack, troops would not become overcome by thirst. Where this was not possible troops would have to rely on the water they carried.

The force would split into four equal units each responsible for one side of the roughly square campsite. Their small tents, known as '*tente d'abri*', would be set out in a line along the side of the square they were responsible for with mules of the whole unit tethered in the centre together with the HQ and senior officers. On the order '*aux murailles*' walls of rocks and stones would be built to a height of around 45 cm parallel to the line of tents. Where rocks and stones were not readily available a trench would be dug and earth from that piled up on the outer edge to create an earth parapet. These simple, but effective, temporary defences provided cover from enemy fire and helped prevent a sudden rush attack on the resting troops.

Once the temporary camp had been built work, and where conditions allowed, work parties would be sent out to gather water, if required, and fuel for fires. From sunset sentries would patrol the sides of the camp whilst the remainder of the force rested.

In the event of attack the sentries on all four sides would fire outwards on the assumption an attack was coming on all sides. This fire, plus the shouts of '*aux armes*', would raise the rest of the unit to defend the camp.

The construction of low walls built from rocks and sand provided cover from enemy fire and helped prevent a sudden rush attack on the resting troops. Initiative by NCOs was very much expected in the field as small subunits were often operating in positions detached from the main force.

The duration of training would vary according to the aptitude of the individual but between three to four months was typical before being posted to a rifle company in an operational battalion.

Even there the recruit would be expected to learn from their more experienced comrades.

The quality of officers in the Legion had always been a particular issue and, at best, could be regarded as uneven. This was, in part, due to the rather unfashionable reputation of the Legion amongst the general military in France who perceived it as little better than a labour corps. By the start of the twentieth century, it is certainly true that there were a number of good quality officers but there were also a significant number who were simply regarding a short time in the legion as a way of gaining some operational experience before pursuing a more traditional career path back in the regular army.

Officers in the Legion had to be French nationals and came from two sources. First there were those who volunteered for service with the Legion after finding life as a regular officer in the metropolitan army in France extremely dull. Commanding conscripts in some provincial French town with nothing but daily routine and the occasional field exercise had little to offer those who sought the challenges and excitement of active service where the dangers of actual campaign were very real. Unlike conscripts, who were constantly changing and who the officers never really got to know, the regular soldiers of the Legion were a different breed who required careful handling and fine leadership skills. Those officers who managed this well quickly earned respect from their men and many made full careers in the Legion. However, others found it almost impossible to establish their authority and found life very difficult.

The second source of officers was from within the ranks. Whilst officially a foreigner could not hold a commission those who had served the required five years to become a French citizen, who had advanced swiftly up the ranks and had a good service record could apply for a commission. Furthermore, unlike in the British army where ex rankers who held battlefield or quartermaster commissions were regarded with some disdain by their regular counterparts, in the Legion there was no such stigma. The difficulty of getting the commission was widely recognised and admired and such officers could go on to long and active careers.

A major would command a battalion, supported by a small HQ staff, that would consist of four companies of around 250 men commanded by a captain and two lieutenants. The company would be subdivided into half companies (*peletons*) of about 100 men, platoons *(sections)* of around 50 and, the smallest operational unit of around 25 men, called squads (*groupes*).

Whilst the Legion was rightly proud of its route marching ability operations in North Africa required even greater speed of movement and endurance if they were to cope with the highly effective hit and run tactics being employed by the Moroccan tribes and with the need to support camel trains that were regularly required to resupply distant outposts. To provide for this role the concept of mounted companies (La Montee) was introduced. Their purpose was to cover great distances fast and, to do this, they were provided with mules which would carry the campaign equipment of two Legionnaires, rations for six days, fodder for the mule and water. It would also carry one of the two men to whom it was given, enabling one to ride, and rest, whilst the other marched. Officers and senior NCOs would have a mule of their own and additional mules would be taken to carry additional baggage and act as replacements. Using this method, the mounted companies could cover almost 80.5 km a day a distance considerably greater than could be achieved on foot alone. They would also arrive at their destination in greater strength as the number of dropouts normally expected during a long march on foot was considerably reduced.

This rate of progress could be sustained, with some short breaks, for up to two weeks at a time providing a combination of swiftness of movement expected from cavalry units with the addition of the far greater fire power and tactical expertise provided by infantry. As operations continued in Morocco the mounted companies became to be regarded as elite units. Almost certain to see more action than others they quickly attracted volunteers keen to escape routine service and see more action. They were, however, worked very hard. When not involved in military operations they were often used for construction work during quiet periods and this plus the demands of climate and terrain soon exhausted those involved. A two-year posting was about the maximum any mounted company soldier could take.

On operations the standard tactical unit would be the half company *(peleton)* consisting of around 100 men divided into two platoons led by an officer. This was then divided into two sections of 25 led by a sergeant and two corporals. The marching formation would be arranged to suit the terrain or other operational requirements but often would be single or double file led by the officer in charge. Between the two columns would be the units pack mules carrying ammunition, rations and water. Far ahead of the advancing column would be an advance guard of mounted Spahi troops, or mounted Arab irregulars known as goumiers, who were responsible for checking the route ahead for traces of the enemy, seeking out suitable campsites and waterholes and generally covering the advance.

Within the marching column the soldier on foot would usually march on the right side of his mounted companion but, at times of perceived risk, these men may be positioned to provide a screen to the right and left of the column or be formed into a single skirmishing group to operate ahead of the column when approaching difficult terrain or possible ambush sites.

In the event of contact with the enemy the mounted soldiers would dismount and join the others in forming a defensive line facing the attack. If the attack was considered to be more serious, then a rough square would be formed. Suitable terrain would be included in the defence where possible and the mules and supplies would be placed in the centre of the formation. To prevent mules from bolting during the action one man in eight would be allocated to looking after them. Whilst this clearly reduced the firepower of the formation it prevented the disastrous loss of vital resources.

The strength of the defensive square is well illustrated by the action at the Zafrani waterholes in July 1900. On that day a mounted company from 2RE was on escort duty for a supply train of camels from Igli following the course of the Oued Zousfana. Some miles north of the waterholes at Zafrani the advance party spotted a war party of some 500 warriors of the Dawi Mani tribe. Sending his second in command back to warn the main convoy the officer in charge, Captain Serant, ordered his men to form a square on a small hill just off the main track.

Shortly after his forward screen of mounted Spahi game galloping back to join the square hotly pursued by three large groups of mounted warriors whose speed carried many into the centre of the square where they were shot down and killed. The shattered side of the square quickly reformed and, from then on, the efficiently controlled fire held off subsequent attacks. In stark contrast Lieutenant Pauly and his platoon who had returned to join the fight were caught in open ground some distance from the main square and overwhelmed with the loss of eight dead and many more wounded.

Of course, the failure of the Arab attack was as much due to their own poor tactics as the steadiness under attack of the French soldiers. Outstanding riders mounted on superb horses the tribesmen preferred to fight on horseback firing their single shot weapons from the saddle. Excellent shots though they were had they dismounted and used their superior numbers to fire aimed shots from a distance the result may well have been different. It was a lesson that took a while to learn.

There were, of course, issues with the mounted company concept. It required a huge amount of water for both mules and men, and the mules themselves were very valuable and attractive targets for the Moroccans. Furthermore, once combat was taking place the safety of the mules was a major issue requiring almost a fifth of the soldiers in the column to secure them. On balance the speed, and more importantly, distance of movement that the mounted company was capable of was its saving virtue provided that commanders in the field used this rather than deploying them on more sedentary convoy protection duties. There still however remained the problem of overuse. Despite the double pay and elite image volunteers did not come forward in great numbers and, of those that did, many would not serve for more than a year. Whilst those in favour pointed to the low attrition rate of the units this was mainly because there was a greater element of selection of those applying to join. Certainly by 1913 even General Lyautey himself was considering the viability of the mounted companies.

Chapter 3

Conquest and Consolidation

Regular armies are cumbersome organisations operating at slow speed and heavily reliant on supply chains and logistical support that inevitably hamper swift action. In essence they are designed to engage with enemies organised in a similar way and where, in some circumstances, the result of one battle can completely destroy an opponent and provide a decisive result. However, where an opposition does not have the logistical restraints of a conventional army, where it is a master of the terrain in which it operates and where it has speed and fluidity of movement the situation has always been, and remains to this day, extremely challenging. This was certainly the issue facing the French who also faced the added difficulty of extreme heat during the summer months.

From 1890 to 1906 two battalions of the Foreign Legion, plus their associated mounted companies, were regularly rotated on tours of duty to the disputed borderland region between Morocco and Algeria known as the 'Sud Oranis'.

In addition to intercepting mounted raiding parties their mission was to survey the region to gather information for the production of detailed mapping, build wells and roads and, finally, to establish temporary, and later permanent, fortified posts to guard the wells and from which further patrols could be launched. Domination of ground and control of vital supply and communication routes would become essential if the French were to complete their mission and, in a way so similar to the legions of ancient Rome, a series of outposts and isolated forts would need to be constructed. By 1900 permanent forts had been established at Igli and Taghit some 300 km southwest of Ain Sefra. Later, other posts would eventually become major bases with large garrisons whilst others would always remain small and temporary in nature. The eventual network of outposts used in conjunction with the ability of the Legion to move troops great distances and speed was envisaged as a way of controlling large areas of ground with a minimal number of troops.

As a secondary role the outposts would provide visible symbols to the local populations that their area was under French control whilst it was also hoped that such posts would become focal points for the development of trade and commerce: 'The mountain tribes believed in the right and might of the strongest and a display of arms had to be shown to them.'[1]

Despite some early success in the southeast, resistance to the French was breaking out all across Morocco. In 1907 a series of incidents, riots and hostage taking resulted in the occupation by the French of Oujda and Casablanca as a new front was opened up along the Atlantic coast of western Morocco. The Sultan, Abd al-Hafid was already heavily in debt to the French government and could do little to prevent further encroachment of his territory. However, some tribal leaders did attempt to fight back. The most noteworthy was Ma al-Aynayn who, in 1910, led his warriors over the High Atlas in an attempt to seize Casablanca back from the French. His forces were never going to be a match for the French, and he was heavily defeated at Tadla on the 23 June long before getting anywhere near Casablanca.

Early in 1911 an uprising against the Sultan in Fez was quickly stamped out by the French who then proceeded to occupy the capital. It was this action that led to concern being expressed by other European powers, most notably the Germans, who dispatched a gunboat to Agadir resulting in what became known as the Agadir Crisis. It was quickly resolved, and military operations moved steadily across the country following a similar approach to the operations in the south and east. By 1912, under the so-called Treaty of Fez, Morocco officially became a French Protectorate, and the Sultan was forced to abdicate in favour of his brother and hand over control of the Government to General Lyautey. This did not end resistance and fighting continued in other areas across the country. For a short period, the city of Marrakesh was seized by Moroccan resistance forces led by a popular tribal leader called Ahemed al-Hiba who declared a jihad and promised to drive the French out of Morocco. His inevitable defeat came at the Battle of Sidi bou Othman, some 40 km north of Marrakesh, where superior firepower and modern weapons quickly devastated his ill-disciplined and poorly armed force.

Despite living in an almost constant state of inter-tribal war the Moroccan tribes faced a significantly more challenging enemy with the French. The rapid hit and run tactics used to steal sheep and camels from rival tribes were less effective against columns of well-armed French soldiers and particularly useless against the fortified positions and forts.

Individual warriors were undoubtably brave but lack of military cohesion, controlled tactics and, most importantly, a good supply of modern weapons and ammunition were significant obstacles to success in battle particularly during the early years of the French occupation.

A rifle of any type was a highly sought-after item and a distinct sign of status. There was an active trade in smuggled weapons, but hose purchased would have been very expensive and many tribesmen would have had to carry older, and in some cases almost obsolete, weapons. As time passed modern breach loading rifles became more abundant as weapons were stolen from the French, retrieved from the battlefield or, more often, obtained from

---

1 Zinovi Pechkoff, *The Bugle Sounds, Life in the Foreign Legion* (London: Appleton, 1926), p.53.

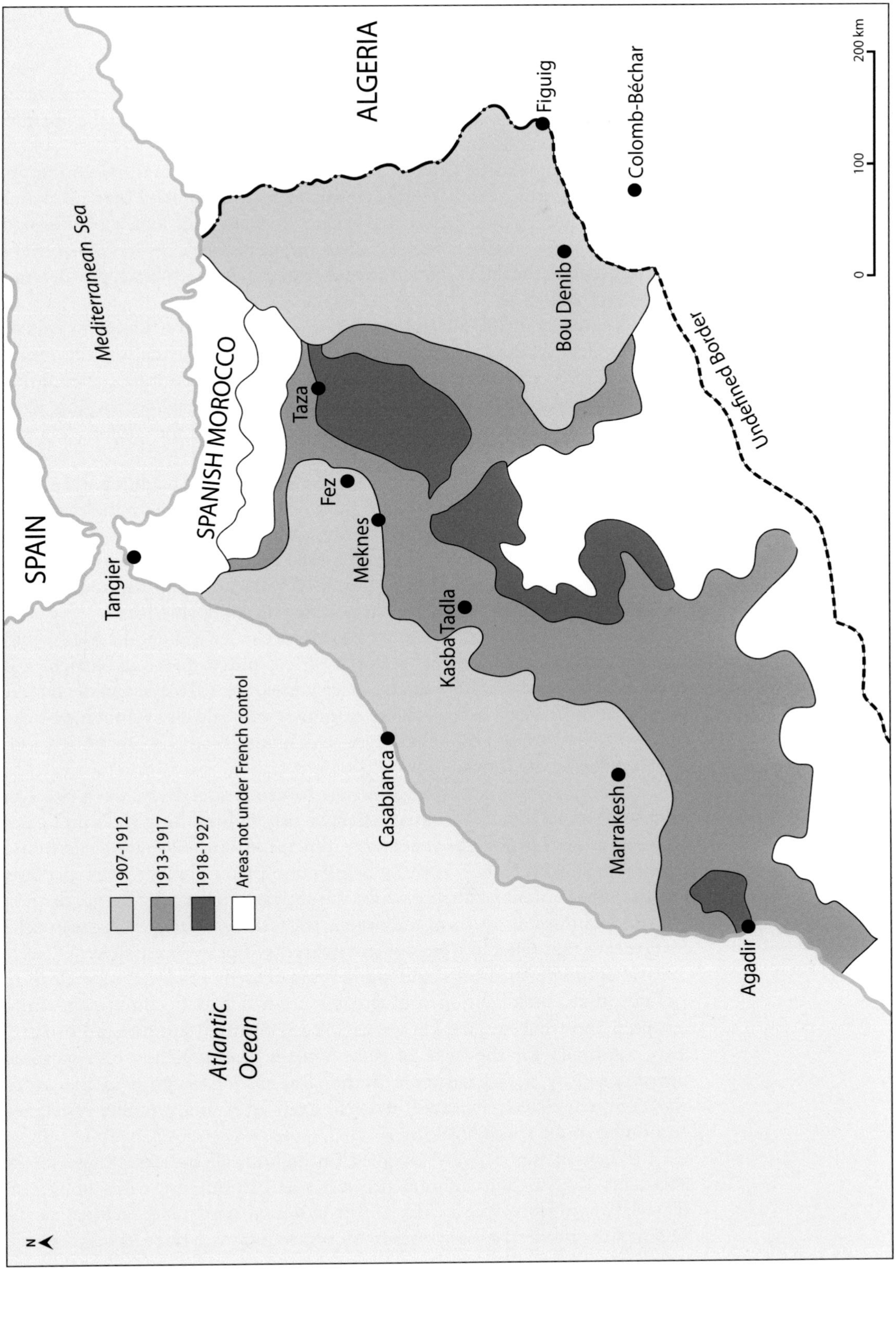

The French conquest of Morocco: 1907–1927.

the sultan's own forces who were less careful in guarding their weapons and not beyond selling them to the highest bidder. It has been estimated that between 1901 and 1902 more than 2,000 rifles were obtained this way. Later, during fighting in the Rif Mountains in the 1920s, a huge amount of weapons, including machine guns and artillery, were taken from the Spanish who suffered several catastrophic defeats.

The most frequently used rifle was a version of the 1871 11 mm Remington, made in Spain, which readily became available as time went by. Martini Henry rifles, Winchesters, and Lebels also became more readily available although ammunition less so and it was not uncommon for warriors to collect spent cartridge cases from fields of action and reload them with black powder and homemade bullets.

Possession of a rifle did not mean the owner was proficient with its use. In general, individual marksmanship was poor with firing, on the move, when mounted on either camel or horse, much preferred to static, aimed shots. Even those on foot would often fire from the hip whilst charging. Even so high French casualties in some engagements show that not all fire was ineffective.

For close contact fighting the *koummya* was the traditional fighting dagger used by the Moroccan tribesmen. With a contoured handle, curved double-edged blades and exaggeratedly upturned scabbard tips they were deadly in proficient hands and much feared by the French. Worn visibly at the left side, at waist level, it was suspended vertically, with the scabbard tip forward, by a long woollen sling worn across the right shoulder.

Some warriors of high status may also have carried a single-handed sword called a *nimcha*. Very specific to North Africa, and Morocco in particular, it was a type of scimitar with a single, sharp edged, curved blade and decorative wooden handle. The best ones were extremely valuable and would have been handed down through the generations with quality blades being refitted with new handles many times.

Artillery, and the knowledge of how to use it effectively, was always in very short supply and without an effective way of breaching walls and gates assaults on forts would have been very difficult. Almost always a siege would be inevitable with forts effectively being cut off from outside help and then subjected to harassing rifle fire whilst the attackers waited for the garrison to run out of ammunition, food, and water. The remote locations of many of the forts meant that relief in time was not guaranteed or even possible.

The sporadic uprisings and underlying dissent made it very clear to Lyautey that consolidation and greater control had become even more essential and what became known as 'the pacification' commenced in 1912. This continued for the next 14 years until a final rebellion and national uprising led by the charismatic Berber leader Abd-el-Krim in the north was comprehensively defeated in 1926. Even after this sporadic resistance continued in the south until 1934.

The Legion was actively involved throughout all the campaigns across Morocco. Whilst their fighting prowess was of immense value, they also played a significant role in the construction of roads and fortified posts. Much of the modern road system in Morocco today can trace its origins back to routes surveyed and constructed by the Legion and the famous Tunnel du Legionnaire located on the main N13 road at the southern end of the Ziz Gorge remains a tribute to what can be built with little, or no, heavy machinery. To this day it remains a vital part of the main route north from the Sahara and its construction is marked by a plaque stating: 'The mountain barred the way. Nonetheless the order was given to pass … The Legion executed it'

Further south, at the Source de Bleu Meski, the recreation area and swimming pool built by the Legion continues in daily use to this day.

One of the advantages of the unique method of recruiting into the Legion was that it brought within its ranks men with a diverse range of skills and abilities. Architects, masons, carpenters, plumbers, and electricians could be found within the Legion's units, and it was to these men that the construction of forts, watchtowers and other civil engineering projects would fall.

Chapter 4

Construction of Outposts

It is unclear as to whether forts and smaller outposts were built to a fixed pattern in the manner adopted by the Romans 2,000 years earlier. However, the current archaeological evidence does reveal several design features common to many posts across North Africa and written records from the period appear to support this. Any unit tasked with constructing a fort would need to consider factors including location, size and shape of the area most suitable for construction, availability of building material, and time available to complete the process.

Location was of primary importance as no military building was simply built at random in the landscape. However, perfect sites would not always be available. The larger forts would be positioned in locations where they would best support operations in the region around it. Access to the site would be important for the delivery of building material and later, once in operation, for resupply. At times a location would be regarded as so important that a road would need to be constructed to gain access to the chosen site. Where possible the defensive importance of a selected location would be considered but this may have been outweighed by other factors such as visibility, access to natural water supply or ease of construction. Watch towers and smaller blockhouses would require line of site to their nearest neighbours to enable the effective use of signals

The popular image of a Foreign Legion fort comes straight from the opening scenes of the novel Beau Geste. 'The tri-colour flew merrily from the flag staff, and the fort looked absolutely normal – a square grey block of high, thick mud walls, a flat castellated roof, flanking towers and a lofty lookout platform.'[1]

It has become a lasting image which may, or may not, have been witnessed first-hand by Wren whose claims to have served in the Legion have never been verified. However, others whose service has been verified provide similar descriptions. In 1928 ex-Legionnaire T. Victor wrote:

1 Percival C. Wren, *Beau Geste* (Hertfordshire: Wordsworth Classic, 1994), p.7.

> In the centre of the post were five sickly palm trees and the water well …
> It had high stone walls around it. Stones were collected from the hamada and carried by Legion labour to the fort which had also been constructed by Legion labour and designed by architects who were legionnaires. In the centre was a high watchtower flying the tricolour on a staff.[2]

His reference to the internal water well is of note as it is a fact that not all forts and outposts had their own, natural, water supply relying instead on storage tanks filled on a regular basis with water gathered from nearby sources. Major Pechkoff wrote of such a post: 'There is an outpost not far away where an officer and thirty men have to remain. It is built on a very high peak and has no water. Water must be carried there every eight days on mules.'[3]

In the hot climate of Morocco this was, of course, an 'Achilles' heel' which would quickly be exploited by the Berber warriors. However, the fact that the French would be well aware of this suggests that the location of an outpost was of overwhelming importance and that the French higher command had supreme confidence in the ability of their supply chain to keep the forts resupplied with water. Although writing about a later period the *Daily Mail* journalist G. Ward Price, one of the very first journalists to be embedded with military units on active service, wrote:

> As the forts have to be sited pre-eminently for defence they are invariably posted on a hill top and their water supply has to be brought to them from the nearest stream … The requirement for water under normal conditions is reckoned to be a gallon a day. To provide for the possibility of the daily replenishment being interrupted by a prolonged attack on the fort a reserve of 40 gallons is kept within two large tanks with it.[4]

Whatever efforts were made to maintain a supply of water the lack of an internal supply would always be an issue that would be exploited by an attacker. Records show that a number of forts were eventually overrun due to lack of fresh water and after attempts to resupply, including dropping blocks of ice from the air, had repeatedly failed.

Ward-Price also provides a description of a fort not unlike that described by Wren:

> The fort was of regulation type and consisted of a square enclosure with a wall nine feet high and each side about 200 yards in length. Projecting towers at the corners rose to a height of about 15 feet. The platform behind the parapet at the top of them was sufficiently roomy for a 3-inch mountain gun to be posted on top of it.
> The walls of the fort were a yard thick, of loose stones plastered and whitewashed. At intervals there are embrasures for machine guns. A fire step runs around the inside of the enceinte.

---

2 T.Victor, *From the Abyss to the Foreign Legion* (London: Sampson, 1928), p.93.
3 Pechkoff, *Bugle Sounds*. p.69.
4 G. Ward Price, *In Morocco with the Legion* (London: Jarrolds Publishers, 1934), p.202.

> The centre of the enclosure is filled with low stone buildings that house the three or four officers, ten non-commissioned officers and the 162 men who form the garrison. Store houses, a cook house, a hospital and a telephone/wireless room lie along the inside of the wall. Sometimes a pigeon-cote for carrier pigeons is provided as well.
>
> On the outside of the walls are built stables and cowsheds as, for hygienic reasons it would be impossible to keep the animals inside the perimeter of the post.[5]

This description is similar to that of a fort built some 10 years earlier and described by the ex-Legionnaire 75645 who wrote:

> Doranov took charge of the construction of a massive tower near the main gates, Dormen continued with the fixing of the roofs while I saw to any odd jobs that arose. We had built 24 rooms inside with store houses for food and ammunition. In one corner of the courtyard, we dug a deep well so that we could have an abundant water supply without going outside the walls.[6]

That the forts were often white in colour is supported by Major Pechkoff who wrote: 'Lime is needed for whitening the walls and two of my outposts have chosen a suitable place between their walls and the barbed wire to excavate and build a lime kiln.'[7]

All such contemporary accounts are supported by contemporary imagery and the archaeological record and are consistent with the vernacular architecture of the region.

As to whether forts were built to a specific plan the record is less clear. Without doubt troops in the field would have had access to manuals of military engineering and construction of defences was part of an officer training syllabus and the Foreign Legion in particular had considerable construction expertise within its ranks. The French *Engineer Journal* (Revue Du Genie) contains many articles and diagrams of military fortifications, but these often represent an ideal. The archaeological record shows that whilst many were constructed with the key features mentioned above the precise layout would vary from place to place and would appear to very often be dictated by the location selected for construction. Ex Legionnaire 75464 wrote: 'We measured out a square and marked down the foundations for the walls with the usual bastion at each corner. We had built so many forts for the legion that we knew the work inside out.'[8] Additional information on the construction process comes from the records of Major Pechkoff:

> As soon as the place was chosen some of the men were given axes to cut down trees. Others with hammers and picks were to break the rocks and clear the ground that tents might be pitched. Gangs of men went to work … masons,

5 Ward Price, *In Morocco*, p.201.
6 Ex-Legionnaire 75464, *Slaves of Morocco* (London: Sampson Lowe, 1938), p.208.
7 Pechkoff, *Bugle Sounds*, p.74.
8 Ex-legionnaire 75464, *Slaves of Morocco*, p.194.

> stonebreakers and miners who drilled the rocks in order to dynamite them and men with picks and shovels who traced the outline of the post. Other men with picks and shovels located an appropriate place and then dug holes in the ground to make limekilns whilst others cut down more trees to make firewood to feed the ovens, where stone was being transformed into lime.[9]

Both the archaeological and written records indicate that the tower was a significant feature in the forts. Given that the location of the forts was chosen for the views provided of the terrain around them the height of any tower would significantly increase the range of observation and, with the use of signal lamps and heliographs that were used for transmitting messages, range of communication. 'A sentry was always posted in the tower, being protected from Arab snipers by a sentry box made of stone which came as high as his shoulders. To celebrate our arrival the sentries in the tower were sniped at for the first twenty four hours, almost without a five minute interval'.[10]

That some forts had additional towers is confirmed in the literary and archaeological record. 'At some distance from the fort are generally built one or two watchtowers from which a more extended view of the environs can be obtained … Such towers are always in view of the main fort'.[11]

Construction of the larger, better designed forts could only take place in an area of relative calm where building could be completed uninterrupted and not all outposts were constructed in the formal manner described above. In some instances, especially along old trading routes that pre-dated French interest in the region, existing buildings called Bordj would be often utilised with hastily constructed defences added as required.

> The location which had been described to us as a strong point was simply a collection of mud huts grouped around an oasis consisting of a water hole and a few palms. The fortifications comprised a ring of rather dilapidated trenches, and equally dilapidated moat, about four feet wide, and a straggling barbed wire entanglement plentifully ornamented with bully beef tins.[12]

During the Rif uprising in north-western Morocco time and terrain simply would not allow the construction of the formal type of outposts. Constructed in considerable haste, simple posts would be created with walls of stacked rocks, sandbags, stone filled boxes and oil drums enhanced with an outer ring of barbed wire for additional defence. Empty tin cans would be hung on the wire to create noise when moved and hence give some advance warning of any attempt to approach the outpost.

All legionnaires were aware of the value of hard defences and were taught during basic training to construct dry stone walls, known as 'Muraille's d'Afrique' around every night camp when units were on active service in the field.

---

9 Pechkoff, *Bugle Sounds*, p.27.
10 Victor, *From the Abyss,* p.152
11 Ward Price, *In Morocco*, p.207.
12 John Harvey, *With the French Foreign Legion in Syria* (London: Greenhill Books, 1995), p.93

Chapter 5

Life in the Outposts

For those serving in the remote forts and outposts it would be boredom that would be the main threat to the welfare of the troops stationed there. These first impressions by Zinovi Pechkoff are probably similar to those of many: 'My heart sank when, from afar, I saw the post of Ouaouizeght where I am to spend the next five months, completely isolated from the rest of the world.'[1]

With regard to life in the outposts that is perhaps best described by Legionnaire John Harvey (not his real name):

> We were utterly and completely fed up with our existence in the desert outpost. Our chief occupation was grousing. We grumbled at the heat, the flies, the heat and each other. And especially we grumbled about the Director of Ordnance whose chief object in life was apparently to keep us short of supplies. The Captain sent indent after indent, but something always seemed to go wrong. If he asked for socks, it was more than likely that we received bully beef. The worst scandal of all was the way in which we were starved of ammunition.[2]

Boredom, discontent, and the availability of cheap wine were a dangerous combination. Excessive drinking, although common amongst off duty soldiers of most armies, was a particular issue in the Legion and Pechkoff wrote of his experience:

> There are no distractions in the outpost. One is confined to its four walls. But outside the post, built against the wall, there are three canteens. The men go there on the days after they receive their pay and they spend all their money. For about two days every fortnight almost everybody is drunk, and one has to have untiring energy in order to control these men. [3]

Being drunk and disorderly was part of being a Legionnaire and there are many accounts of men rising, falling and rising again through the ranks due to alcohol consumption

1 Pechkoff, *Bugle Sounds,* p.69.
2 Harvey, *With the French Foreign Legion*, p.109.
3 Pechkoff, *Bugle Sounds,* p.78.

The extreme boredom, stress and general living conditions produced an effect on the troops that eventually became known as 'cafard'. This metaphorical beetle that began to eat away at men's brains was widely regarded as the root cause of many desertions and potential mutinies and it affected all ranks. German Legionnaire Erwin Rosen described his experience at the start of the twentieth century:

> All idiocy in the Legion is called cafard. A legionnaire is gloomy, sitting sullenly on his bed for hours speaking to no one. If you ask him what is the matter he will answer you with a gross insult. He sits thinking all the time and does the queerest things. He has the cafard.
>
> His madness may turn into a senseless explosion or a fit of fury: men suffering from cafard will run a bayonet through their comrades' body, without any reason, without any outward cause. Sometimes they rush out into the desert, sometimes they tear every piece of their outfit into rags, just to vex themselves and others thoroughly.[4]

For some serving in remote outposts the stress and boredom could result in suicide or desertion. Both have become part of the folklore associated with the Legion. Writing in 1904 about his time as a Legionnaire in the 1880s John Patrick Le Poer described service in remote outposts:

> These are suicide stations, if I may call them so ... When one man shoots himself an epidemic seems to set in; men hear every day in hut or tent or guard room the ill-omened report; soon they go about looking fearfully at one another, for no one knows but that he is looking into the eyes of a comrade who has made up his mind to die. The corporal counts his squad, fourteen, fifteen – ah, there were sixteen yesterday.[5]

For others desertion was seen as an acceptable option. Such action may stand a chance of success if the deserter could gain easy access to a safe haven in relatively short time but from the remote outposts in the mountains and deserts of Morocco the chances of success were very slim. Writing of desertion from the station at Bou Denib in the 1920s Legionnaire Jaques Weygand wrote:

> Although there may have been an even chance of success in deserting when passing through a port or when stationed in a town or near to the Mediterranean coast only the unbalanced would attempt it from a starting place like Bou-Denib. The only patch open lay in the direction of Colomb-Bechar, and that was neither easy nor safe. The rest of the surrounding country for many miles was either desert or rebel territory.

---

4 Erwin Rosen, *In the Foreign Legion* (London: Duckworth, 1910), p183.
5 John P. Le Poer, *A Modern Legionary* (London: Methuen, 1904), p.89.

> Journeys of pathetic folly, most likely to end up in the lock-up of a Native Affairs Office, whose informers are always on the alert, or the alternative of a slow and painful death, for even the strongest cannot fight thirst.[6]

These were all issues well known to the higher command and one of the responsibilities of the officers chosen to command the forts and outposts was to ensure that the troops under their command were kept as well occupied as possible.

A typical day of a Legionnaire on garrison duty would consist of:

Table 2

Time	Activity
0500	Reveille
0500–1030	Parade, flag raising, sentries relieved, dawn recce patrol, animals fed and watered, inspection of defences, construction and repair work, disposal of rubbish, general administrative duties.
1030–1230	Rest, midday meal and distribution of lemon juice.
1230–1630	Continuation of duties, patrols, training, laundry (Wednesdays only)
1630	Rompez
1630–1800	Free time, sport, bathing (where possible)
1800	Evening Meal
2000	Retreat
2000–2030	All men inside the fort. Paths through outer wire closed. Gates closed. Flag lowered.
2030	Roll call
2100	Lights out

Where conditions allowed field exercises would be carried out. Sunday morning would be allocated to kit cleaning and Sunday afternoons would be free for all those not otherwise allocated guard duties. Pay would be given on the 15th and 30th of each month.

Good commandants would try to make provision for their men and often books would be collected to create a small library and newspapers would, where possible, be delivered twice a week. Such items would be brought in by despatch riders from the nearest large supply base which could be anything up to 80.5 km away and frequently delivery of these items would be subject to ambush. Infrequently parcels, mail and rations could be delivered by patrolling aircraft.

Pechkoff refers to the planting of gardens near to his outpost: 'We have planted a vegetable garden near to the post and, although the men were sceptical about planting in June, it has come out wonderfully'.[7]

The home-grown vegetables would clearly have been a welcome addition to the standard military rations that would form the daily diet of the garrison. Food supplies would be held in the larger forts and one of the roles of the

6 Jaques Weygand, *Legionnaire: Life with the Foreign Legion Cavalry* (London: Harrap,1952), p.182.

7 Pechkoff , *Bugle Calls*, p.73.

commanding officer would be to ensure that food was distributed to the outlying observation towers and more remote sangars that supported the fort. Stocks of tinned rations ('boeuf boulle' and sardines) would be supplemented with sugar, flour, lard, and wine. Bread could be made at most forts and livestock, for fresh meat, would be kept in buildings and compounds situated close to, but outside, the fort. A ration of lemon juice would be issued daily to maintain Vitamin C levels and prevent the onset of scurvy.

As time went on trade with friendly locals would add variety and there are many references to traders establishing successful businesses outside the forts. Known as 'soukiers' they were issued with passes and regulated by the general staff who allowed them to supply other luxury items such as soap and cigarettes to the troops.

Such luxuries would cost money and any Legionnaire with money in addition to regular pay was in a very fortunate position:

> Having money in my pocket, I soon became popular; half a dozen hungry looking, ill clad Germans introduced themselves to me as aspirants, like myself, to military renown in the ranks of the second regiment of the French Foreign Legion. I cannot say I felt proud of my future brothers in arms, rather the reverse. However, I gave them something to eat and drink, and thus made them for ever my most obedient slaves.[8]

The arrival in the post of a little cash or postal order for an individual would have a similar effect: 'Then there is joy in the land. For a day, or a few days, or even a week, the prodigal son with the postal order lives like a king. He has his boot cleaned for him and would not dream of making his own bed as long as the money lasts'.[9]

Low pay and low morale inevitably led to theft. This would range from items of clothing and equipment to cash and valuables. Known in Legion slang as 'decorating' it was widespread even though punishment, both official and unofficial, was harsh for those caught:

> His face was black, so terribly was it bruised. A blow from a bayonet had split his cheek and a stream of blood flowed over his blue jacket. The guard came up and the fellow was carried into hospital. The man lay in hospital for weeks. That was the end of it. The nights lynch law was not inquired into. The punishment of the thief rests in the hands of his comrades.[10]

In the larger garrison towns Legionnaires would visit local bars and the use of prostitutes, although discouraged, was common. Eventually some effort was made to control this issue, and try to ensure the medical health of the men, with the introduction of the Bordel Militaire de Campagne (BMC) – essentially an officially regulated mobile brothel that would provide 'entertainment' for the troops.

---

8 William Stamer, *Recollections of a Life of Adventure* (London: Hurst and Blackett, 1866), p.84.
9 Rosen, *Foreign Legion*, p.108.
10 Rosen, *Foreign Legion*, p.113.

In the more remote outposts, where the BMC would not be able to visit, encounters with local village girls was inevitable. Legionnaire Ernst Lohndorff wrote of sexual encounters with local girls whilst he was stationed in a remote outpost on the Algerian/ Moroccan border:

> The oasis dwellers are blessed abundantly with children, especially girls, and they do not scruple in the least to sell us their half-grown daughters, who are about 13 years old but already mature women. For a few hours spent alone with the daughter of an Arab in his tent we pay five boxes of wax matches or a tin of sardines.[11]

Whilst sexual liaisons with local girls were officially discouraged, links with local communities of a more formal nature were actively encouraged as part of a 'hearts and minds' programme.

Not all Moroccans were hostile to the French and in the more peaceful regions closer relationships would develop and be encouraged. Pechkoff wrote of one such event:

> I was invited today to a feast given by the Caid of the region. In an orange grove on a cleared place on the grass, carpets were spread. There were two big carpets where fifty men could easily sit. We were met by the elder men of the village in snow white attire and with snow white turbans. We laid aside our arms and accompanied by these older men, and by other guests, we went into the orange grove. The Caid himself met us, but he did not follow, because he had to supervise the roasting of the mutton, of the chickens, of the wild game and look after the sweets that were being prepared for his guests.[12]

Homosexuality is also recorded as being a part of garrison life, particularly in the more isolated posts where, according to Beric: 'Inaction and boredom stimulate the force of desire, promiscuity facilitates approaches, ambient immorality excuses it.'[13]

He claimed that such activities created a bad atmosphere that, on occasion, led to desertion or suicide. His views on homosexuality are from a time when it was illegal, and his claims are not widely supported by others. Certainly, the issue was never regarded as a major problem in the way that alcohol abuse or theft was.

Whatever activities were engaged in there is no doubt that garrison duty in the remote outposts was essentially routine and tedious in the extreme and, for many who had joined the legion to seek action and adventure, very disheartening. For many, action when it came, would be a welcome relief. John Harvey wrote with some relief: 'The period of suspense was over at last. The enemy was here. All was tense with excitement.'[14]

---

11 Ernst Lohndorff., *Hell in the Foreign Legion* (London: George Allen and Unwin, 1931), p.257.

12 Pechkoff, *Bugle Calls*, p.121.

13 Raoul Beric, *Les routiers: La Légion Etranger: Source d'admiration et de pitié* (Paris Édition Moderne, 1907), p.127.

14 Harvey, *Foreign Legion*, p.114.

Chapter 6

Under Attack!

The forts and outposts constructed by the French served both strategic and tactical purposes. Large garrisons, such as the one at Kasba Tadla, were located in strategically significant positions often within, or very close to, existing Moroccan towns and cities such as Fez, Meknes, Marrakech, and Casablanca. Operating as major administrative centres, supply stores and training bases they would act as the support hub for units being deployed into operational zones further out. In these relatively peaceful locations garrison life would continue much as it would in metropolitan France but for the outposts further out in the frontier areas danger would be ever present.

During the early years of French occupation, the local tribes lacked effective artillery and other methods of forcing entry into the forts so the garrisons would have felt relatively secure from attack. With their modern weapons and protected by the hard cover afforded by the outpost the greatest threat most garrisons faced was that of a protracted siege. However, for the outposts built without internal water wells the cutting off of any water source would be an ever-present danger.

Sniping, small-scale attacks and attempts at infiltration were a constant hazard at the more remote posts. Sometimes the threat would be quite subtle.

> Often the Berber come and lie quietly in the vicinity of the post hoping to get something at daybreak if not at night. A sentry becomes sleepy after an hour of watching. Then the brigand who is watching the fort swings a rope and there have been occasions when men have been pulled from the bastion with their gun, sometimes killed, sometimes not, but always robbed of everything they had.[1]

At other times a more direct assault may be made: 'I leapt to my feet as I heard the sous officers crying "Aux armes! Aux armes! Prenez la garde, Legionnaires". Then I heard a blood curdling yell and I knew the sentries had been shot … I could see a rising wave of faces as the Arabs scaled the walls and bastions'.[2]

---

1 Pechkoff, *Bugle Calls*, p.109

2 Ex-Legionnaire 75464, *Slaves of Morocco*, p.112.

During the early years of the French occupation of Morocco major assaults on the outposts were rare. One of the most serious took place at Boudenib in southeast Morocco in August 1908.

In early 1908 reports of a gathering of Berber tribes in the region intent on moving north against the settlement at Colomb Bechar resulted in the despatch by General Vigny of troops to locate and intercept this force. Amongst the troops sent were four-foot companies of the 2RE and two mounted companies from 1RE On the 16 April the French force was attacked in its makeshift marching camp and stiff fighting followed. For a time, the result hung in the balance but the determined resistance by the French, and the lack of fighting spirit by the tribesmen, eventually resulted in the withdrawal of the Berber with the estimated loss of around 100 killed. However, the French too had 120 casualties, including 19 killed, and this was the greatest single loss in any engagement yet.

Whilst the Berber force dispersed, taking with them captured horses, mules, crates of ammunition and tinned foods, the attack was a wakeup call to General Vigny who immediately assembled a large force to pursue the enemy and finish the job.

In early May intelligence reports reached him of the gathering of between 800 to 2,000 tribesmen at Boudenib.

Located a few kilometres east from the southern end of the Tazuguerte Pass and set amongst some of the most desolate and inhospitable terrain in Morocco, a concentration of palm trees surrounded a large kasbah and an area of cultivated farmland and scattered dwellings. The Oued Guir flowed just to the north of the settlement and to the south of this the barren, rock strewn plain, interrupted by large rocky outcrops and small hills known as '*gara*' stretched south to the horizon.

After further intense fighting in, and around, the settlement and oasis, the French finally occupied Bou Denib in mid May 1908. Once again, the Berbers dispersed into the desert whilst the French immediately set about fortifying the location by building a walled redoubt just north of the Oued Guir. Located about a mile to the northwest of the palm groves and kasbah the redoubt was hastily constructed using earth from deep ditches to form ramparts in a rough square shape with bastions at each corner to house the artillery. The site today is covered by the modern town and no trace is visible. They also reinforced an existing tower being used as a local police post near the kasbah in the oasis.

To these earthwork defences were posted some 1,600 colonial troops, hundreds of horses and mules and two batteries of 75 mm and 80 mm field guns respectively.

Views to the south, where any impending attack was most likely to come, were blocked by a number of steep sided, flat-topped hills known as '*gara*' in Berber. To enable better observation of approaches from this direction the French constructed a blockhouse on a prominent '*gara*' about 2 km from the redoubt on the south side of the river. The remains of this structure can be seen today and these, plus imagery from the period, show a five sided, high walled, structure of irregular shape with outer defences consisting of low rough stone walls, bastions for artillery and barbed wire entanglements.

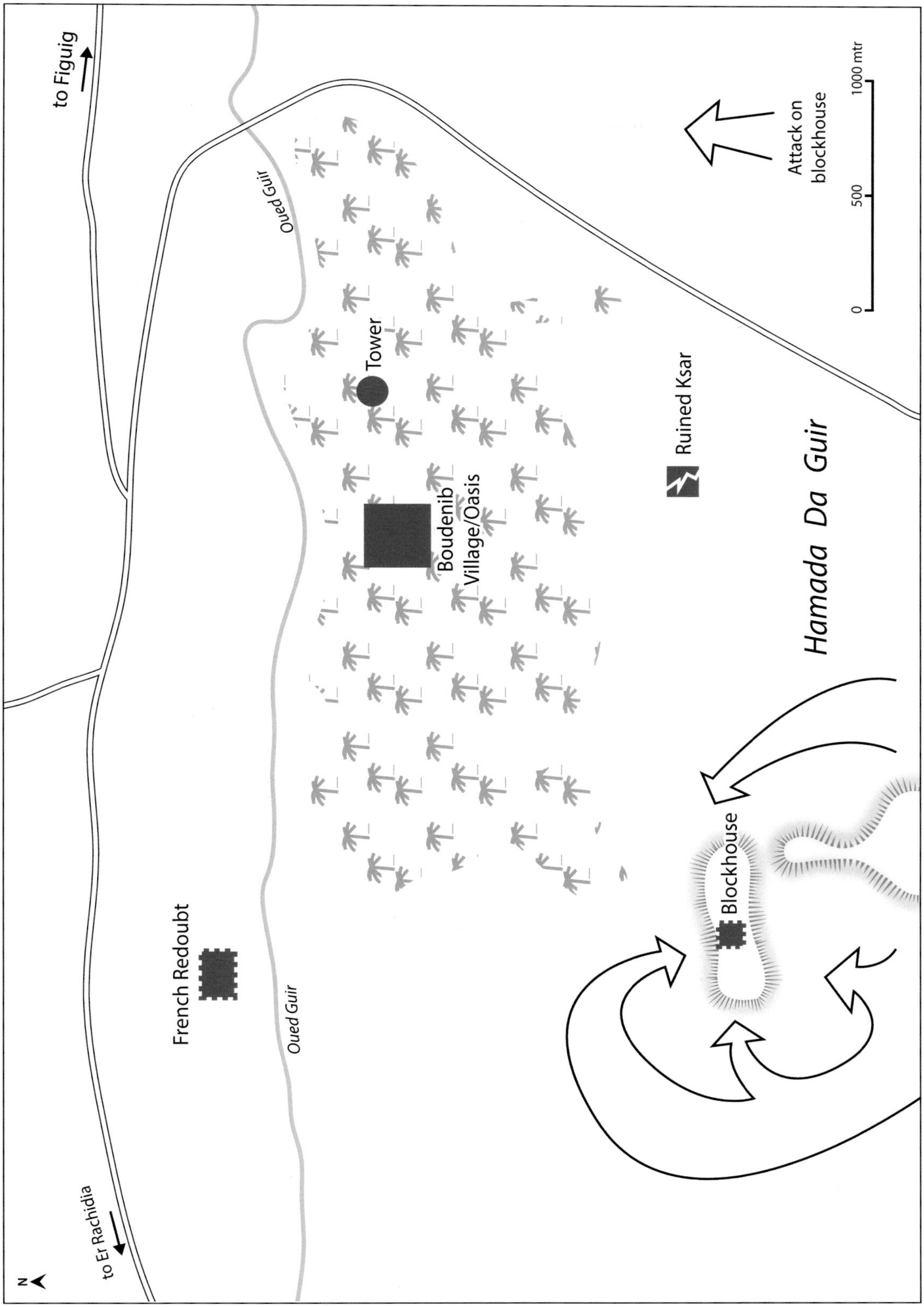

The oasis at Boudenib.

Built onto a levelled rock platform it was surrounded on all sides by near vertical cliffs with a single access route up a very steep path on the southern approach. Unlike the more temporary main redoubt to the north the blockhouse was constructed from dressed stone and was an altogether more permanent structure. In sight of the main redoubt, communication between the two was via an optic telegraph system set up on the roof on the north side of the building and clearly visible in photographs.

Posted to the blockhouse was a force of some 75 men, of whom about half were legionnaires and half locally recruited skirmishers under the command of a Lieutenant Vary and Sergeant Koenig. Their role was to watch for enemy movement and to keep the garrison in the main redoubt, under the command of a Major Fesch, updated on all activity.

Whilst the French had been preparing their defences the Berber had fallen back to an area close to the Tazzougerte Pass in order to reorganise their forces which had continued to grow in number as recruits flocked to the call to arms. Tribes joined from all over eastern Morocco and by mid-August the size of the harka was reported as being close to 20,000. Their intention was to return to Bou Denib to overwhelm the French forces and avenge the earlier defeat.

Late in the afternoon on 31 August the first signs of enemy activity were spotted from the blockhouse. They reported a large concentration of Berber warriors forming up to the north and west of the redoubt. Tented camps were being set up and a large force of cavalry and infantry was clearly gathering for an attack. By the next morning the redoubt was surrounded on three sides by a mix of mounted warriors and men on foot and by mid-afternoon further Berber forces were also massing in the desert to the south of the blockhouse. This force was invisible to the men in the redoubt who were already preoccupied by fire from the enemy forces around them and amongst the palm groves. However, the observers in the blockhouse had a relatively clear view, although sometimes obscured by smoke, of the enemy positions around both themselves and the redoubt and there was a constant exchange of information between the two sites.

Late in the afternoon of the 1 September a single rider in a white *djellaba* approached the blockhouse and issued a challenge of single combat to the garrison commander. With the challenge unanswered several hundred tribesmen began to attack the blockhouse by scrambling up the steep sides to the east, west and south in an attack that was unrelenting for 18 hours.

With only light weapons the defenders were hard pressed to hold the position. When the enemy was found to have infiltrated the outer walls and barbed wire defences the defenders used explosive charges and grenades thrown down from the walls to clear the area. Even then a number of attackers were able to make their way inside the walls of the blockhouse before being killed in desperate hand to hand combat.

From surviving transcripts of the communication between the blockhouse and the redoubt, and from eyewitness reports, it is known that Lieutenant Vary repeatedly called for artillery support from the 75 mm and 80 mm guns at the redoubt. With ammunition becoming dangerously low it was the artillery fire directed onto the blockhouse and surrounding area

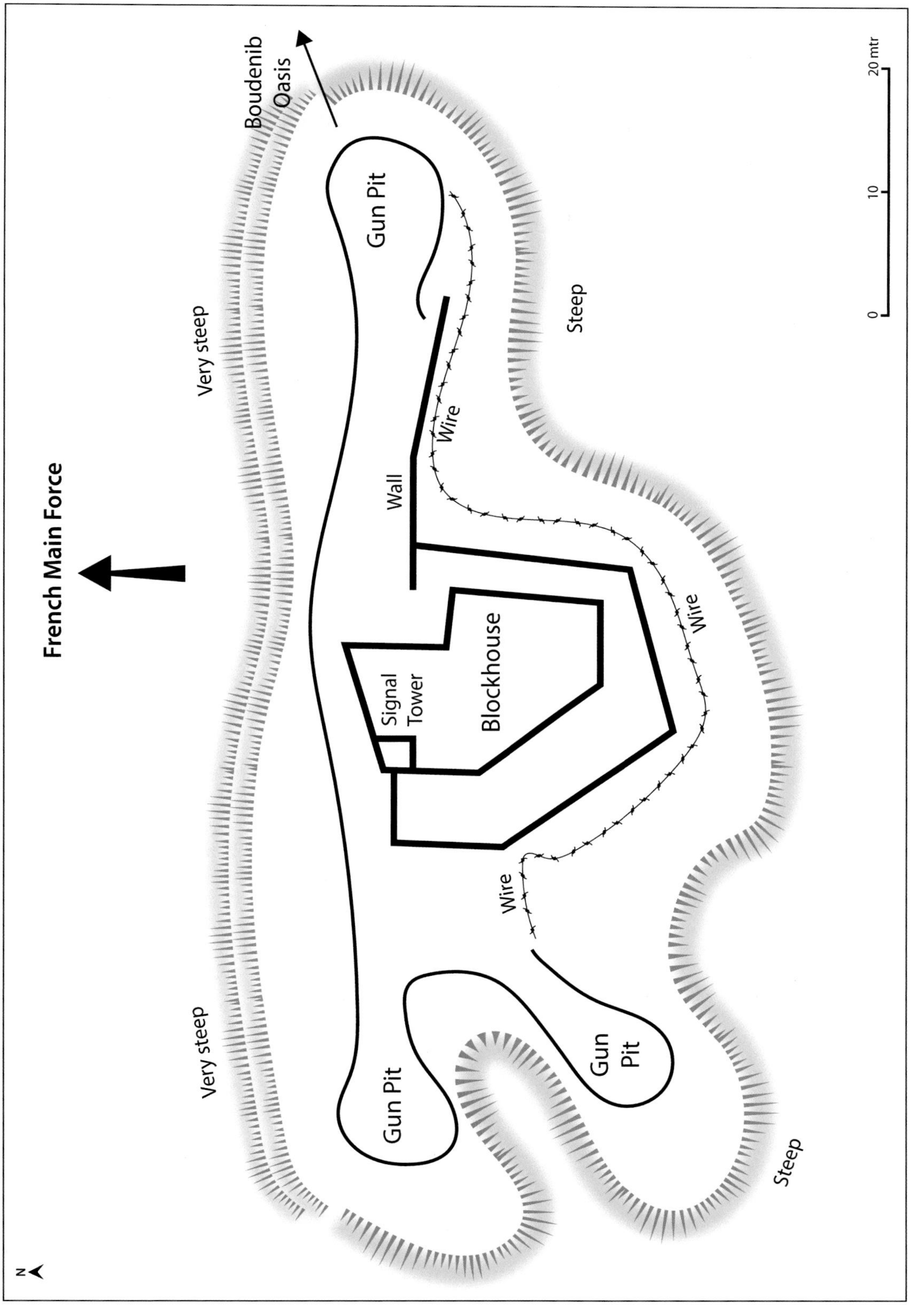

Plan of Boudenib blockhouse defences.

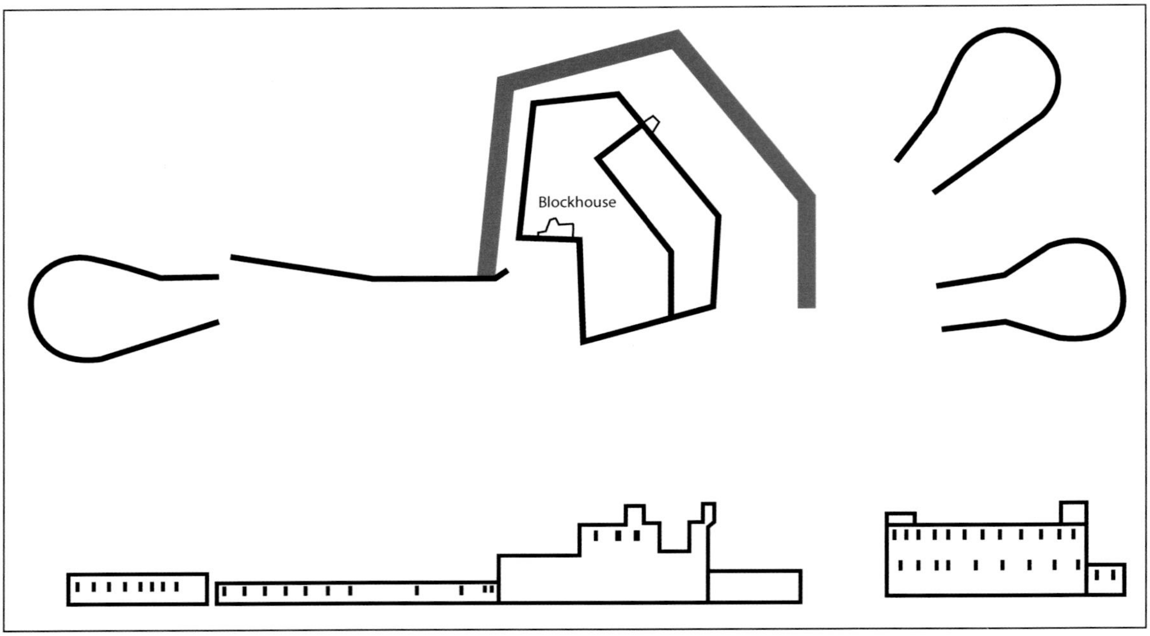

Blockhouse Plan.

that kept the Moroccans from overwhelming the position. Just before dawn the attack began to cease in intensity and gradually the Moroccans broke contact and moved back to their initial assembly areas. They had suffered heavy casualties with a 173 dead being left around the blockhouse and many more wounded making their way down the precipitous sides of the '*gara*'. The defenders had only one man killed and 25 wounded.

The heroic defence of the blockhouse was quickly seized upon by the French as an opportunity for publicity and propaganda. Despite all that had been happening in Morocco the campaigns were largely unknown back in metropolitan France where there were still large numbers of politicians opposed to further colonial expansion. The story of Lieutenant Vary and his gallant Legionnaires struggle against seemingly overwhelming odds was quickly picked up by the press and it was reported widely around the world including a front cover article in the popular magazine *Le Petit Parisien* and several articles in *The New York Times*.

Although the story reported in the press was undoubtedly embellished for the sake of an exciting read, the facts of the event were supported by an archaeological survey of the site carried out in May 2012 which confirmed not only the construction and layout of the blockhouse but also the evidence to confirm the reports of the assault. See Appendix I.

The successful defence of the blockhouse was down to a number of important factors. Without doubt the courage and military proficiency of the defenders and the calm leadership of Lieutenant Vary played a crucial role but, without the artillery support from the nearby redoubt the outcome may very well have been different. Crucial to victory was the location of the structure. Situated on a high hill, surrounded by steep cliffs and with access routes well covered any assault would always have been difficult and costly.

Chapter 7

Siege at Taghit

The positioning of a fortification, no matter what its size, is critical and the French military engineers did not always get it right. On rare occasions tactical or strategic factors may trump position but, where possible, military surveyors would seek a location providing the best position for defence and observation. At Taghit they got it very wrong.

The fort at Taghit was one of a number of posts located along the 193 km Zousfana river valley. The valley, which connected the major garrison and regional administrative centre at Ain Sefra to the north with Beni Abbes in the south was generally broad but, for a 11.3 km stretch between mountains of Ben Goumi and the vast sand desert of the Grand Erg, the river entered a steep sided gorge some 200 metres wide. At its narrowest point, some 50 metres wide, a ksar had been built on some high ground overlooking the palm groves and river below totally dominating the gorge. It was an excellent defensive position. The later fort built by the French in close proximity to the ksar was not.

Designed more as a fortified police station than a military fortress it was built as a base from which patrols would be sent out to deal with raiders and small warbands from the Tafilalet who regularly raided the nearby farms and villages. It was certainly not designed to withstand a siege. The pentagon shaped structure had been built behind the ksar with no views of the river or valley floor and with many of the approaches in dead ground. To make matters worse two sides were completely dominated by high ground enabling any attackers to fire directly into the position. Critically there was no internal water supply. Water for the post came from wells some distance away. For some protection the path to and from the wells was walled and covered with a rudimentary roof providing limited cover for the water parties but, in a desert location where water is more valuable than bullets, the post was indefensible.

In an attempt to rectify the situation, and provide at least some observation, a small blockhouse, connected to the main post by a very steep track, was constructed nearby to house a signal lamp and telescope but space there was very confined and although it could hold a few of troops, and be crammed with as much ammunition as possible, it would be impossible to reinforce if any assault took place. In August 1903 it did.

At that time the permanent garrison of about 300 soldiers and two 80 mm mountain guns, under the command of a Captain Susbielle, consisted of a mix of locally recruited irregulars and a half company of infantry from 1st Bats d'Af. Sometimes confused with the Legion Etranger, this unit was originally established in 1830 as a place for troublesome left-wing revolutionaries and other socially undesirables who were deported to Algeria and conscripted into military service. By 1903 recruits also included criminals and delinquents who were offered military service in lieu of harsh penal sentences. Nicknamed '*les joyeux*' they were often troublesome and mutinous in times of peace but often surprisingly effective when it came to fighting.

The initial attack came on the morning of 17 August. It was not entirely unexpected as Susbielle had sent out patrols in the previous days to locate the enemy forces and also, if possible, link up with a legion patrol from the 22nd mounted company of 2RE under the command of a Lieutenant Pointurier who had been aware since the 15 August that a large war band was on the move and making its way towards Taghit. He immediately sent word to Susbielle to prepare for an attack and with information rapidly passing from post to post along the valley through the use of signal lamps and telegraph he received on the 17 August orders to take his half company Legionnaires to reinforce the garrison at Taghit. Knowing that the fort was almost certain to be attacked that day he knew his men would have to move as fast as possible to get there before it was too late.

By eight in the morning on 17 August the warband was in sight of the palm groves and ksar at Taghit. A target too tempting to pass the advance party of the harka charged into the palm tree to assault the ksar. Although the ksar was empty they encountered stiff resistance from the locals who were quickly reinforced by Captain Susbielle who despatched his eighty irregulars, under the command of a Lieutenant Ganay, to join the battle. Although an intense firefight commenced little damage was inflicted although the plan of drawing the attackers away from the ksar and up towards the fort began to work. Their retreat was covered by additional troops sent out from the fort who formed a thin line across the valley. The Moroccans launched one of their typical, uncontrolled attacks onto this line.

Charging forward, firing as they ran, followed by a hasty withdrawal to reload was repeated many times and was largely ineffective. Had Susbielles irregulars been better soldiers, or had they had a machine gun, then many of the attackers would have been killed. As it was, they slowly withdrew back towards the fort in a controlled manner. It was at this point that the defenders were able to deploy the two 80 mm mountain guns. Mounted on small wooden wheels these tiny artillery pieces were little more than knee high when assembled but they were light and easily carried on a mule and the loud bang they made was itself enough to stop the attack in its tracks.

The harka fell back down the hill towards the palm trees and river and the initial assault was over. Around 8,000 Moroccans set up camp for the night leaving the tiny French garrison to contemplate their fate the following day.

As dawn broke on the 18th Lieutenant Pointurier and his legionnaires arrived having force marched almost 45 km overnight. They were just in time as the assault began again shortly after their arrival. Again, the fort was best defended by troops outside the walls. The Bats de Af formed a line some distance to the south whilst their flanks were protected by the irregulars. Much to their displeasure the Legionnaires of 2RE were held in reserve. The 80 mm guns were used to fire airburst shells some 80.5 km ahead of the line with the aim of preventing a surge against the defenders. Fighting continued in the palm trees and close to the ksar throughout the day. As dusk came the French retired in good order back to the fort having suffered minimal casualties.

During the early hours of the 19 August, a large fighting patrol was sent out under cover of darkness to locate the Moroccan camp. It was closer than anticipated and within only a few 100 metres the advance sections encountered a strong Moroccan force advancing up towards the fort. As the French fought a fighting withdrawal back to the fort, they inflicted heavy casualties on the Moroccans. However, they continued to advance and, for the first time it appears they realised the vulnerability of the fort to fire from above. Whilst some moved into the palm grove and village beneath the fort others, armed with captured rifles, began to pour fire into the fort from the high ground on two sides. Although the fort provided some cover for the defenders many of their animals were shot and use of the path to get water was denied. Lieutenant Susbielle posted marksmen on the battlements to try and disrupt the firing from the hills above, but the lack of an internal water supply could easily have been decisive had the Moroccans realised the issue and pressed home their siege.

With sunrise on the 20 August the call to 'Reveille' by the bugler in the fort was met with a hail of rifle fire from the sand dunes above the fort and the garrison prepared for another hard fight. Shortly after, a small force of reinforcements approached the fort's entrance at speed and were able to gain entrance at the cost of two wounded. This arrival of reinforcements, plus the heavy casualties already sustained, appears to have forced a decision not to press on with the attack. By mid-morning firing from the heights had ceased and when a small patrol was sent out from the fort it was discovered that the Moroccans were breaking camp and preparing to withdraw. The assault on Taghit was over. The French had four men killed and 10 wounded. They had expended over 45,000 rounds of rifle ammunition and fired a 103 artillery rounds. The attackers had over 400 killed and many more wounded and the warband had moved south.

Gallant though the defence had been the vulnerability of a badly positioned fort was revealed and it could be argued that it was the Moroccan failure to exploit the flaws from the start that led to their defeat. They failed to exploit the high ground overlooking the fort, they failed to prevent entry to and from the gates for troops to access open ground, they failed to prevent reinforcements getting through and, perhaps crucially, they failed to exploit the lack of internal water from the start. Without a properly coordinated plan of attack and, importantly, without artillery to breach the walls, success was always going to be unlikely, but lessons were learned and such mistakes would not be made in the future.

Chapter 8

Fort at Tazougerte

In comparison with the poorly located fort at Taghit the fort at Tazougerte was a textbook construction and something straight from the pages of Beau Geste and Hollywood films. Its remote location and superb construction has left it largely intact, unlike many others which have almost entirely disappeared or been converted to other uses, and, as such, it is worthy of detailed examination.

Located in southeast Morocco some 25 kilometres northwest of Boudenib the fort was built on a high plateau on the eastern side of the Oued Guir river valley. It commanded the southern entrance to the valley and overlooked the main route running west to east from Er Rachidia, where the Foreign Legion had built a base around a natural spring for rest and recuperation, to Boudenib and then Figuig in the east.

It is an important strategic and tactical location as the valley is one of the few giving access from the sand desert of the south to the more fertile regions of the north. The river itself flows above ground as far south as Boudenib although for much of the summer it is little more than a shallow stream. It supported numerous small villages along the base of the valley and there was a small oasis and settlement at the base of the cliffs beneath the fort. When the river reaches Abadla it frays out into a number of narrow streams creating an alluvial plain that was a major source of wheat and barley for the local tribes.

The width of the valley ranges from between 100–500 metres and the near vertical sides on both sides rise several hundred metres to what is still considered one of the most hostile environments in southeast Morocco. Known as the Hammada du Guir, it is a bleak and waterless plateau about 108 km at its widest. During high summer the heat is almost unbearable, and it remains to this day completely uninhabited. In the cooler spring and autumn periods local herdsmen would traverse the plateau with their flocks of sheep and goats but there was not much food to sustain them.

At the northern end the steep sides gradually become lower as the valley widens out to form a desolate plain of rocks and sand. To control the northern approaches to the valley a fort was built at Atachana. This was connected to Tazougerte fort, some 20 km away, via a line of signal towers built along the top of the cliffs on the eastern side of the valley.

An artist's reconstruction of the fort at Tazougerte. (Illustration by Anderson Subtil © Helion & Company)

Fort at Tazougerte.

Obvious care was taken when positioning the fort. It was constructed on a narrow spur of rock with effective use of the natural terrain features to enhance its defences. The northern wall effectively cuts off the spur from the plateau and runs from one cliff edge to the other. The walls to the west and east were constructed to precisely follow the edge of the cliffs.

To the south there was a small plateau that was covered by the southern wall. There was no access to this area other than via the fort as on three sides the cliffs were vertical. It was in this area that a large, and very deep, well was constructed to supply fresh water to the garrison. Water would also have been available from the river below although the steep and very narrow track linking the fort to the river would have been hazardous even at the best of times.

Linked to the fort, providing forward observation and covering what would have been dead ground, two identical watchtowers were constructed that would have been linked to the fort by signal lamp and telegraph. The paths to these towers were clearly marked with rocks enabling movement of men between the locations in darkness without danger of falling over the cliff tops.

The fort and its outlying watchtowers had outstanding views for miles in all directions, totally dominated the southern end of the Oued Guir valley and was well protected from any possible attack.

The overall plan of the fort was dictated by the spur of rock on which it was built. Roughly rectangular in shape, approximately 22 m by 42 m, with the main entrance to the north and a secondary entrance to the south. Overall construction was from roughly shaped stone blocks covered with a thick, whitewashed, plaster. Windows and doors had well made, dressed, stone lintels although palm wood was also used for some. There is a clear difference between the construction of the main fort and the fort's tower which is identical in style and construction to the outlying watchtowers. The style matches very closely the buildings described by numerous writers of the time, in particular Ward Price and Zinovi Pechkoff.

The Entrance (1)

The main entrance to the fort is located in the northern wall. It is only 2.3 m wide and there remain no traces of the original gates. There is no clue as to the height of the gate but steps on the parapet on either side suggest there may have been a walkway over the gate. It is known that some forts had decorative lintels over their main gates bearing either the name of the fort or a regimental crest. The entrance is well protected with embrasures allowing fire from the walls on either side. Enfilade fire across the gate and wall is provided from the western facing wall of a two-storey tower in the northeast corner which projects out beyond the walls. In the event of the gate being breached direct access to the fort is prevented by a wall located immediately behind the gate which has two firing embrasures.

To the right of the main entrance is a small building most likely to have been a guardroom. This building has three entrances, two from the inner courtyard and one reached via the parapet on the north wall. A small window in the east wall of the building allowed observation of the main gate and of anyone passing through into the fort.

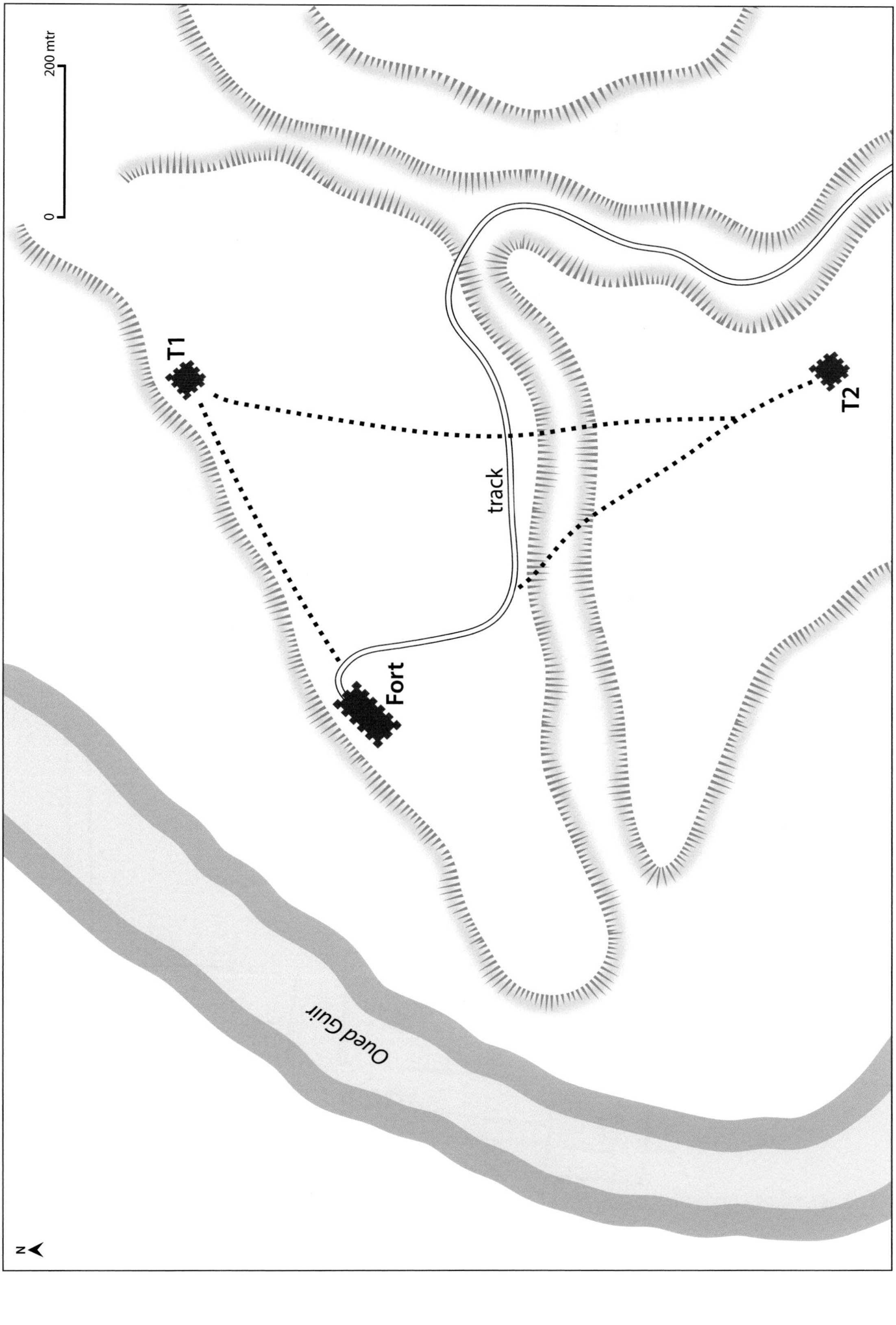

Location of Tazougerte fort and associated watch towers.

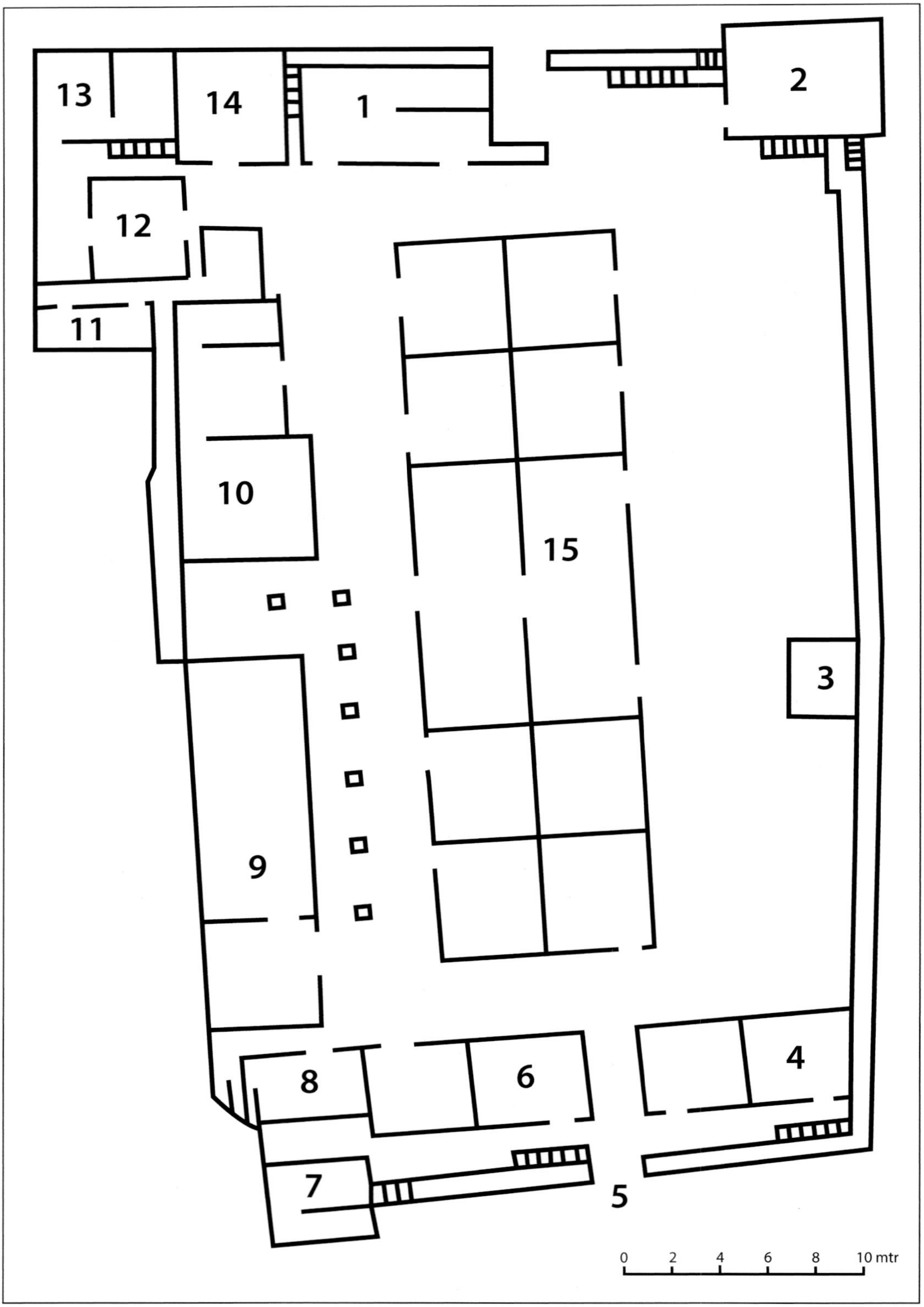

Plan of Tazougerte Fort.

North East Tower (2)
Projecting almost 2 m beyond the main wall this two storey, roughly square, tower overlooks the main entrance enabling enfilade fire across the front of the fort. The size of the top floor would have been sufficient to house a small artillery piece or heavy machine gun. Access to the top floor is via steps from the walkways on the north and east wall.

East Wall (3)
Just over 40 m long the wall is built right on the edge of a vertical drop. The walkway is protected by a 2 m high wall containing 36 firing points along its length. Roughly halfway along there is a platform of indeterminate use. It may have been for a water tank which were known to have been put into other forts or it may have been a platform for heavy weapons or artillery.

Building (4) – Probable Store
The fort would have needed to hold a large supply of rations and essential ammunition and equipment which Ward Price confirmed after his visit to Fort Tilmi: 'The fort contains a six month supply of food consisting of flour, rice, peas, beans, lard, tinned meat, coffee, sugar, wine and barley'.[1]

A rectangular structure, it is divided into two rooms of equal size with an entrance to each room from the main courtyard. There are no windows suggesting use as a store.

South Entrance (5)
Located centrally in the southern wall the entrance, and only 1 m wide, the entrance was clearly for access on foot only. It leads to a small plateau surrounded on the other three sides by vertical cliffs. Towards the centre of the plateau a large well was dug to provide water for the fort.

Building (6) – Probable Store
Of similar size to building four, the two structures are situated in such a way as to create a passageway leading to the southern entrance. Again, no windows but entrance from the main courtyard and from the south.

Southwest Tower (7)
The smallest of the fort's corner towers, it is a two storey building with access to the first floor via steps from the walkway on the wall. Entrance to the ground floor is through a narrow door which was one of the few to have a wooden lintel rather than stone.

Building (8) – Probable Store or Latrine
Located at the base of the southwest tower are a series of very small, interconnected rooms that may have been part of the stores or they may have been latrines.

---

1 Ward Price, *With the Legion*, p.207.

Above: Tower in the northeast corner. The second largest tower it projects beyond the north wall to provide enfilade fire across the entrance. The large dressed stone blocks used for construction are clearly visible.
Left: An example of a vertical break between two walls. The lack of bonding might suggest this is a later addition
Facing page top: The approach to the main entrance.
Bottom: A view of the interior of the fort as it looks today.

The East wall.

The south wall showing pedestrian entrance and southwest tower.

Building (9) – HQ Building
A large rectangular building consisting of two rooms. A small, square windowless room provided access to a much larger, rectangular room which has four windows facing onto the courtyard. The building is unique within the fort as it has a covered veranda in front which indicates a building of status – possibly the commanding officer's office/ accommodation.

Building (10) – Armoury
A block of rooms with a single entrance from the courtyard. Entrance was via a small, covered yard leading to a large internal window. This opening creates a type of counter arrangement that could have been used for the dispensing of weapons or rations to those queuing outside. A raised area running round the interior wall is indicative of the type of arrangement found in many military armouries where weapons are stored in racks and issued when required.

Building (11) – Latrines
A very small building located behind the armoury and right on the cliff top. Holes at the base of the wall above the vertical drop suggest the building may have housed latrines with the human waste being passed directly out of the fort and into the valley below.

Building (12) – Unknown
There is no obvious function for this building. Doors on the east and west side allow access from the courtyard to a small passage. There are large rectangular windows on either side of the doors.

Building (13) – Unknown
Building 13 consists of two rooms entered by a single door reached either from the passage to the rear of building 12 or from a passage leading from the entrance to the main tower. A flight of steps leads to the flat roof and on the north and west side a wall with firing loopholes was constructed which can be clearly seen from outside the fort. These walls may have been a later addition to the fort.

Building (14) – The Tower
A crucial component of any fort, this one consists of three square rooms and a roof area. Entrance to the ground floor is via a door in the south wall. The largest room in the tower is windowless for defensive reasons. The room provides access to the floors above via a hatchway in the roof that would have been reached by a ladder that could have been pulled up after use to prevent access to the top of the tower should the ground floor be entered by attackers. The position of the hatch is different for each room.

Getting progressively smaller toward the top of the tower, first and second floor rooms have large windows located centrally in each wall. Positioned around each window there are embrasures allowing protected firing from within. On the rooftop a low wall encloses the top of the tower with four firing embrasures on each side that would have provided cover for lookouts on the roof.

View of the interior looking south from the main tower. Armoury and HQ building along the west wall.

Interior of the fort viewed from the South East. The columns are the remains of the HQ building.

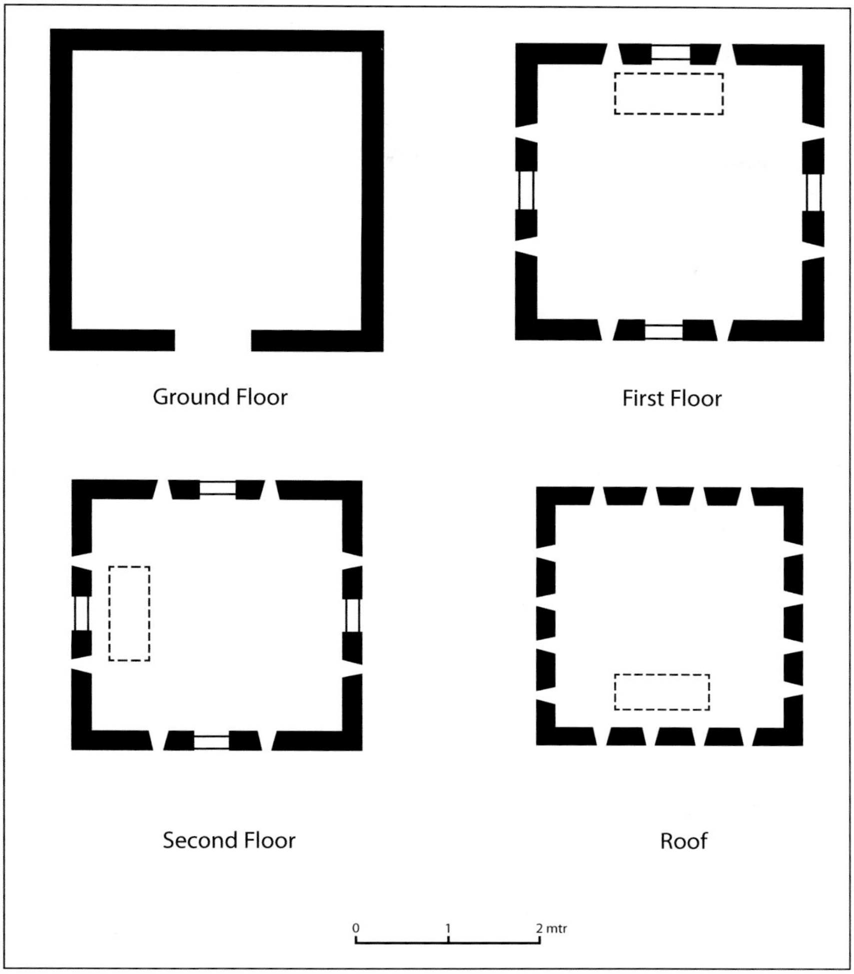

Floor plans of the main tower.

At Tazougerte the tower has been constructed in a far superior way to the rest of the fort and it is almost identical to the two watchtowers located away from the fort suggesting they were built at the same time. It is the only part of the fort where steel girders were used as part of the frame and the exterior plasterwork is of greater quality to that used elsewhere. The stonework of the walls has not been properly bonded into the north wall of the tower which could indicate that the existing tower is a later addition replacing an earlier tower that was lower and like the towers in the northeast and southwest. This suggests an upgrade to the fort at a time when it became of even greater strategic importance.

Building (15) – Accommodation Block
The largest single building occupies the centre of the fort. It consists of 10 rooms each with their own entrance. The central two rooms are exactly double the size of the other rooms and they are connected via an internal door.

We know from the description of Fort Timli by journalist Ward Price: 'The centre of the enclosure is filled with low stone buildings that house the three or four officers and ten non-commissioned officers.'[2]

The roof is slightly pitched and would have been thatched with palm leaves.

Associated Buildings

To the north of the fort there are the remains of a number of small buildings and terraces. These would almost certainly have been used for housing livestock and we know from Zinovi Pechkoff that occupants of forts would often establish small gardens for vegetables and flowers.

Leading away from the fort in a generally easterly direction there is a well-constructed road. Following a precipitous, descending and winding route this eventually reaches the valley floor close to the junction of the main road running east to west between Boudenib and Er Rachidia (now the N10) and the road heading north that follows the valley floor. This track would almost certainly have been used for resupply of the fort and for the delivery of the steel girders used in the construction of the towers.

Zinovi Pechkoff, describing the construction of a similar fort in the Atlas Mountains wrote:

> 'A road had to be made to bring up the guns, mules, horses and men'.[3]

The Watchtowers

Two watchtowers were constructed to support the fort. Built in view of each other and the fort,

tower one is about 5 m to the northeast of the fort whilst tower two is approximately 7 m to the southeast. They are positioned to enable increased observation of the valley and the plateau. In construction style they are identical to that of the main fort tower although they do not have access at ground floor level. Instead, access is at first floor level. Designed to stop access by an attacker the entrance would have been reached by a ladder that would have been pulled up by those inside. Both towers have a hook located at the top of the tower and above the door onto which a pulley could have been fitted to pull up the ladder and any other supplies such as rations and ammunition that would be required by the occupants.

At both of the towers the main windows are protected with metal bars.

Ward Price described a similar layout at Fort Timli:

> At some distance from the fort are generally built one or two watchtowers from which a more extended view of the environs can be obtained. These have a platform on the top twenty feet above the ground with a chamber for shelter below it, which is connected to the ground only by a ladder that can be pulled up after them by the occupants …

2 Ward Price, *With the Legion*, p.201.

3 Pechkoff, *Bugle Calls*, p.26.

Central accommodation block – east side.

It can be seen that careful attention has been paid to the creation of doorways and windows.

Central accommodation block viewed from the southwest tower.

Remains of a range of buildings located outside the north wall.

Watchtowers were built to support the main fort.

> Such towers are always in view of the main fort, and the machine guns of the garrison are manned morning and evening to protect, if necessary, the movement of the lookout men between the watchtower and the fort.[4]

The watchtowers are connected to each other, and the fort, by trackways, created by double lines of stones, that lead directly to the entrances at the different locations. No literary sources have so far been found that refer to this but clearly troops moving between the towers and the fort would have been exposed to sniper fire and ambush. It was standard practice for legionnaires to build low stone walls, known as 'murettes' around night camps so this could have been an extension of that practice. However, at Tazougerte, there is no evidence that the lines of stones were ever more than single stone height so an alternative reason may have been safety. All around the site there are vertical cliffs and steep drops so it may be that the routes between the towers and fort were clearly defined to avoid troops inadvertently falling over the edges if moving at night or in poor visibility. Even today walking on the plateau is very challenging due to loose rocks and scrub. The defined paths have been completely cleared of such obstacles thus increasing the speed at which movement could be made between locations.

There were many similar towers constructed all over Morocco. Usually manned by four to six men under the command of a corporal or sergeant they would occupy the position for a week at a time before being relieved. Their role was observation and communication. In the early years signals would be sent using flags or heliograph (see Appendix III) and later many were also equipped with field telephones. Such positions were always extremely vulnerable, particularly those without an internal water supply.

One of the Legion's most famous members, Prince Aage of Denmark, related to journalist Ward Price of an incident that he experienced at a watchtower near Tadhout in 1924. One morning the men at the watch post failed to respond to the usual signal from the nearby fort and the prince, with an armed patrol of 20, was sent to investigate. They found the access ladder in the down position and blood dripping through the first floorboards. The prince explained:

> As I began to climb the ladder there came from the room into which it led a horrible sound of cackling laughter. I confess that although it was broad daylight and I had 20 men with me I felt scared of going up. It was almost dark inside as I put my head through the opening in the floor. Then I made out the body of the German corporal, lying with his throat cut from ear to ear. It was his blood that stained the ground beneath the tower, Meanwhile, in the corner of the room, crouched a Russian, gibbering and crooning to himself. He had gone completely mad.
>
> Of the other two men there was no trace and the rifles, equipment, ammunition and Verey light signalling pistol of the post had all gone, and the lantern for lighting the little room lay smashed on the floor.[5]

4 Ward Price, *With the Legion*, p.207

5 Ward Price, *With the Legion*, p.208.

Unlike many forts and outposts, the remote and inaccessible location of the fort at Tazougerte has resulted in it being exceptionally well preserved. Although the roofs of the buildings have disappeared the fort stands much as it did when first constructed and during the archaeological survey investigators were surprised at the remarkable number of artefacts found within and around the site. Ration tins, cartridge cases, hobnails from boots, belt buckles, buttons, barbed wire and even an expended bullet were located during field surveys.

The siting of the fort, its textbook style and its solid construction is a testament to the skilled builders who, despite building in a very harsh and dangerous environment, had the time to complete the outpost to the highest standard. It is indicative of the operation being carried out in what must have been regarded as a relatively safe, pacified zone, where work could continue without great risk of interruption from attack.

During times of crisis, where positions needed to be built in hostile environments, significantly quicker building techniques would be required, and lower standards of structure accepted.

Ration tins found in the remains of the fort.

A collection of artefacts found within the fort including the heel of a boot, grenade fragments, cartridges, and a magazine clip.

Chapter 9

Rebellion

In 1925 the French faced a critical situation against an opponent unlike that they had faced before. Whilst French interest from the start of the twentieth century had always been on middle and southern Morocco the northern region had been under control of the Spanish. Close to Spain and the Mediterranean Sea the Rif Mountains created a natural barrier inland from the Mediterranean coast that was home to four major tribes who maintained an uneasy relationship with the Moroccan government to the south and a hostile relationship to Spanish.

The Spanish forces based in the region were far inferior to those of the French. Poorly trained, equipped, and led, the majority were scattered through the region in poorly constructed outposts devoid of water, resupply, and support. With the appearance of a highly intelligent and charismatic leader called Abd-el-Krim, who was able to unite the tribes of the region and launch devastating assaults on the Spanish forces, it was very clear that a critical situation was evolving that could have an impact on the whole of Morocco. In 1921 the Rifian forces rapidly overran many Spanish positions resulting in a general withdrawal which quickly became a massacre. Some 15,000 Spanish troops, including their commander in chief General Manuel Silvestre were killed. Three years of indecisive fighting followed as the Spanish attempted to regain control but in November 1924 the Rifians inflicted another massacre on Spanish forces in the central part of the region.

For three years the French had watched events unfolding in the Spanish zone. During that time Abd-el-Krim had declared he had no issues with France and no intention of expanding his campaigns further south. However, as far as the French were concerned, his success against the Spanish was being closely watched by many Berber tribes, many of whom still resented French occupation. Should he succeed in establishing an independent Muslim state in the Rif.

Mountains then a dangerous precedent could well be set for others to follow. Tribes in the

northern sector of French occupied Morocco had already proved difficult and in May 1924 the French crossed over the Ouerrha river, which served as the border between the Spanish zone and the French Protectorate and established a line of hastily built outposts along a 120.7 km line running from

Biban to Taza which the garrisoned with Algerian and Senagalese troops. The area they moved into had not been physically occupied by the Spanish, but it was still a contentious move as far as Abd-el Krim and many of the local population were concerned.

Up until that time the French view of the situation had been that the success of the Rifians was due more to Spanish ineptitude rather than the skill of the tribes and they were supremely confident that their years of experience, their overwhelming forces in Morocco, supported by all the latest military hardware and air support, and the newly created line of blockhouses and outposts along the hills overlooking the Ouerrha river, would be sufficient to deter Abd-el-Krim from any military action against them. In this belief they were mistaken, and by June 1925 the situation was dire. Sixty-six outposts had been constructed and of these 44 had been assaulted, cut off or overwhelmed completely. Pechkoff described the situation: 'First the advance outposts, then those in the rear were surrounded by Riffians. All the outposts on the North bank of the Ouergha River were surrounded and completely isolated from the rest of the world. The Riffians dug trenches around these outposts in order to prevent succour from reaching them'.[1]

The very nature of their remote location made rescue, resupply, and reinforcement almost impossible and even though the outposts were in sight of each other besieged garrisons could do little more than watch their neighbours be abandoned or overrun. The post at Aulai resisted for 22 days under heavy attack before being relieved. Further along the line another blockhouse containing a garrison of thirty was completely overwhelmed and the bodies of the defenders badly mutilated and strung up on the outer barbed wire defences to rot in the searing summer heat.

Pechkoff described similar experiences at other posts: 'At times we would approach a post in ruins and no French flag would be flying. It would be a sign that there was only death within.

We would find the bodies of men who had been killed, stripped of their clothes'.[2]

The small garrisons defending the posts could expect no mercy from the Rifians should the defence fail. Torture or swift execution was inevitable, and, at some posts, survivors chose to kill themselves rather than fall prisoner. The post at Beni Derfoul held out for 61 days but on 14 June, with only six unwounded men left and relief impossible, the commanding officer detonated all of the explosives held in the fort for road construction and blew his post and all remaining defenders to pieces.

The blockhouse at Mediouna was completely surrounded and cut off from relief by a double line of trenches dug around it. In addition, the high ground around the post was in the control of the Riffian forces making any attempt at relief virtually impossible. After several failed attempts the position of the defenders became desperate: 'The position of Mediouna was daily becoming more tragic. And one day they signalled that if it was not possible to free them before the next day, they could defend themselves no longer and would

1 Pechkoff, *Bugle Calls*, p.178.
2 Pechkoff, *Bugle Calls*, p.221.

A triangular fort in the Rif Mountains. (Gallica)

have to blow up the post and themselves with it'.[3] Despite repeated attempts the post was never relieved and the garrison were all killed.

Constructed at roughly 3 km intervals on hilltop positions and always within sight of nearby posts, with whom communication would be made via signal lamps, many of the positions fell far short of the official design described in the military manuals of field engineering. The posts concerned were certainly nothing like the well-constructed forts in the south.

The irregular shapes and sizes would be dictated by the space available on the hilltop and the construction method influenced by available materials and time. Many were very compact. The external ramparts were built from dry stone walls built to a height of around two to three metres. A firing step running along the interior gave access to well-spaced out loopholes and small cavities for the storage and ammunition. The firing position would be well concealed from the enemy outside. In some positions the tops of the walls were given the additional protection of broken glass set in cement. Stakes projecting out from the top of the wall would carry lengths of barbed wire. where available space permitted, wide bands of metal fencing stakes adorned with barbed wire would be planted. To provide some form of early warning against a stealthy approach the wire would be hung with empty tins which would make a noise when moved and alert the garrison.

3 Pechkoff, *Bugle Calls*, p.260.

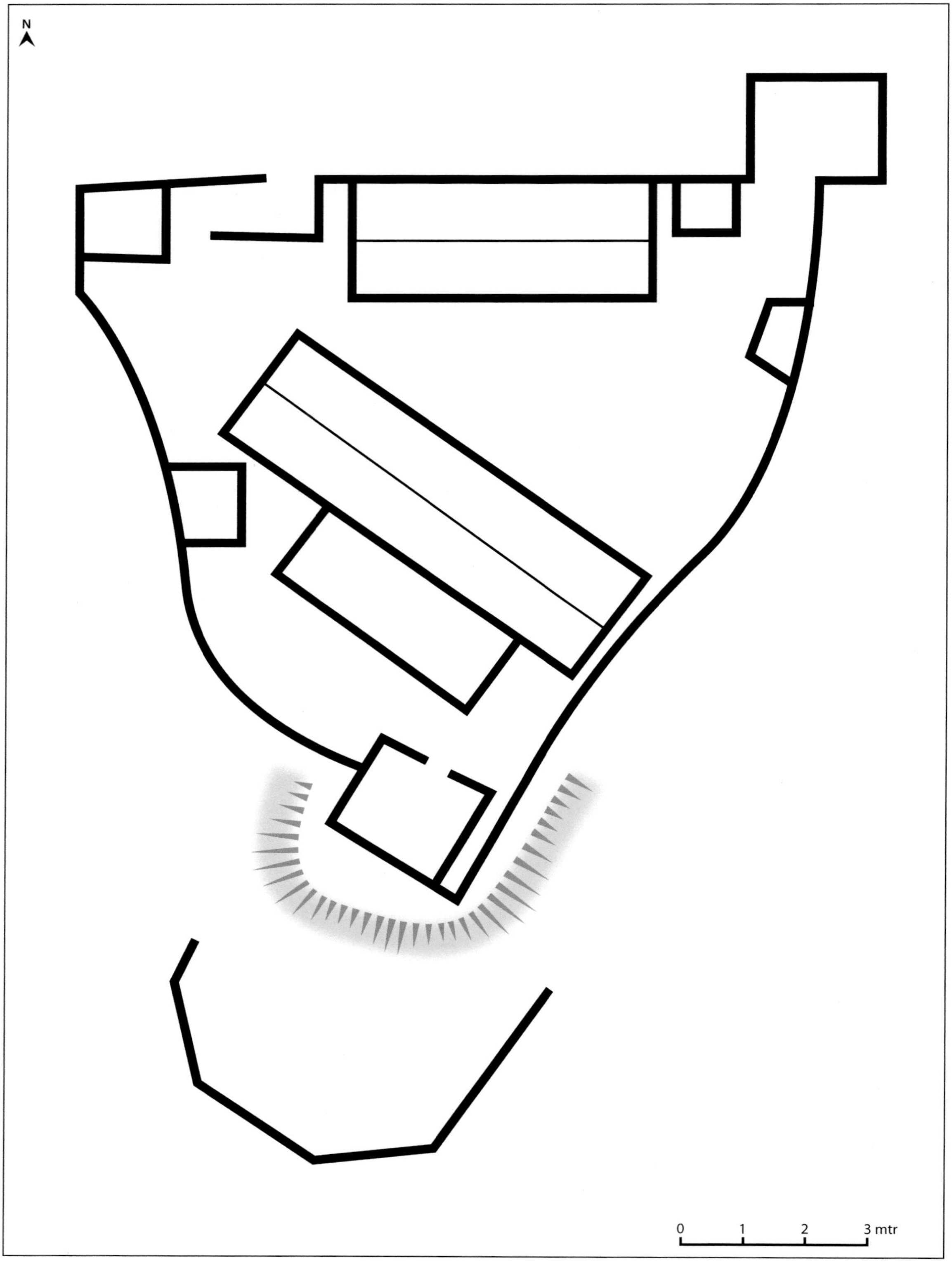

Plan of a triangular fort in the Rif Mountains.

A well-constructed outpost in the Rif Mountains. Note additional wire defences and the 75 mm gun. (Gallica)

Where large stones were in short supply, sections of walls would be constructed from gravel filled ammunition/ ration boxes or sandbags.

Inside there would be a range of buildings housing accommodation, stores, and administration. Again, drystone walling was used when possible, but also boxes and sandbags, with roofing made from wood and corrugated iron. A water tank would hold up to 5,000 L of drinking water and space would be found for latrines, and the very important bread oven.

Where available space permitted, wide bands of metal fencing stakes adorned with barbed wire would be planted. To provide some form of early warning against a stealthy approach the wire would be hung with empty tins which would make a noise when moved and alert the garrison. The entrance to the outpost would be narrow and further protected with additional wire and chicanes of stone walls preventing a direct approach. Where visibility in a particular direction was not possible from the main post, trenches would be constructed to allow protected access to small forward observation positions.

The garrison of Algerian or Senegalese tirailleurs would normally be of platoon strength of some 30 soldiers plus a couple of NCOs and a commander who may or may not be a commissioned officer. Where possible the garrison would have a 75 mm artillery piece and several Hotchkiss machine guns to supplement their standard rifles and grenade launchers.

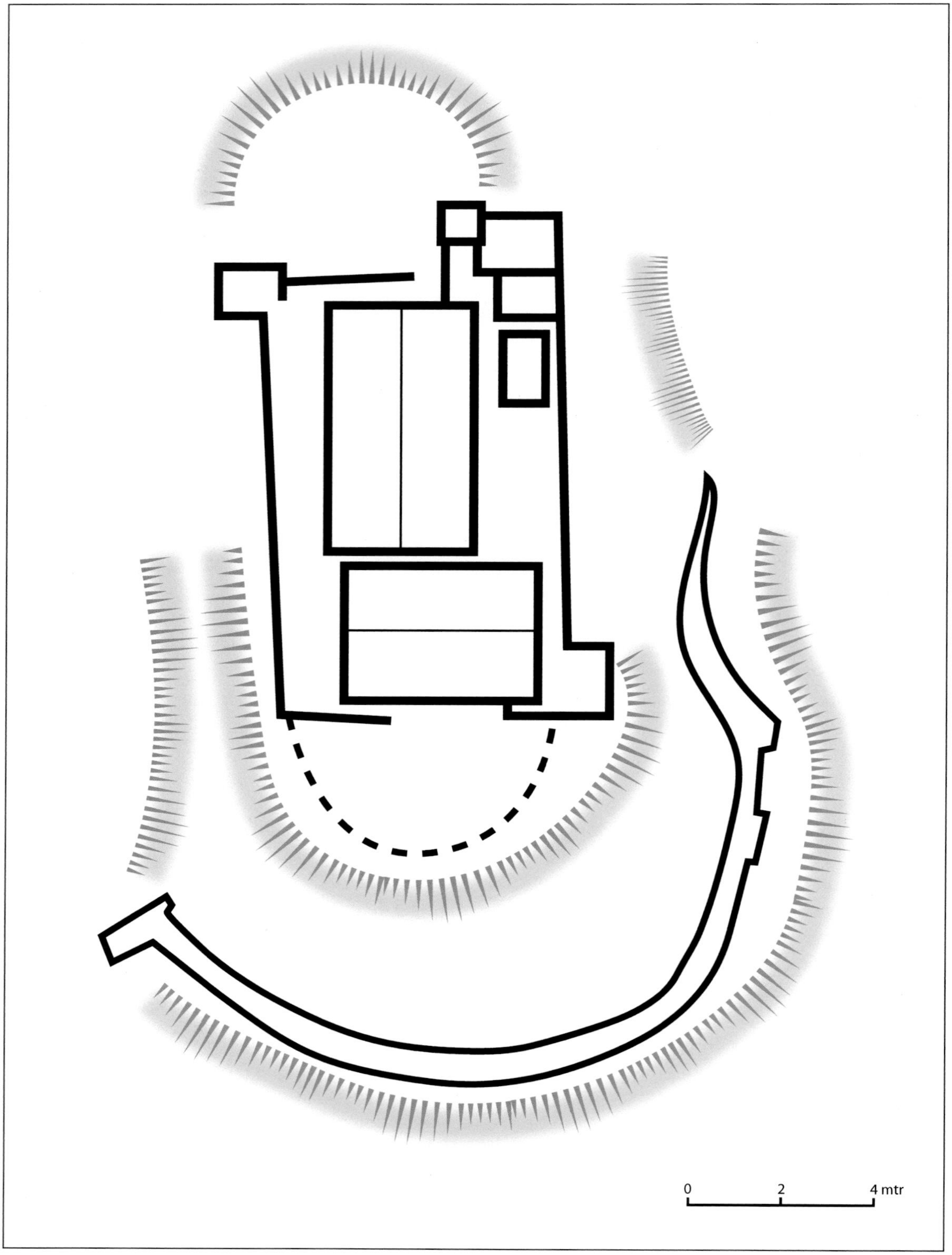

Plan of a rectangular outpost in the Rif Mountains.

As a defensive structure these outposts often proved well capable of withstanding very aggressive assaults. Their weakness came from factors beyond the control of even the stoutest defender. Their isolated positions meant that fire support from neighbouring outposts, and resupply and reinforcement was either exceptionally challenging or impossible. Garrisons could hold until rations and ammunition ran out but under heavy siege that would only be a matter of time. More importantly the lack of a natural water supply was critical as the water tanks provided would inevitably run dry as the garrison fought to survive in scorching summer temperatures. Desperate attempts were made to get water to the besieged garrisons including the use of aircraft: 'Aeroplanes had been sent to furnish water by throwing down blocks of ice, but sometimes these blocks would fall inside the post and sometimes a few yards outside'.[4]

In the high summer heat, the men in the outposts should have been drinking up to 4 L of water a day but with supplies rapidly dwindling this was being reduced to half a litre which was simply not enough to maintain a man. The dry rations and tinned meat added to the problem of thirst and often attempts were made to send out small parties of men to gather water from nearby sources that were often temptingly in sight of the garrison. Almost always these parties would be intercepted and killed, and their mutilated bodies would be left hanging from trees to taunt their comrades.

The delivery of ice from the air was a desperate operation for the pilots involved. The aircraft of the time, typically the Breguet 14 biplane of First World War vintage, struggled to fly in the hot climate where rising thermals above the hot ground made level flight almost impossible. Above the mountain regions other hazards were encountered. The thinner air meant the aircraft needed longer take off runs and, once airborne, they could struggle against fierce currents of air created by the confusing arrangement of mountains and valleys below. Numerous aircraft were lost over Morocco and the climatic conditions often dictated flying operations could only take place in the early morning.

In such conditions to drop ice and messages in the small outposts required a high level of pilot skill which would have been further tested by intense ground fire coming up at them from the Rif forces surrounding the outpost.

A new danger facing the defenders of the outposts was the use of artillery by the Rifian forces. During the earlier operations in southern Morocco artillery capable of damaging the fortifications was almost non-existent but now the situation had changed. Abd-el-Krim's successes against the Spanish had furnished his forces with a number of modern artillery pieces which his men had been taught to use by deserters from the Spanish and French armies. Whilst the limited number of pieces available prevented artillery being used in every attack where it was deployed it was devastating against the drystone walls of the small outposts and several were utterly destroyed by artillery fire. One of the final acts of garrisons facing being overrun was to destroy, or render inoperable, any artillery held at their post to prevent it

4 Pechkoff, *Bugle Calls*, p.200

from falling into enemy hands and being used against their compatriots at other posts.

Operations to relieve beleaguered outposts often involved heavy fighting on very steep approaches entailing heavy casualties. At the outpost of Astar, Zinovi Pechkoff and his Legionnaires reached an empty post where all defenders had been killed and the 75 mm field gun destroyed only to find that they had been drawn into an ambush and immediately under heavy attack themselves. 'We had not been in this outpost for more than half an hour when we were attacked from all sides. We could not believe that there was anyone hiding yet on all sides we saw white and grey burnouses creeping cautiously from one stone to another.'[5]

The attacks continued throughout the next 24 hours before finally coming to an end. As at so many other posts Pechkoff was ordered to demolish the post with explosives and withdraw.

Ultimately the rebellion was doomed to fail. The French and Spanish began to discuss more joint action, and in July 1925, the great French war leader Marshal Petain arrived in Morocco to assume overall command of operations. By the end of that summer there were 160,000 French troops and some 200,000 Spanish troops concentrated in the region. By mid September the French launched an offensive north to retake all ground previously lost whilst the Spanish made an amphibious landing at Alhucemas Bay and began a drive south. Whilst Rifian resistance was initially stiff, lack of food and an outbreak of typhus weakened their ability.

At a tactical level, lessons had been learned and costly daylight attacks were replaced by more night operations. Rifian hilltop positions were simply surrounded and cut off with stone walls and barbed wire rather than directly assaulted, and Moroccan irregular forces were used to harass the Rifian forces.

Further combined operations were carried out in the central region of the Rif in April and May 1926 and Abd-el-Krim finally surrendered to the French on 27 May. He was immediately offered an annual pension of 100,000 francs and exile to a large estate on the island of Reunion.

With the defeat of Abd-el -Krim most resistance throughout Morocco came to an end. However, it would be another seven years before Lyautey considered the pacification of Morocco completed.

The last region to resist was in areas of the High Atlas where Berber resistance leaders took up arms against the French and continued the struggle from their mountain strongholds. The climax to this came in 1933 at the mountain of Djebel Baddou where a force of 2,000 warriors and their families prepared to fight a French force of some 25,000.

The mountain stronghold was regarded by both sides as being virtually impregnable. Neither French artillery or aerial bombing had any significant impact on the Berbers inside their caves.

Commander of the French forces was determined to take the mountain by storm and ordered an assault by a force of Moroccan mercenaries led by

---

5 Pechkoff, *Bugle Calls*, p.249.

Captain Henri de Lespinasse de Bournazel who was famed for riding into battle unarmed and wearing a scarlet tunic. Berber legend claimed that he was invincible and could not be killed but during this attack he was shot and killed by a sharpshooter hidden amongst the rocks. His men faltered and fled in shock and dismay leaving the final assault to be carried out by men of the mounted company of the second regiment Legion Etranger. This attack was also met by a hail of fire from Berbers in well concealed and protected positions on the steep, rocky slopes of the mountain. Only one officer and 12 men returned safely after the ineffectual attack was called off.

The whole assault had been a pointless and expensive waste of time and men. With the mountain effectively cut off and access to water and food denied it was only a matter of time before the tribes would be forced to surrender.

After six weeks of siege the Berber resistance ended, and the conquest of Morocco was completed. It had lasted almost 40 years and cost an estimated 100,000 dead. Less than 20 years later, in 1956, the French Protectorate came to an end and the sultan King Mohammed V took control of an independent, but not fully unified, country.

Chapter 10

Aftermath and Decline

Sporadic resistance continued well into 1935 but the role of French forces in general, and that of the Legion in particular, was changing. Active service was being replaced by more sedentary policing and garrison duties. The Foreign Legion was beginning to receive some criticism for its performance at this time, but this was largely due to the way it was being used. From being frontline troops engaged in the thick of battle it was now being split up into small units destined for garrison duty or construction work. Road building, including the famous Tunnel du Legionnaire near Er Rachidia, bridge construction and numerous other building projects were given to the men of the Foreign Legion who carried out the arduous work with pride. It did however diminish their combat readiness and performance, and many felt that they had become nothing more than a uniformed construction company.

Whilst there continued to be a need for the construction of forts and outposts the focus was now switching to Algeria as legion mechanised units used locations such as Fort Trinquet and Fort Zouerat as patrol bases from which they could keep vast areas of the western Sahara under a watchful eye.

A significant number of those built earlier in Morocco were abandoned when no longer required. Many had only ever been built as temporary structures and they rapidly fell into decay with many of the materials used to build them being taken for the construction of other buildings by locals from nearby villages. Some, such as those built during the Rif uprising, had been destroyed by their own garrisons prior to departure.

The outpost of Astar, scene of very heavy fighting during the Rif Uprising, has now almost entirely vanished with only very slight traces left to show what had once been there. Roughly 3 km northwest of the small town of Taounate (34.32.9 N, 4.38.24 W) the post was constructed on a pear-shaped hill about 400 m high. The site is now covered with olive groves. The outer walls of the post have entirely gone, almost certainly reused for local farm buildings and walls. However, traces of the internal buildings, outer trenches and the gun emplacement described by Pechkoff remain clear to see.

Due to the quality of its construction and remote location the fort at Tazougert remains in a remarkable state of preservation. Located just off the N10, midway between Boudenib and Er Rachidia at (32.031316 N, 3.3628

W). Although it easy to locate and visible from the road, requires a steep climb on foot to reach the site. The access road built by the legion starts close to the junction of the Oued Guir valley road, the R601, with the N10 and winds its way up to the fort. Rocky, steep in places and with a high, vertical drop on one side it is just passable with a four-by-four but only with an experienced driver. Initial visits to this site were carried out by the author on foot and, later, off road motorcycle.

In comparison, its sister fort built a few miles away to the north, at Atachana, was built on the valley floor to a much lower standard and has now almost entirely disappeared into the sand and gravel plain that surrounds it. The site can be found at the northern end of the Oued Guir valley (32.220928 N, 3.821266 W). Follow the R601 until reaching a junction and then follow the left branch heading towards the R708. A few surface remains are visible on the left after about 28 km, but aerial imagery reveals a very clear ground plan showing how extensive the fort was originally. It remains to be properly surveyed and there is likely to be much of interest to be found.

Very little now remains of the blockhouse at Boudenib whilst the fort it supported has long since vanished beneath the expanding new town. The surviving remains of the blockhouse are located south of the N10 at Boudenib (31.5659 N, 3.3628 W). Despite being visible from the main road access requires some challenging navigation through the narrow streets of the old town and palm groves followed by a very steep climb to the summit. The easiest approach is from the east and south, but this can only be reached on foot.

An easily accessible ruined fort, with a local hotel nearby, is Fort Bou Jeriff. Located close to the Atlantic coast, about four hours south of Agadir (29.081966 N, 10.331371 W) is well worth a visit. Yet to be fully surveyed it is one of the largest forts in Morocco and is still sufficiently preserved to give a real understanding of what it would have been like in its heyday. Zinovi Pechkoff wrote with foresight:

> The men of the Foreign Legion are the ones who always construct the outposts. After a few years we shall go farther but these outposts will remain in the rear. They will be dismantled. They will serve as shelter for passing caravans. Around them market places will be established and the people will forget that there was a time when the towers carried guns.[1]

1 Pechkoff, *Bugle Calls*, p.64

Appendix I

Boudenib Blockhouse Survey

Survey of Blockhouse at Boudenib

The blockhouse at Boudenib is of particular importance as it is one of very few sites whose history is well documented. Subjected to a major attack in September 1908 it stands as a testimony to the courage and tenacity of the legionnaires who defended it and the Moroccans who attacked it.

The story of the attack has been well documented but none of those who wrote about it were actually able to visit the site. Despite its clear visibility access to the site presented numerous difficulties and it was only after several attempts that a recce team using off road motorcycles managed to find a suitable route to the site in 2011.

This initial reconnaissance was followed a year later by a team of students from the Archaeology Department of Worcester University who completed a detailed survey of the site in May 2012.

Although very little remains of the blockhouse today there are numerous contemporary photographs and detailed drawings providing a very clear picture of how the structure looked in 1908.

With design and layout restricted by the space available on the summit of the hill the building appears to have been of two storeys flanked to the east and west by sandbag and rock enclosures – two to the west and one to the east – designed to hold artillery. Whilst this would have considerably increased the firepower available at the post there is no mention, or evidence, of any guns being positioned there at the time of the attack.

With regard to the main structure the remains of the west wall are very clear but now stand at a much-reduced height. On the south side a small room with loophole windows survives intact and these are visible in contemporary photographs.

To the east, traces of the low walls that created the outer enclosures remain, but large sections have disappeared.

Fieldwork being undertaken by students from Worcester University.

The west side of the blockhouse. The tallest structure is part of a small tower housing a signal lamp.

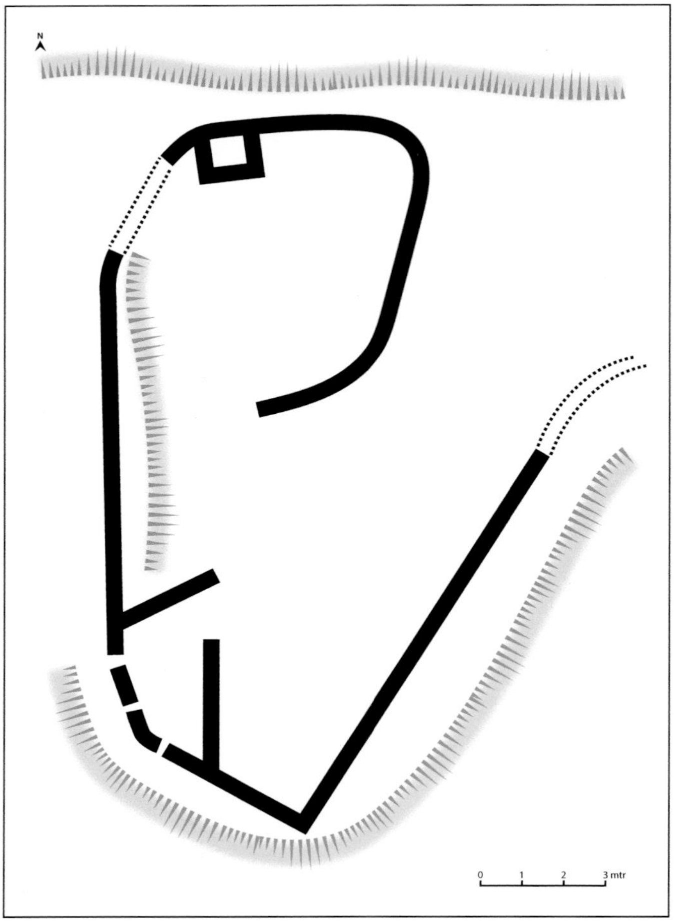

Plan of the remaining walls of the blockhouse.

Remains of the interior. This small room is on the west side of the blockhouse.

The view to the east of the oasis at Boudenib.

The view to the south.

Traces of Battle

Reports of the assault on the blockhouse tell of an unrelenting firefight lasting almost 18 hours. The heroic 'last stand' by massively outnumbered defenders is reminiscent of the more well-known actions such as the British stand at Rorke's Drift during the Zulu War of 1879 or the Foreign Legion stand at Camerone Farm in Mexico in 1863 and, almost certainly, the story would have been elaborated upon by press reporting at the time. As such, one of the aims of the archaeological survey was to ascertain if there was any evidence remaining to support the story.

Documentary evidence tells of the main attack on the blockhouse coming from the south and the geography of the hill on which the blockhouse was positioned clearly supports this. The approaches from the north and east are almost vertical and they are clearly very exposed to artillery fire from the main redoubt. The western approach is also very steep but would have been slightly easier to climb and is more sheltered from view from the redoubt. The approach from the south is indeed the most logical route for any assault being completely out of view of the redoubt, screened from artillery fire and much easier to ascend via a number of clear tracks.

The steepness of all the approaches would not have provided any suitable firing positions from which the attacking force could fire directly onto the blockhouse. This could only be achieved towards the top of the slope and once the flat plateau was reached. Likewise, it would have been very difficult for the defenders to acquire targets coming up the steep sides unless they left the main building and went to the top of the slopes. This fits well with the reports that attackers were able to get very close to, and at one point, inside the defences before being repelled by explosive charges and grenades being dropped down from the top of the walls to the base of the walls.

Once attackers reached the plateau on top of the '*gara*' they would have been able to find numerous suitable firing positions behind large rocks and holes in the ground. An area survey with metal detectors located numerous spent cartridge cases at a number of obvious firing positions that have remained in place since the attack. The plateau was also covered with a significant quantity of artillery shrapnel confirming the reports that Lieutenant Vary called for artillery fire directly onto his position to deal with the overwhelming numbers outside the blockhouse. Grenade fragments were located around the base of the walls confirming the reports that defenders actually rolled grenades down the outside of the walls.

Remains of barbed wire fences to the south and west were also found although these could have been put up at a later date. The blockhouse was reinforced soon after the action and remained in use for a long time afterwards.

The isolated position of the blockhouse has resulted in the remarkable preservation of evidence of the attack, and which confirms the reports of the action.

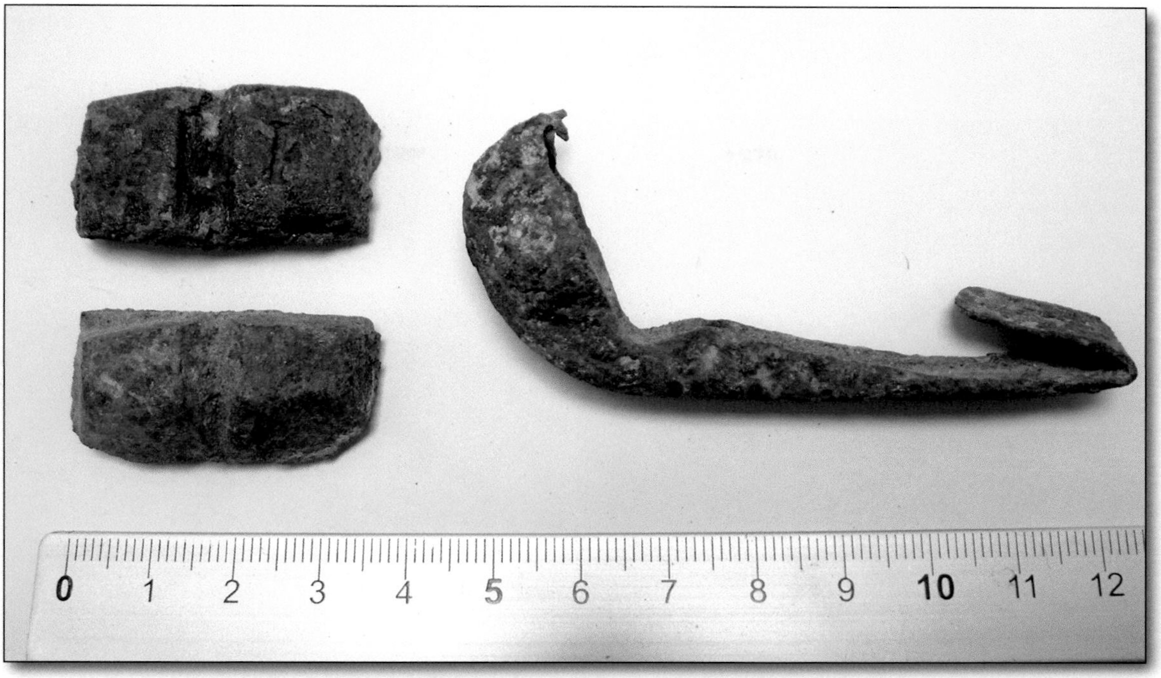

Remnants of an F1 fragmentation grenade found close to the west wall.

This expended bullet was found about 50 m to the southwest of the blockhouse.

Remnants of barbed wire entanglements.

Appendix II

Military Units in Morocco

In addition to the Foreign Legion and the Bataillon d'Affrique there were a wide range of units within the French army in Morocco. These included volunteers from the local population (spahis, goumiers and tirailleurs); regiments largely made up of French settlers doing their military service (zouaves and chasseurs d'Afrique). The divisions were not absolute and volunteers or conscripts from mainland France might choose to serve in the spahis and tirailleurs, while Arab volunteers might appear amongst the ranks of the zouaves.

Tirailleurs – Light Infantry

Recruited from a number of west African colonies they provided fierce and courageous light infantry troops to the French army. The title Senegalese was applied to all such units, regardless of where they were actually recruited, in honour of the first black Tirailleur regiments formed in Senegal in the 1850s.

During the First World War the much-reduced French garrison in Morocco consisted largely of battalions of *Tirailleurs Sénégalais*, who were not affected by the divided loyalties of locally recruited troops and who could be more readily spared from service on the western front than French troops. Very often used for garrison duties they would generally replace the Foreign Legion garrisons who had constructed the forts. During the uprising in the Rif, when 8,000 Berber fighters attacked a line of French outposts recently established in disputed territory north of the Ouerghala River, the majority of these posts were held by Senegalese and North African tirailleurs. Tirailleurs continued to play a major part in subsequent operations in both northern Morocco (until 1926) and southern Morocco (until 1934). In one of many engagements, the 2nd battalion of the 1st regiment of *Tirailleurs Sénégalais* won 91 citations for bravery during fighting around Ain-Gatar on 22 June 1926.

Spahis – Cavalry

Prior to 1914 there were four regiments of Spahis in the French army, three based in Algeria and one in Tunisia. During their period as mounted cavalry the Spahis generally comprised Arab and Berber soldiers commanded by French officers. However, there were always a certain number of French volunteers in the ranks and by the 1920s about 20 percent of the rank and file were French. In addition, a fixed number of commissioned positions up to the level of captain were reserved for Muslim officers. NCOs were both French and Muslim.

In contrast to the North African tirailleur units the mounted spahis were drawn from amongst the higher social classes of the Arab and Berber communities. This was a tradition dating back to the establishment of the corps when recruits were required to provide their own horse.

Moroccan Goumiers

These were indigenous Moroccan soldiers who served in auxiliary units attached to the French Army of Africa, from 1908 onward. While nominally in the service of the Sultan of Morocco, they served under French officers and French higher command.

Algerian goumiers were employed during the initial stages of the French intervention in Morocco, commencing in 1908 but, after their terms of enlistment expired, they were replaced by Moroccans. Retaining the designation of goumiers, the Moroccans served in detachments under French officers, and initially mostly Algerian NCOs, both of whom were usually seconded from the Spahis and Tirailleurs. Moroccan *sous-officers* were in due course appointed.

They were used to patrol recently occupied areas and they also served as scouts and in support of regular French troops. In 1911 they became permanent units.

As part of the agreement reached at The Conference at Algeciras the French had initially agreed not to recruit local troops but, with the outbreak of the First World War this restraint was lifted and the French enlisted large numbers of regular Moroccan tirailleurs, spahis and artillerymen. The goumiers had however proven so valuable that they continued their dual roles as tribal police and combat troops.

Zouaves

A class of light infantry serving from 1830 onwards. The zouaves, along with the indigenous Tirailleurs became some of the most decorated units of the French army.

It was initially intended that the zouaves would be a regiment of Berber volunteers from the Zwawa group of tribes in Algeria and some 500 were recruited in August and September 1830. Twelve years later, zouaves began to be recruited almost exclusively from Europeans, a policy which continued until the final dissolution of these regiments after the Algerian war.

Chasseurs d'Afrique

These were a light cavalry corps first raised in 1831 from regular French cavalry posted to Algeria. For most of their history they were recruited from either French volunteers or French settlers in North Africa doing their military service. As such they were the mounted equivalent of the French Zouave infantry. In the 1920s they gradually converted to armoured cars.

Appendix III

Foreign Legion Weapons used in Morocco

Lebel Rifle

The Lebel Model 1886 rifle (also known as the '*Fusil Mle 1886 M93*', after a bolt modification was added in 1893), was an 8 mm bolt-action infantry rifle that entered service in the French army in 1887. It was a repeating rifle that held eight rounds in its forestock tube magazine, one round in the transporter and one round in the chamber. The rifle was the first military firearm to use smokeless powder ammunition. The Lebel rifle was a durable design capable of long-range performance. In spite of early obsolete features, such as its tube magazine and the shape of 8 mm rimmed ammunition, the Lebel rifle remained the basic weapon of French infantry during the First World War (1914–1918) and in Colonial service long after. Altogether, 3.45 million Lebel rifles were produced by the three French state factories between 1887 and 1916.

Berthier M1906/ 15 Rifle

Named after its inventor, André Berthier, a French civilian engineer working on the Algerian railways, the Berthier's three-shot vertical-feed Mannlicher-type en bloc magazine could be loaded far faster than the Lebel it was designed to replace. The Berthier carbine was adopted by the French army on March 14, 1890, and a short rifle version of the Berthier rifle was adopted in 1907.

VB Rifle Grenade

The Viven-Bessières rifle grenade, named after its inventors, was also known as 'VB grenade', and officially referred to as the '*Viven-Bessières shell*' in the French army instruction manual. It was an infantry weapon in use with the French army from 1916 onwards and extremely popular in Morocco where, when facing overwhelming odds, it was regarded as a force equaliser.

Because of heavy recoil, and to increase range, the grenade was fired with the rifle butt placed on the ground at an angle of 45 degrees. This would give a range of around 190 meters and to simplify the calculations, a special firing-rack was also provided which could be used when time permitted.

F-1 Fragmentation Grenade

The F-1 grenade was first put into mass production by the French State in 1915 during the First World War and was soon adopted by many countries around the world. Variants are still in use. Operated by a percussion cap system and shattering into 10 large fragments the design was proved to be very functional, especially due to its stability compared to other grenades of the same period. It was popular in Morocco particularly for the defence of forts and outposts where, in extreme cases, they were simply rolled down the outside of walls to stop rush attacks.

Mle 1914 Hotchkiss machine gun

Designed for the 8 mm Lebel cartridge, it became the standard machine gun of the French army during the latter half of the First World War and for many years afterwards. Mounted on a stable tripod it was gas actuated and air-cooled and operated by a three-man crew. Early versions were fed with 8 mm rounds held in strips of 24. This system, whilst effective, slowed the rate of fire as the gun had to be continually reloaded after short bursts quickly used up the 24 rounds. Later versions were belt fed which could encounter issues in the sandy conditions of Morocco.

De Bange 80mm Field Gun

Developed in France by Colonel Charles Ragon de Bange in 1877, and adopted by the French army that same year, the gun was specifically designed for use by horse artillery units. The gun lacked a recoil mechanism, meaning that it moved backward at each firing, necessitating re-aiming every time, which considerably slowed the rate of firing. However, it was light and rugged and could easily be stripped down for carriage on mules or wagons. Its small size made it ideal for use in forts and outposts across Morocco as well as by troops on campaign in challenging mountain terrain.

Canon de 65 M modele 1906

This very small, robust but lightweight French gun was designed specifically for use in mountains and entered service with the *régiments d'artillerie de montagne* in 1906. It was one of the first soft-recoil guns in service. The carriage of the Mle 1906 was hinged and could be broken down into four

Hotchkiss machine gun crew. Bundesarchiv, Bild 102-723 / CC-BY-SA 3.0.

mule loads for transport making it ideal for use in Morocco. It had an effective range of over 6 km and was very easy to use even by untrained operators.

Matériel de 75 mm Mle 1897

Designed as a quick-firing field artillery piece it was adopted by the French army in March 1898. Used as an anti-personnel weapon system for delivering large volumes of time-fused shrapnel shells on enemy troops advancing in the open. This made it particularly useful in Morocco and many were situated in the forts and outposts across the country.

It was the first field gun to include a hydro-pneumatic recoil mechanism, which kept the guns trail and wheels perfectly still during the firing sequence. Since it did not need to be re-aimed after each shot, the crew could reload and fire as soon as the barrel returned to its resting position. This also meant it was particularly suited to use in the confined spaces of the towers, firing platforms and redoubts of the forts. In typical use, the French 75 could deliver 15 rounds per minute on its target using either shrapnel or melinite high-explosive, with a range of up to 8,500 metres (5.3 miles) away. Its firing rate could reach close to 30 rounds per minute, albeit only for a very short time and with a highly experienced crew.

Bréguet 14 TOE

A French biplane bomber and reconnaissance aircraft of the First World War it was built in very large numbers and it continued in use by numerous air forces for many years after the end of the war.

The Bréguet 14 was among the first mass-produced aircraft to use large amounts of aluminium, rather than wood or steel, in its structure. This allowed the airframe to be both lighter and stronger, in turn making the aircraft fast and agile.

There were a number of variants including a special version developed for the harsh conditions encountered in North Africa. Designated '14 TOE' (*Théatres des Opérations Extérieures*), these saw extensive service in Morocco.

Appendix IV

Signalling Equipment

The rapid flow of information and intelligence was vital to the French if they were to be able to respond quickly and effectively to unfolding developments. The network of watchtowers and forts enabled information to be passed around the system rapidly in a time before modern radio and satellite communications.

Climatic conditions in Morocco meant that the heliograph was a particularly effective method of swift communication over long distances – up to 60 km. The equipment works by reflecting the rays of the sun by means of mirrors. Using a key to actuate the mirror the operator can move the sending mirror into a position that reflects the light towards any receiving station which, in ideal conditions could be many miles away. Releasing the key returns the sending mirror back to its original position thus preventing any light being sent. By working the key morse code messages can be transmitted to receiving stations. As with morse sent by telegraph communication is quickly established and a high rate of transmission can be kept going for extended periods of time.

Where the angle between the sun and the receiving station is less than 90 degrees a single mirror system can be used but to provide 360 degree cover a second mirror is required. Called the duplex mirror it reflects the sun's rays from the first mirror onwards to the receiving station.

In the nineteenth and early twentieth centuries the heliographs were completely manual, relying entirely on the operator to track the sun as it moved across the sky as well as aligning the mirrors to send the message. However, the French developed heliographs that used clockwork heliostats to automatically follow the sun's movement and by 1884 all French military units were equipped with Mangin apparatus that used clockwork heliostats and could also use lantern light as well as sunlight thus enabling signalling at night. It was actually possible, in certain conditions, to use moonlight as well, but signal range was greatly reduced.

Although restricted by weather conditions and cloud cover this was not generally an issue in Morocco. The greater problem was having sufficient posts to maintain a line of sight. In addition, the delicate nature of the equipment, which was easily broken, required skilled operators to be really effective. However, unlike later field telephones that relied on connecting wire which could be cut the heliograph signals could not be interrupted or stopped and, for this reason, the system stayed in use far into the twentieth century.

Appendix V

Locating and Surveying Forts

There are many forts to be found and investigated and, with careful planning and preparation the undertaking is well within the capability of the enthusiastic investigator.

Morocco is a very straightforward country to visit with an excellent infrastructure supporting tourism. Customs formalities are minimal and, while French is the most widely spoken foreign language, English is well understood in many areas. Vehicle hire, including four-by-four, is very easy and guides readily available if required. However, main routes are well marked, tourist maps excellent and satellite navigation means that travel without a guide is not an issue. The people are generally very friendly and helpful and, as long as you follow basic etiquette regarding local customs and the Muslim faith, no problems should be encountered.

Whilst initial desk-based research is essential at the outset there is no substitute for actually visiting Morocco and trying to locate sites on the ground. The remote locations of many of the forts and outposts means that easy access today can be challenging but not impossible. For many locations a four-by-four or off-road motorcycles will offer the best form of travel but, if inexperienced, great care should be taken when travelling off the beaten track in remote desert or mountainous regions.

A particular issue with locating sites today is simply the problem of relating French maps of the period with modern maps. The spelling of names is often very different today and early mapping was not nearly so precise in recording geological features. What were once isolated villages are now sprawling urban developments. Modern roads and railways have replaced the old tracks and trails and large-scale intensive farming, and, in particular on the hills, olive groves, have turned what were once arid regions into areas of specialist food production.

In several parts of Morocco, and especially in the Rif Mountain region, large areas were flooded as part of hydroelectric projects commissioned in the 1960s and many sites were lost to the rising waters.

French military records are not as helpful as one might expect although this is not surprising as they regarded most sites as purely temporary and there was no requirement for those, other than local commanders responsible for supply and reinforcement, to have precise details of locations.

Further contributing to the difficulty of locating sites is the lack of local knowledge and oral tradition. With hardly anyone alive today who was old enough to remember the campaigns and forts, memories have faded, and many Moroccans today have little or no knowledge or interest in their colonial past.

What appear to be small forts are often visible along many of the main routes through Morocco but often these have been converted into other uses and are privately owned. It is also sometimes not always easy to distinguish between vernacular Moroccan buildings, buildings built by the French and more modern ones as construction techniques are often the same and it is only subtle style features that can distinguish them. Modern route maps often show symbols representing forts, but they do not differentiate between the types of fortification, age or type and the accuracy of the location shown is not always accurate.

For the location of fort sites in the Rif Mountains the most interesting source of potentially very useful information is the detailed work by Henri Clerisse who produced a definitive history of the campaigns in the Rif Mountains called *The Rif war and the Taza Spot 1925–1927*. Packed with contemporary photographs, detailed maps and with a preface by General Lyautey it is one of the most authoritative works on the subject at the time and is still a valuable source of information. Unfortunately, whilst of great value in showing general positions and areas worthy of further investigation, the maps showing the location of forts and blockhouses are not of sufficient scale or accuracy to provide reliable, precise locations for visiting today.

Google Earth coverage of Morocco is good and, used in conjunction with historic and modern mapping, it is often possible to identify the traces of fort sites on the satellite imagery. The site at Atachana, for example, is very clear in the satellite imagery which actually reveals considerably more of the plan of the fort than can be seen on the ground today.

Use of satellite and low altitude aerial imagery takes time and patience, and it is often easy to confuse other sites with possible forts. Cross reference with other sources is important and final confirmation of any potential site found can only be confirmed with a ground survey.

When searching for archaeological sites the planning phase is critical. Often referred to as a desktop survey, this is the stage when the meticulous study of maps, air photographs, satellite imagery and primary sources will reap rewards once in the field. If it is not done well a huge amount of time will be wasted at a later date.

Once a possible site has been identified verification can then be carried out with field surveys. A preliminary visit to the site should be used to confirm the desk-based research and establish the existence of a potential fort. Called a level one survey, this will confirm the precise location as well as access points and other factors, including current ownership, that may affect later field work. Whilst it may be possible to take a few pictures and make some initial sketches and notes, anything more prolonged and detailed may well require permission from local, or national, authorities. It is critical to check this as sites, particularly those close to the eastern and southern borders, may well be in sensitive areas where investigation could be prohibited.

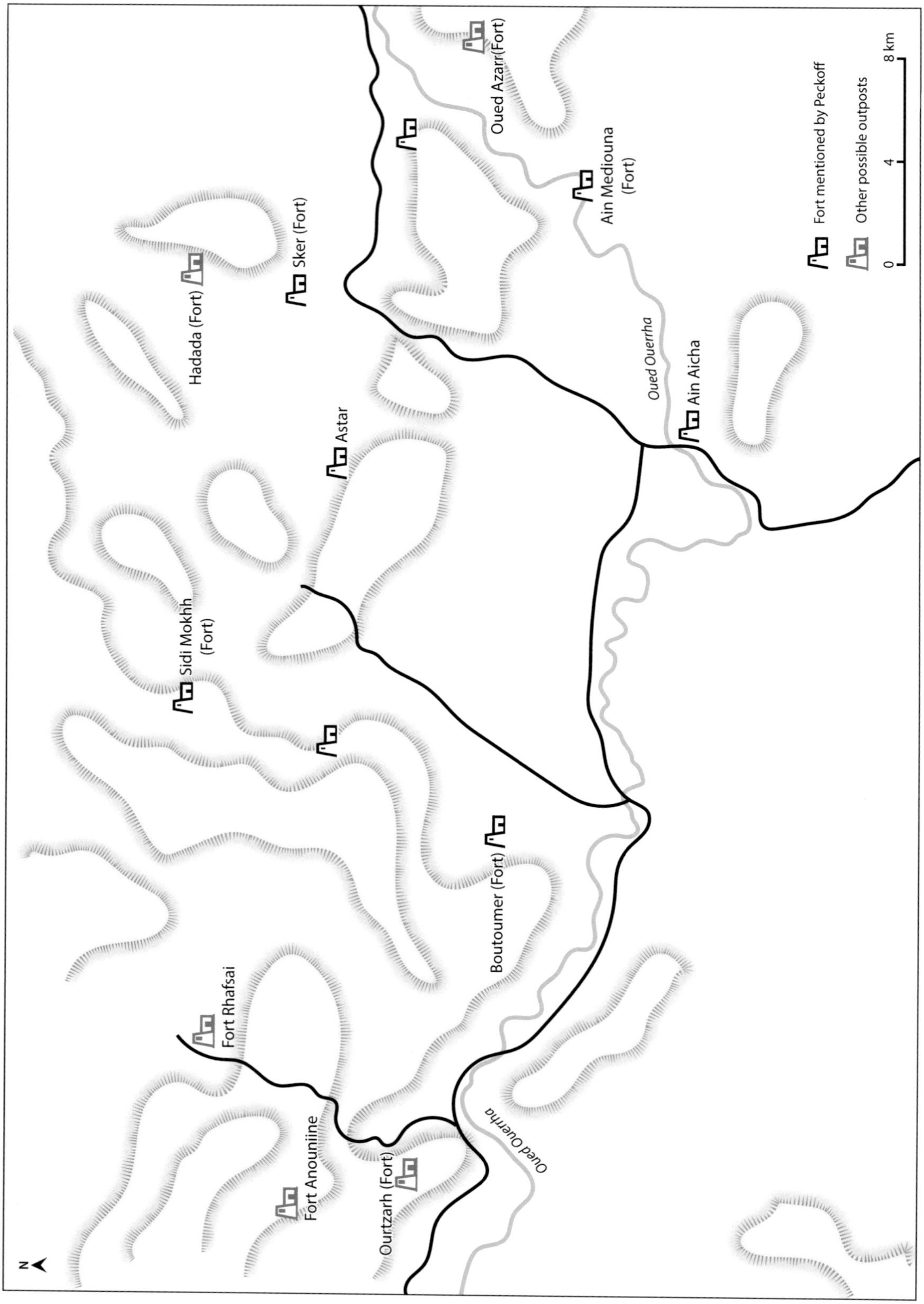

Possible blockhouse locations marked onto a modern map.

Walking the site as part of the initial survey.

On the assumption that all the necessary permissions have been gained it will be possible to proceed with a more detailed level two survey. This should record the following information:

a. Location,
b. Statement of building type including, if possible, construction date, function and construction materials,
c. Tactical and strategic importance of the location,
d. Evidence of links to other possible sites in the area,
e. Plan of site,
f. Floor plans and elevation drawings of internal/ external structures,
g. Drawing of architectural features,
h. Reconstruction drawings of what the structure may have looked like when complete,
i. Photographs of all aspects including all buildings (interior and exterior), decorative features, functional features, surrounding area and any other associated features,
j. Sketch maps of the immediate and extended areas around the site.

Should any artefacts be found that are clearly related to the site their location on the site should be recorded precisely onto a site plan and they should be photographed, in situ, with a scale before being moved. Any items moved should be clearly labelled with reference to their type and location on the site plan.

Recording artefacts found on site.

The following equipment is suggested for site surveys:

a. Measuring tapes (50 m and 20 m),
b. Pedometer,
c. Clinometer,
d. Range pole,
e. Compass,
f. GPS,
g. Camera,
h. Record sheets/ pencils/ notebooks/ maps,
i. Laptop and solar charger,
j. Hard hats.

Drones with cameras are very useful for getting aerial views of sites and reaching high points that may be inaccessible or dangerous to reach on foot. However, operating a drone may require permission and this needs to be checked in advance. Even taking a drone into Morocco can raise concern and it is best to gain a permit or written permission.

Survey equipment will need to be carried onto the site and this needs to be considered if the site being investigated requires a lengthy walk or climb to reach.

Some sites can only be reached on foot.

Safety should be taken seriously, and care should be taken when surveying ruined buildings. A first aid kit is essential as is suitable clothing and footwear for working in the hot climate of southern Morocco.

Once survey work has been completed it is important to record all results and produce a written report. Even if the report is limited in scope and detail, it may provide other interested parties to carry out further research.

Appendix VI

Fort Zinderneuf 1939 Film Set

In 2011 Professor Seth Mallios led a team from San Diego State University to the location of the film set of Fort Zinderneuf that had been constructed for the 1939 film Beau Geste.

The site had been located by documentary film maker Frank Thompson in the Californian desert and it was felt that applying archaeological technique to the recording of the site would be an interesting project. The fort site was located on government land, so special permits were needed to study the location and the archaeological survey team were not allowed to do any excavating or remove any artifacts from the site.

Unlike the remains of many real forts in Morocco there were no visible standing remains but the site was identified from the post demolition debris field which contained various artifacts including broken glass and blank cartridge cases from the rifles used during the making of the film. The survey team also found the heel of an old boot, which may have been part of a film costume, and pieces of what might have been the flooring from the fort. The similarity of these artifacts to those found at fort sites in Morocco is remarkable.

The outline of the foundation of the fort was clearly visible marked by wooden posts still firmly planted in the sand.

Site of the Fort Zinderneuf film set. Courtesy of Seth Mallios. San Diego State University.

Bibliography

Primary Sources

Aage de Denmark, Prince. *My Life in the Foreign Legion* (London: Nash and Grayson, 1928).
Beric, Raoul. *Les routiers: La Légion Etranger: Source d'admiration et de pitié* (Paris Édition
Moderne, 1907).
Cooper, Adolphe R. *March or Bust* (London: Robert Hale and Company, 1972).
Ex-Legionnaire 17889., *In the Foreign Legion* (London: Duckworth, 1910).
Ex-Legionnaire 75464. *Slaves of Morocco* (London: Sampson Lowe, 1938).
Harvey, John. *With the French Foreign Legion in Syria* (London: Greenhill Books, 1995).
Le Poer, J. P. *A Modern Legionary* (London: Methuen, 1904).
Lohndorff, E. *Hell in the Foreign Legion* (London: George Allen and Unwin, 1931).
Lyautey, L.H. *Vers le Maroc: Lettres du Sud-Oranis,1903–1906* (Paris: Armand Colin,1937).
Magnus, M. *Memoirs of the Foreign Legion* (London: Martin Secker, 1924).
Pechkoff, Zinovi. *The Bugle Sounds, Life in the Foreign Legion* (London: Appleton 1926).
Rosen, Erwin. *In the Foreign Legion,* London: Duckworth, 1910).
Stamer, William. *Recollections of a Life of Adventure* (London: Hurst and Blackett, 1866).
Victor, T. *From the Abyss to the Foreign Legion* (London: Sampson, 1928).
Weygand, J. *Legionnaire: Life with the Foreign Legion Cavalry* (London: Harrap,1952).
Ward Price, G. *In Morocco with the Legion* (London: Jarrolds Publishers, 1934).

Secondary Sources

Clerisse, Henri. *The Rif war and the Taza spot 1925–1927* (Paris: Desgrandchamps, 1927).
Dunn, Robert E. *Resistance in the Desert* (London: Croom Helm Ltd, 1977).
Gilbert, Adrian D. *Voices of the Foreign Legion* (Edinburgh: Mainstream Publishing, 2 9).
Hoisington, William A. *Lyautey and the French Conquest of Morocco* (London: MacMillan, 1995).
Mahuault, Jean-Paul. *L'épopée Marocaine de la Légion Étrangère 1903–1934* (Paris:
L,Harmattan 2 5).
Parker, John. *Inside the Foreign Legion* (London:Judy Piatkus Ltd, 1998).
Porch, Douglas. *The Conquest of Morocco* (New York: A F Knopf Inc, 1982).
Porch, Douglas. *The Conquest of the Sahara.* New York: A F Knopf, 1984).
Porch, Douglas. *The French Foreign Legion* (New York: Harper Collins, 1991).
Wellard, James. *The French Foreign Legion* (London: Rainbird Ltd, 1974).

Windrow, Martin. *The French Foreign Legion* (Oxford: Osprey Publishing, 1971).
Windrow, Martin. *French Foreign Legion 1914–1945* (Oxford: Osprey Publishing, 1999).
Windrow, Martin. *Our Friends Beneath the Sands* (London: Weidenfield and Nicolson, 2010).
Wren, Percival C. *Beau Geste* (Hertfordshire: Wordsworth Classic, 1994).
Young, John R. *The French Foreign Legion* (London: Guild Publishing, 1984).

Technical Guides

Andrews, Donald. *The Survey and Recording of Historic Buildings* (Oxford: AAI&S, 1995).
Bowden, Mark. *Unravelling the Landscape* (Stroud: Tempus Publishing, 1999).
Hutton, Barbara. *Recording Standing Buildings* (Sheffield: University of Sheffield, 1988).
Morris, Richard K. *The Archaeology of Buildings* (Stroud: Tempus Publishing, 2000).
Swallow, P. *Measurement and Recording of Historic Buildings* (London: Donhead Publishing, 1993).
Wood, J. *Buildings Archaeology* (Oxford: Oxbow Books,1994).

Morocco Guides

Marquet, Catherine (ed.). *Morocco:Eye Witness Travel Guide* (London: Dorling Kindersley, 2002).
Scott, Chris. *Morocco Overland* (Hindhead: Trailblazer Publications, 2009).
Stabler, J. *The Desert Drivers Manual* (London: Stacey International, 1998).
Stannard, D. *Morocco: Insight Pocket Guide* (Singapore: APA Publications, 2007).

Books in this series:

1. *The Battle of Majuba Hill: The Transvaal Campaign 1880–1881* John Laband (ISBN 978-1-911512-38-7)
2. *For Queen and Company: Vignettes of the Irish Soldier in the Indian Mutiny* David Truesdale (ISBN 978-1-911512-79-0)
3. *The Furthest Garrison: Imperial Regiments in New Zealand 1840–1870* Adam Davis (ISBN 978-1-911628-29-3)
4. *Victory Over Disease: Resolving the Medical Crisis in the Crimean War, 1854–1856* Michael Hinton (ISBN 978-1-911628-31-6)
5. *Journey Through the Wilderness: Garnet Wolseley's Canadian Red River Expedition of 1870* Paul McNicholls (ISBN 978-1-911628-30-9)
6. *Kitchener: The Man Not The Myth* Anne Samson (ISBN 978-1-912866-45-8)
7. *The British and the Sikhs: Discovery, Warfare and Friendship c1700–1900* Gurinder Singh Mann (ISBN 978-1-911628-24-8)
8. *Bazaine 1870: Scapegoat for a Nation* Quintin Barry (ISBN 978-1-913336-08-0)
9. *Redcoats in the Classroom: The British Army's Schools For Soldiers and Their Children During the 19th Century* Howard R. Clarke (ISBN 978-1-912866-47-2)
10. *The Rescue They Called a Raid: The Jameson Raid 1895–96* David Snape (ISBN 978-1-913118-77-8)
11. *Hungary 1848: The Winter Campaign* Christopher Pringle (ISBN 978-1-913118-78-5)
12. *The War of the Two Brothers: The Portuguese Civil War 1828-1834* Sérgio Veludo Coelho (ISBN 978-1-914059-26-1)
14. *Forgotten Victorian Generals: Studies in the Exercise of Command and Control in the British Army 1837–1901* Christopher Brice (editor) (ISBN 978-1-910777-20-6)
15. *The German War of 1866: The Bohemian and Moravian Campaign* Theodore Fontane (ISBN 978-1-914059-29-2)
16. *Dust of Glory: The First Anglo-Afghan War 1839–1842, its Causes and Course* Bill Whitburn (ISBN 978-1-914059-33-9)
17. *Saarbruck to Sedan: The Franco-German War 1870–1871 Volume 1* Ralph Weaver (ISBN 978-1-914059-88-9)
18. *The Battle of Lissa 1866: How the Industrial Revolution Changed the Face of Naval Warfare* Quintin Barry (ISBN 978-1-914059-92-6)
19. *The Zulu Kingdom and the Boer Invasion of 1837–1840* John Laband (ISBN 978-1-914059-89-6)
20. *The Fire of Venture Was in His Veins: Major Allan Wilson and the Shangani Patrol 1893* David Snape (ISBN 978-1-914059-90-2)
21. *From the Atacama to the Andes: Battles of the War of the Pacific 1879–1883* Alan Curtis (ISBN 978-1-914059-90-2)
22. *The Rise of the Sikh Soldier: The Sikh Warrior Through the Ages, c1700–1900* Gurinder Singh Mann (ISBN 978-1-915070-52-4)
23. *Victorian Crusaders: British and Irish Volunteers in the Papal Army 1860–70* Nicholas Schofield (ISBN 978-1-915070-53-1)
24. *The Battle for the Swiepwald: Austria's Fatal Blunder at Königgrätz, the climactic battle of the Austro-Prussian War, 3 July 1866* Ernst Heidrich (ISBN 978-1-915070-49-4)
25. *British Military Panoramas: Battle in The Round, 1800–1914* Ian F.W. Beckett (ISBN 978-1-915113-84-9)
26. *Onwards to Omdurman: The Anglo-Egyptian Campaign to Reconquer the Sudan, 1896–1898* Keith Surridge (ISBN 978-1-915070-51-7)
27. *Hungary 1849: The Summer Campaign* Christopher Pringle (ISBN 978-1-915113-80-1)
28. *Line in the Sand: French Foreign Legion Forts and Fortifications in Morocco 1900-1926* Richard Jeynes (ISBN 978-1-915113-83-2)